Bluetooth for Java

BRUCE HOPKINS AND RANJITH ANTONY

Technical Reviewer: Andrew Stringer
Editorial Directors: Dan Appleman, Gary Cornell, Simon Hayes, Karen Watterson, John Zukowski
Assistant Publisher: Grace Wong
Project Manager and Development Editor: Tracy Brown Collins
Copy Editor: Ami Knox
Compositor: Impressions Book and Journal Services, Inc.
Artist and Cover Designer: Kurt Krames
Indexer: Valerie Robbins
Production Manager: Kari Brooks
Manufacturing Manager: Tom Debolski

Distributed to the book trade in the United States by Springer-Verlag New York, Inc., 175 Fifth Avenue, New York, NY, 10010 and outside the United States by Springer-Verlag GmbH & Co. KG, Tiergartenstr. 17, 69112 Heidelberg, Germany.

In the United States, phone 1-800-SPRINGER, email orders@springer-ny.com, or visit http://www.springer-ny.com.
Outside the United States, fax +49 6221 345229, email orders@springer.de, or visit http://www.springer.de.

For information on translations, please contact Apress directly at 2560 9th Street, Suite 219, Berkeley, CA 94710. Phone 510-549-5930, fax: 510-549-5939, email info@apress.com, or visit http://www.apress.com.

The source code for this book is available to readers at http://www.apress.com in the Downloads section.

First and foremost, I dedicate this book to the Lord Jesus Christ, without whom I could not have written this book. I also dedicate this book to my loving wife, Schrell, and my two wonderful children, Lydia and Bruce Jr.
—Bruce Hopkins

Dedicated to my parents, Prof. Antony Mampilly and Prof. Kochurani Mampilly.
—Ranjith Antony

Contents at a Glance

Contents

Appendix B javax.obex *265*

Appendix C Java Bluetooth Development on the PalmOS Platform *269*

Appendix D BlipNet 1.1 API *273*

About the Authors

 **Bruce Hopkins** is a 6-year Java veteran with experience in distributed computing and wireless networking. He has an electrical and computer engineering degree from Wayne State University in Detroit and has interest in robotics, microcomputing, and electronics. He has worked in Java since JDK 1.0a, and his research studies include distributed computing, clustering, encryption, and pervasive computing. He currently works as an independent consultant in the Metro Detroit area.

 **Ranjith Antony** earned his bachelor of technology degree in computer engineering from the College of Engineering, Chengannur, Kerala, India, an institute affiliated with Cochin University of Science and Technology. He became a lecturer in the Department of Computer Engineering of the Government Model Engineering College, an institute affiliated with Cochin University of Science and Technology. In June 1998, he joined Atinav as a software engineer. Presently, he is working as a senior technical manager and is managing the Bluetooth-related Java products from Atinav.

About the Technical Reviewer

Andrew Stringer was educated at the Dublin Institute of Technology in computer science and software engineering, receiving a bachelor of science degree. Andrew joined Rococo Software in 2001 as a trainer and consultant in the field of wireless software development. Andrew has great experience in developing and delivering courses with J2ME and also with Java APIs for Bluetooth Wireless Technology (JABWT). Andrew lives in Dublin, Ireland.

Acknowledgments

I PERSONALLY WANT TO THANK all the people who helped me in writing the book that you're holding. Never in a million years would I have thought that I would be working with Gary Cornell and John Zukowski, both of whom are very respected Java authors. I'm very grateful that Gary and John accepted my proposal way back in January of 2002. For that matter, I want to thank the rest of the team at Apress including Tracy Brown, Ami Knox, Kari Brooks, and Wanshun Tam. More honor, however, goes to Tracy. Many thanks to Andrew Stringer from Rococo for tech reviewing this book; I never knew that I could have been wrong so many times. It's good to have an expert at your disposal.

Bluetooth equipment isn't cheap, so I also want to acknowledge all the great companies around the world (literally) that gave Ranjith and me hardware loans and technical assistance. For instance, Jeff Day and the rest of the team at 3Com (including Ken Morley, Brent Nixon, and Randy Rollins) were very helpful in providing us with Bluetooth adapters and tech support. Mahendra Tailor from TDK Systems in the UK was very helpful in providing us with equipment as well. Rococo was very kind to allow us to have an extended evaluation period in order to write the chapter on Bluetooth simulation. Thanks to Geraldine, Karl, and the rest of the team in Ireland. Lim Siong Huat from Mobiwave in Singapore was very helpful in allowing us to use their protocol analyzer for the security chapter. Peter Duchemin from Smart Network Devices in Germany was very helpful in getting me the inside scoop on their Micro BlueTarget. I also want to thank Niels-Christian Gjerrild from Ericsson in Sweden for hardware and documentation on the Ericsson BlipNet system. North of the border, in Canada, I also received assistance from Dr. Steven Knudsen regarding the integration of Jini and Bluetooth.

This is my first book, so I definitely have to thank all the wonderful teachers at Grant, Cass Tech, and WSU who helped me to get here. You'll never forget a good teacher, and I've had many in my lifetime. I want to thank personally Mrs. Smith, Mrs. Parent, Mr. Walker, and Mrs. Cowan from Grant School. At Cass Tech, I had the pleasure to study under Mr. Miller, Mr. Raymond, and Mrs. Ashford. Dr. Steve Kahn was a little disappointed that I didn't finish my degree with the Mathematics Department after I joined the Emerging Scholars Program, but he deserves to be mentioned. I also want to thank Dr. Chaudhary for giving me the opportunity to study and research with him in the Parallel and Distributed Computing Lab at Wayne State. Very few students were eligible to work in the undergraduate research program, and I'm grateful to Bill Hill for allowing me to be a part of it.

I wouldn't be the person that I am today without the spiritual guidance of my pastors at Bethlehem Temple Church. Many thanks to the late Bishop Jackson, the late Bishop Porter, Elder Clark, and the whole church family.

I'm the youngest of seven children, so each one of my siblings played a role in shaping my life and career. Thanks to Theresa, Valerie, Darlene, Barbara, Mark, and Tyrone. I definitely have to give special thanks to Mom and Dad, because they've dealt with me for 26 years of my life. They did an excellent job raising all seven children with college educations. Thanks to Thaddeus Johnson for being a good friend. In order to stay smart, you have to hang around smart people.

Finally, I want to thank my wonderfully sweet wife, Schrell. She was very patient and understanding while I wrote this book. She is truly a virtuous woman.

—Bruce Hopkins

Numerous people have provided assistance, advice, and encouragement during the preparation of this book. Major contributors of material, ideas, insights, solutions, and explanations that have found their way into this book include James Jose, Salman Ali, Rajesh Rabindranath, Sudhin Latheef, Vaishali Patil, and Sajith M Nair. Besides them, my teammates at Atinav, especially George Mathew, Cipson Jose, and Dinkar Raj, have contributed suggestions, fixed program bugs, and made imperceptible contributions too numerous to mention. I am also grateful to Mr. Lim Siong Huat and his colleagues at Mobiwave for extending their support by providing timely advice and necessary equipment. Without him, the chapter on Bluetooth security would not have materialized.

—Ranjith Antony

Introduction

IN THE NEAR FUTURE, Bluetooth wireless technology will be embedded into nearly every consumer electronics device. Devices like mobile phones, PDAs, laptops, desktops, calculators, watches, keyboards, mice, printers, scanners, cameras, and video game consoles are just a sample of what device manufacturers will be embedding with Bluetooth. Today, Bluetooth chipsets can be purchased (in mass quantities) for $5, so it's only a matter of time before many of your personal devices become Bluetooth enabled.

With Java, you get the ability to create applications that are agnostic of their underlying hardware platform. As you can see, this makes Java the perfect programming language for Bluetooth! Regardless of the hardware or OS used for your PDA, mobile phone, watch, etc., you can use the same programming language to create your Bluetooth applications. This book is all about how to create wireless applications using Java and Bluetooth.

How This Book Is Organized

Here's an overview of what's covered in this book:

Chapter 1: Introducing Bluetooth: If you're completely new to Bluetooth, then this chapter is for you. In Chapter 1, we give a brief introduction to Bluetooth, with a general explanation of what you can do with the technology.

Chapter 2: Bluetooth 1.1: In this chapter, we dive right into the dirty details of the Bluetooth protocol. Here we define the roles and relationships between the Bluetooth stack, Bluetooth profiles, and Bluetooth hardware. If you've seen Bluetooth terminology before, but you don't know the difference between SDP and SDAP for instance, then this chapter will help clear things up.

Chapter 3: Before You Get Started: Chapter 3 is very appropriately named because it covers all the loose ends that need to be addressed before we show you how to integrate Bluetooth and Java.

Chapter 4: Understanding the Java Bluetooth API: This chapter covers the full life cycle of a Bluetooth application (whether you're using Java or not). This chapter also shows you how to use the javax.bluetooth package of the official Java Bluetooth API (the JSR-82) in order to create Bluetooth applications.

Chapter 5: Bluetooth with J2ME MIDP: The first complete example of a Java Bluetooth application is explained in Chapter 5. Before we present the code, however, we provide a short review of the J2ME MIDP.

Chapter 6: Creating a Bluetooth Print Server with JPS API: Now with a complete example under your belt, things will start to get pretty exciting. In Chapter 6, we introduce you to the Java Printing API and show you how to create a Bluetooth print server.

Chapter 7: Java and OBEX: Chapter 7 covers the foundation of the OBEX protocol and provides an example on how to transfer files using the javax.obex package of the JSR-82.

Chapter 8: Using a Bluetooth Simulator: As you might have guessed, this chapter is all about how to create Java applications that interact with virtual Bluetooth devices. In this chapter, the entire Bluetooth network is simulated in software.

Chapter 9: Bluetooth Security: Chapter 9 covers the security measures provided by the Bluetooth specification in order to make wireless applications more secure.

Chapter 10: Wireless Embedded Systems with the Micro BlueTarget: The primary focus of Chapter 10 is the Micro BlueTarget by Smart Network Devices. In this chapter, we explore the possibilities of creating applications with a fully functional computer that fits in your hand and includes an implementation of the JSR-82.

Chapter 11: Enterprise Bluetooth Applications with the Ericsson BlipNet: In Chapter 11, we introduce you to enterprise Bluetooth applications and show you how to construct them using Java and the Ericsson BlipNet.

Chapter 12: Bluetooth and Jini: In the final chapter of the book, we provide an overview of Jini network technology and describe how to implement Jini and Bluetooth together.

Appendix A: javax.bluetooth: Appendix A is a handy reference that contains all the method signatures of the javax.bluetooth API.

Appendix B: javax.obex: Appendix B is a handy reference that contains all the method signatures of the javax.obex API.

Appendix C: Java Bluetooth Development on the PalmOS Platform: Appendix C provides a quick overview of how to get started creating Java Bluetooth applications on the Palm OS platform.

Appendix D: BlipNet 1.1 API: Appendix D contains full descriptions of the classes, exceptions, and interfaces that comprise the BlipNet API. This appendix will be really useful to have on hand when developing BlipNet applications.

Intended Audience

So who are you? This book really has two audiences. If you're a Java developer, then this book assumes that you're an intermediate Java developer with little or no experience with Bluetooth. You'll get the most out of this book if you've written a few Java classes on your own (especially J2ME applications).

If you're a Bluetooth developer, then this book becomes useful to you after Chapter 2. If you've never used Java before, then we'd suggest that you read the first few chapters of a J2ME book before you read this book.

The Code

The source code for this book is available at http://www.apress.com in the Downloads section. The book's companion Web site, http://www.javabluetooth.com, also contains the source code, as well as other useful resources such as a list of recommended Bluetooth hardware for running the examples.

CHAPTER 1

Introducing Bluetooth

SIMPLY STATED, BLUETOOTH is a wireless communication protocol. As such, you would use Bluetooth to communicate to two or more other Bluetooth-capable devices. In this sense, Bluetooth is like any other communication protocol that you may use every day like HTTP, FTP, SMTP, or IMAP. Bluetooth is also like these protocols in that it has a client-server architecture. In Bluetooth, the one who initiates the connection (the client) is the master, and the one who receives the connection (the server) is the slave.

The purpose of this chapter is to give you an introduction to Bluetooth. We'll briefly compare it with competing technologies like Infrared and 802.11b and explain where Bluetooth fills the gaps that these other technologies leave open. Next, we'll show you what Bluetooth can do and where it is currently used in applications today, just in case you're unfamiliar with the capabilities of the technology. Finally, we'll wrap up this chapter with a few scenarios for how Bluetooth will be used in the near future.

Bluetooth vs. Infrared

Of course, wireless communication between two computers is not new. PDAs have been able to do that for years using infrared technology. One drawback to infrared is that the devices involved must be a few feet apart, and most importantly, the infrared transceivers must see each other "eye to eye." If either of those conditions are not met, then the transmission will fail. Bluetooth overcomes the first limitation by having a nominal range of about 10 meters (30 feet). Bluetooth overcomes the second limitation because it works like a radio, so transmissions are omnidirectional. Consequently, there are no line-of-sight issues when communication occurs between two Bluetooth devices.

Bluetooth vs. 802.11b

If you've heard of Bluetooth before, then you've certainly heard of 802.11b (the wireless LAN protocol), another wireless communication protocol. Bluetooth and 802.11b were created to accomplish two different goals, although both technologies operate in the same frequency band: 2.4 GHz.

NOTE   *Having both technologies operate at the same frequency range does not mean they'll interfere when placed in range of each other, according to a Forrester Research study conducted in 2001. Go to* http://www.forrester.com/ *for details on that report.*

The goal of wireless LAN (802.11b) is to connect two relatively large devices that have lots of power at high speeds. Typically, this technology is used to connect two laptops within 300 feet at 11 Mb/s. This technology is also useful for network administrators who want to extend their LAN to places where it is either expensive or inconvenient to run cables.

On the other hand, Bluetooth is intended to connect smaller devices like PDAs and mobile phones within a range of 30 feet at a rate of 1 Mb/s. Slower data rates and shorter ranges allow Bluetooth to be a low-power wireless technology. Compared to 802.11b devices, some Bluetooth devices can easily consume 500 times less power, which can make a huge difference in the battery life of many mobile devices.

Bluetooth is also intended to be used as a cable replacement technology. If you have multiple peripherals connected to your computer using RS-232 or USB, then Bluetooth is the ideal solution if you want to use those devices wirelessly. It's almost impossible to connect peripherals to your computer using 802.11b technology (well, except for printers). Bluetooth even has a built-in capability for wireless audio communication.

Can either technology replace the other? Hardly. Bluetooth will never replace 802.11b because it's bad at handling the following:

- Large file transfers between devices

- Long-range communication (only Class 1 Bluetooth devices have a range of 300 feet)

CROSS-REFERENCE   *See "Bluetooth Device Power Classes" in Chapter 2 for details about power classes.*

On the other hand, 802.11b will never replace Bluetooth because

- 802.11b can't be used to communicate to peripherals.

- 802.11b requires too much power for communication.

- 802.11b is overkill for small data transfers.

- 802.11b wasn't designed for voice communication.

In the wireless communication arena, there is no technology that is best suited for every possible application. Either Bluetooth or 802.11b can be used for wireless communication between computers. Both have their place in the market and can perform in their niches well. Newer wireless LAN protocols like 802.11a and 802.11g will further clear the distinction between Bluetooth and wireless LAN because they extend 802.11b's bandwidth limitation to 54 Mb/s.

Bluetooth Devices on the Market Today

Now, let's take a look at Bluetooth devices that you can get at any consumer electronics store today. We'll highlight the problems that Bluetooth solves and give some scenarios for using this technology. If you're already familiar with common usage scenarios of Bluetooth devices, then feel free to skip this section.

Wireless Data Transfer: PDA to Phone

Almost everyone owns a mobile phone nowadays. These devices are very convenient, compact, and cute (well, at least some of them). However, they suffer from two major limitations:

- Mobile phones have limited memory for phone book entries.

- Data entry on mobile phones can be cumbersome.

We've all been there before. Entering data on a mobile phone is very tedious because you're dealing with a nine-button keypad to type alphanumeric text. Also, mobile phones don't have a lot of memory for storage, so you're limited to only 50 or 100 entries. On top of that, you'll also need to truncate some names when adding phone entries, so "Aunt Clarissa Johnson" becomes "Ant Clrssa Jnsn."

If you own a PDA, then you probably agree that PDAs are also useful devices. They can store thousands of contact entries, and they are a lot better for entering data compared to mobile phones. Since you can't store your entire contact list on your mobile phone, you probably have it stored on your PDA. Unfortunately, it's a little inconvenient to look up a phone number on the PDA and then manually dial the number on the mobile phone.

With a Bluetooth-enabled PDA and a Bluetooth-enabled mobile phone, you can keep your entire contact list on the PDA where it's far more convenient. Don't even bother to store phone numbers on your phone. Whenever you are ready to dial a number, you just look up the number on the PDA and send the phone number over to the phone; no wires, no hassle. Figure 1-1 is a picture of one of HP's advanced Bluetooth-enabled PDAs.

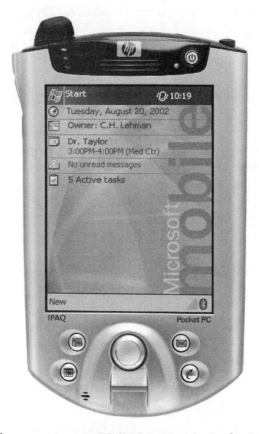

Figure 1-1. The short antennae on HP iPAQ 5400 series Pocket PC allows it to communicate via Bluetooth and 802.11b. For added security, this model also includes a fingerprint reader.

Connection Sharing: Laptop to Phone

If you're a programmer and you have a laptop, you know how cumbersome it is to get a dial-up Internet connection on your mobile phone. You may have an Internet-ready phone, but you may not have the right cable. Maybe you have the right cable (which isn't cheap), but you need additional software to establish the dial-up connection. Sometimes, you need to connect two cables together to accomplish this feat. Bluetooth eliminates all the hassle from this scenario by creating a standardized method for wireless dial-up networking. You can even keep your wireless phone at your hip or in your purse while you surf the Web on your laptop. The same applies for PCs or PDAs that want to use your phone to connect to the Internet. This is really convenient whenever your broadband connections at home go down for servicing. You can simply place your wireless phone in the vicinity of your PC and that's it, you're connected.

Personal Networks: PC to PC

Bluetooth is great for connecting two PCs together at a moderate speed. If you want higher speeds or if you need to transfer large files, then you're better off using Wireless LAN technology. On the other hand, Bluetooth is good at creating small, personal networks. So this is a great technology if you're having an impromptu meeting with coworkers. Bluetooth also has the added capability to discover new devices when they enter your network.

Cable Replacement: PC to Peripherals

You can imagine Bluetooth as functioning like any other protocol to connect to your peripherals, such as serial (RS-232), parallel, USB, or Firewire. In the near future, your personal computer will be equipped with a Bluetooth "port" in the same manner that it currently features a serial and USB port.

You can use Bluetooth to connect to your peripherals wirelessly and effortlessly. Have you ever been to a remote location with a laptop and wanted to use a printer to print out some files? If you don't have the right printer driver or the right cable, then you'll need to give your file to someone who does have it. If that person doesn't have the right program to read your file, then you're out of luck; no printing for you. If you had a Bluetooth laptop and that printer was a Bluetooth printer (regardless of the manufacturer), then you'd have no problem. With Bluetooth, you can ask the printer for the right driver if you don't have it, and then you can print your file with no problem.

The Power User

So what if you're a power user? You most likely have a PDA, a wireless phone, a printer or two, a scanner, an MP3 player, a digital camera, and a DV camera. The back of your computer probably looks like a rat's nest of wires and cables. Some devices you may leave disconnected until you really, really need them. Bluetooth solves all this by allowing you to have virtually an unlimited number of peripherals wirelessly connected to your computer. The only limitation is that you can only have seven active connections at the same time. That should be fine because it would be quite rare for you to print, scan, upload pictures, and sync your PDA all at the same time.

Interoperability: Any Device to Any Device

In the previous scenario, your non–Bluetooth-enabled devices are definitely not interoperable. In other words, if you want to send a picture from the camera to the PDA, then you'll need to use the computer to interconnect them. The same also goes if you want to scan a document and send it to the printer (i.e., to act like a copier) or send it to the PDA; you'll always need your PC to be the "man in the middle." Of course, you can buy a cable or two to do some of those tasks, but those cables are rare and expensive. Bluetooth solves all this by allowing your devices to communicate among themselves with no hassle and with no cables. It's essentially the universal cable!

Bluetooth in the Small Office or Home Office

In the small office setting, how do you share peripherals like a printer among users? Let's say you have a $300 printer that you want two users on your network to share. Your cheapest option is to buy a print server—but that's another $300! You might as well buy another printer for that kind of money. With Bluetooth, if both your users are in range, no print server is needed because both users can connect to the printer as if it were a local printer. For that matter, the printer should be able to print for every Bluetooth user within range; but remember that it can only handle seven active connections at the same time.

Bluetooth for Voice Applications

Now, Bluetooth is great at transferring data wirelessly, but it also has the capability to transmit voice and sound as well. So if you had a Bluetooth headset, you could use the same headset to answer calls on your Bluetooth-enabled wireless phone as well as answer calls on your Bluetooth-enabled home phone. You could also use the same headset to listen to your Bluetooth-enabled portable radio.

Bluetooth can also be enabled in your car so that if you're driving and you receive a call on your wireless phone, you can simply transfer the call to the hands-free system built right into the car. Your phone stays on your hip, or in your briefcase. You can also use the same technology to initiate a call in your car without touching your phone at all. In either case, if you've arrived at your destination and you want to continue the conversation, you just transfer the call back to the phone.

Bluetooth for Wireless Gaming

Of course, you can use Bluetooth for wireless gaming. It's always a hassle when you want to connect two handheld video game systems and play against a friend. Most cables were about 6 feet long, so if both players were on a school bus, they needed to sit right next to each other to play. With Bluetooth, you just have to come within range of your opponent to play.

Okay, we're grownups now. But what do you do if you're in a boring meeting and you have some time to kill? With Bluetooth, you and your equally bored colleague can both get out your PDAs and play a game of checkers. PDAs are business tools, so no one will ever know if you are taking down notes or getting double jumped. Figure 1-2 shows a Bluetooth-enabled mobile gaming device that could revolutionize the portable gaming industry: the Nokia N-Gage.

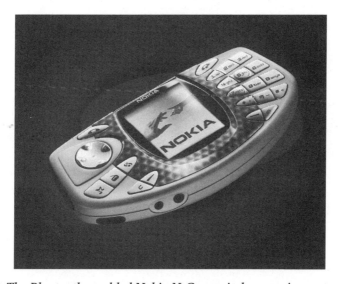

Figure 1-2. The Bluetooth-enabled Nokia N-Gage wireless gaming system

Devices of the Future

So, what kind of devices, applications, or innovations can we expect to see in the future that involve Bluetooth? Well, here are just a few that we can think of:

- Bluetooth locator system

- Personalized family car

- The new arcade: a restaurant lobby

The following sections describe these in more detail.

Bluetooth Locator System

Let's start off with a Bluetooth-enabled home, which means that wherever you go in your home, you are within range of the wireless network. With a Bluetooth-enabled home, you have the ultimate locator system. All your Bluetooth-enabled devices can never be misplaced if they are within the bounds of your home. If an item ever gets lost, all you need to do is go to your PC and start up the Bluetooth locator system program. For basic systems, you tell the program what device you are looking for, and the device will beep until it is found. For advanced systems, the Bluetooth locator system will display a map of your house and show you which room has your lost item. This solution is ideal for people who always misplace small but essential items like PDAs, wireless phones, keys, TV remotes, watches, and baby pacifiers!

Personalized Family Car

In this example, let's start off with a Bluetooth-enabled car. With a Bluetooth-enabled car, all you need to do is to set the mirrors, seats, and radio stations just once and store your preferences on a Bluetooth-enabled device that you carry with you all the time, like a wireless phone, PDA, or a watch. It wouldn't matter if someone else used your car, because all your preferences are stored on the device you keep with you. After someone uses your car, all you need to do is upload your preferences from your Bluetooth-enabled device (like your watch—see Figure 1-3) and be on your merry way.

Figure 1-3. Although the Fossil Wrist PDA doesn't contain any Bluetooth hardware, it does come preloaded with a Bluetooth-enabled OS: the Palm OS 4.1. Palm OS is a registered trademark of Palm, Inc.

The New Arcade: A Restaurant Lobby

Finally, let's say that sometime in the near future, you (and several other people) are waiting for a seat at a restaurant. While you are waiting for your table, the hostess gives you a little gaming device to help you kill time. This Bluetooth-enabled device not only lets you play games against the computer, but you can also play games with other people in the lobby! When your table is ready, your game unit vibrates automatically, so the hostess doesn't even need to call you. When you turn your device in to the hostess, your score is automatically uploaded to the high scores list. If your score is good enough, you may even win a free meal.

Summary

Bluetooth is a great technology for wireless connections between power-conservative computer devices. It is also a great cable replacement technology for PCs and laptops. It can function as a universal connector between your peripherals and devices, and you may never again need a cable (some of which can be expensive) to connect your devices together.

In the next chapter, we'll dig right in to the Bluetooth protocol. If you're new to Bluetooth, this will be your first introduction to a lot of new terminology. We'll explain to you the components of the Bluetooth stack and the purpose of Bluetooth profiles. When you create your wireless applications, you'll interact with the stack and profiles to send and receive data.

CHAPTER 2

Bluetooth 1.1

THE MAIN FOCUS OF THIS CHAPTER is to describe the inner workings of Bluetooth. The most current revision of the protocol is version 1.1. Almost every device on the market today is compliant with Bluetooth version 1.1, although you might be able to find some devices that use the 1.0B version of Bluetooth. The differences between Bluetooth 1.0B and 1.1 are beyond the scope of this book. The differences are minimal, and they really don't apply to Java programmers.

What can you expect for future versions of Bluetooth like 1.2 and 2.0? Whenever the Bluetooth SIG (the group of companies that developed the Bluetooth spec) plans to release later revisions of the spec, you can expect some things like higher speeds, more profiles, and backward compatibility with 1.1. We wouldn't expect the newer versions to try to compete with 802.11 speeds, but you might see data rates of 4, 8, or even 12 Mb/s. Bluetooth's niche is as a low-power wireless communication protocol, so don't expect Bluetooth 2.0 to be a power hog.

 CROSS-REFERENCE   *See Chapter 1 for a discussion of Bluetooth versus 802.11b.*

This chapter is all about Bluetooth. We'll give you brief history on how it began and how it got its name. Next, we'll show you the radio spectrum and where Bluetooth fits in with devices that you probably already know about. Afterwards, we'll describe the anatomy of a Bluetooth-enabled device by giving a description of Bluetooth hardware, the Bluetooth stack, and Bluetooth profiles. For the remainder of this book, when we refer to Bluetooth, we are referring to the 1.1 version of the spec. Now, let's dig in to Bluetooth!

A Brief History of Bluetooth

Bluetooth got its name from King Harald Blätand (Bluetooth) of Denmark. His most notable accomplishment was that he united Denmark and Norway under Christianity in the 10th century. In 1994, Ericsson conducted the first research studies of a wireless technology to link mobile phones and accessories. Years later in 1997, Ericsson formed the Bluetooth Special Interest Group (Bluetooth SIG) so that other companies could use and promote the technology. At that time, the Bluetooth SIG consisted of the following promoter companies:

- Ericsson

- IBM

- Intel

- Nokia

- Toshiba

Later on, in 1999 after the 1.0 specification was released, the Bluetooth SIG added four more members:

- 3Com

- Agere

- Microsoft

- Motorola

Today, the Bluetooth SIG has well over 2,000 members that are all interested in promoting and improving the Bluetooth standard.

The Radio Spectrum

Wireless communication between computers is either in the form of light or radio signals. Infrared technology is the common way to conduct short range wireless communications and obviously uses light. Conversely, Bluetooth technology uses radio signals. Table 2-1 gives a list of common everyday items that rely on radio signals for communication. As you can see, Bluetooth, cordless phones, 802.11b, and 802.11g fall in the 2.4 GHz range. Hopefully, this will demystify the Bluetooth concept if you are new to all this; it's just a radio.

Table 2-1. Common Radio Frequencies

ITEM	FREQUENCY RANGE
AM radio	535 kHz–1.6 MHz
Garage door openers	40 MHz
Baby monitors	49 MHz
TV channels 2–6	54 MHz–88 MHz
FM radio	88 MHz–108 MHz
TV channels 7–13	174 MHz–216 MHz
TV channels 14–83	512 MHz–806 MHz
CDMA cellular phone	824 MHz–894 MHz
GSM cellular phone	880 MHz–960 MHz
Cordless phones	900 MHz
Global Positioning System	1.227 GHz–1.575 GHz
PCS cellular phone	1.85 GHz–1.99 GHz
802.11b	2.4 GHz–2.483 GHz
802.11g	2.4 GHz–2.483 GHz
Bluetooth	2.4 GHz–2.483 GHz
Cordless phones	2.4 GHz
802.11a	5.15–5.35 GHz

Bluetooth Devices

So, if a Bluetooth device is just a radio, then what do these radios look like? Well, Figures 2-1, 2-2, and 2-3 are just a sample of devices that are Bluetooth radios. Some of these items are used in development kits, while others are meant to be used by consumers.

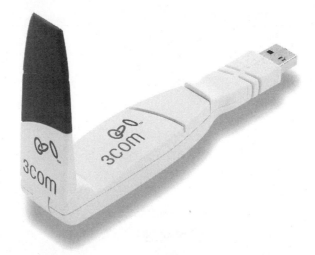

Figure 2-1. The 3COM USB Bluetooth module

*Figure 2-2. The CSR BlueCore 1. This single-chip solution includes
a microprocessor, RAM, I/O controller, and Bluetooth implementation in a single
package! This is most likely the smallest radio that you've ever seen.*

Figure 2-3. The Palm SD Bluetooth card for Palm OS 4 devices. Palm OS is a registered trademark of Palm, Inc.

The examples in this book will use a variety of Bluetooth devices from multiple vendors. The example in Chapter 8, however, uses no Bluetooth devices at all! In that example, we simulate the entire Bluetooth network in software using the Rococo Impronto Simulator.

Point-to-Point and Multipoint

One factor that distinguishes various Bluetooth devices is their connection capabilities. If a Bluetooth device can only support point-to-point communication, then it can only communicate to a single Bluetooth device at a time. Figure 2-4 demonstrates point-to-point communication in Bluetooth.

Figure 2-4. You can only connect to one Bluetooth device at a time if you have hardware that only supports point-to-point communication.

Now, point-to-point communication isn't necessarily a bad thing. If you have a Bluetooth phone, you really only need one connection to your Bluetooth phone. Frankly, it doesn't make sense to have multiple headsets be able to connect to your phone while you are using it.

On the other hand, a multipoint device is able to communicate with up to seven other devices at the same time. Figure 2-5 is a diagram of a multipoint device communicating to other devices within range using Bluetooth technology.

Figure 2-5. You can connect to up to seven Bluetooth devices at a time if you have multipoint-capable hardware.

Bluetooth Device Power Classes

Bluetooth hardware devices are broken up into three power classes. Table 2-2 describes the device classes and their capabilities.

Table 2-2. Bluetooth Device Power Classes

CLASS	POWER RATING	RANGE
Class 1	100 mW	100 meters
Class 2	2.5 mW	20 meters
Class 3	1 mW	10 meters

So as we stated in Chapter 1, Bluetooth devices are not limited to 10 meters in range.

CROSS REFERENCE   *See "Bluetooth vs. 802.11b" in Chapter 1 for details on the initial discussion of Bluetooth's range.*

How can you determine a Bluetooth device's power class, and thereby know its range? The power class is rarely printed on the unit, so here's a hint if you're trying to distinguish the power class of a device that you've never seen before. If that device is powered by batteries, or if it fits in your hand (like a wireless phone or a headset), then it is most likely a Class 2 or 3 device. If the Bluetooth device is built right into the hardware of another unit, and that unit is plugged into AC power, then it is most likely a Class 1 device.

Don't worry about Bluetooth device classes too much; just be aware that Bluetooth can communicate at greater distances than 10 meters.

The Bluetooth Protocol Stack

Your computer is a pretty powerful device. It has a processor, memory, bus, hard drive, and other neat things. The unfortunate thing is that the computer doesn't have the ability to use peripherals by itself. Common peripherals like CD/DVD drives, graphic displays, mice, keyboards, modems, printers, and scanners all need drivers. Your computer needs a driver to instruct it how to use a peripheral. By itself, the computer has no idea how to print to a printer or scan with a scanner. The computer is pretty powerful, but also pretty helpless. The device driver is the controlling agent that helps the computer to communicate with its peripherals.

The Bluetooth stack and Bluetooth hardware have a similar relationship. The Bluetooth stack is a controlling agent (it could be software, firmware, hardware, or a combination of all three) that implements the Bluetooth protocol and also allows you to control your Bluetooth device programmatically. The Bluetooth stack allows you to do these two things:

- Communicate with other Bluetooth devices

- Control your own Bluetooth device

So, if you're familiar with the HTTP protocol stack and how it works, then you can relate to the Bluetooth protocol stack. A Web browser uses an HTTP protocol stack so that it can receive Web content like HTML pages, images, files, and best of all, Java applets. A Web server also uses an HTTP protocol stack to send out Web content to Web browsers over the network. So, like the HTTP protocol stack, a Bluetooth protocol stack will allow Bluetooth clients and servers to send and receive data over a wireless network.

So how do the Bluetooth device and the Bluetooth stack work together? What is their relationship? Well, a Bluetooth device without a stack can be compared to a computer without an operating system. More specifically, it's like a computer peripheral without a driver. Figure 2-6 illustrates this concept.

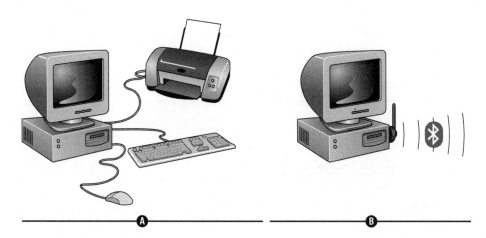

Figure 2-6. A) The computer may be attached to its peripherals, but it can't control them without a driver. B) The computer may be attached to a Bluetooth device, but it can't control it without a stack.

So, in order to communicate with the Bluetooth protocol and to control a Bluetooth radio, your computer uses a Bluetooth stack. Now, let's break down the Bluetooth stack into its individual components and see how they work. Each component of the stack is called a *layer*.

Layers of the Protocol Stack

For application developers, the Bluetooth protocol can be broken up into two main items: layers and profiles. All the layers of the Bluetooth protocol form the protocol stack. Figure 2-7 shows how the following layers of the Bluetooth protocol "stack up":

- Host Controller Interface (HCI)

- Logical Link Control and Adaptation Protocol (L2CAP)

- Service Discovery Protocol (SDP)

- RFCOMM

- Telephony Control Protocol Specification (TCS-BIN)

- Wireless Access Protocol (WAP)

- Object Exchange (OBEX)

- Bluetooth Network Encapsulation Protocol (BNEP)

- Human Interface Device Protocol (HID)

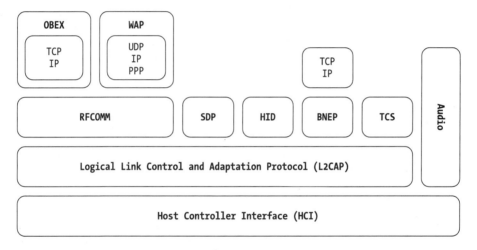

Figure 2-7. The Bluetooth protocol stack

 NOTE *Now, if you're familiar with the Java Collection Framework, then you've heard of* java.util.Stack. *Please erase that idea from your mind completely, or you'll be thoroughly confused here. Bluetooth uses some terms like stack and profile, which unfortunately are used in Java as well. This chapter is all about Bluetooth, so we'll clear up the confusion whenever there is a clash of terminology here.*

You may notice that some of these layers are called "protocols" as well. That's because these items are subprotocols of the Bluetooth protocol stack. Others like TCP/IP, OBEX, and WAP were not originated by the Bluetooth SIG, but they have been incorporated into the Bluetooth protocol. Those subprotocols are known as *adopted protocols*.

Host Controller Interface (HCI)

The Host Controller Interface is a layer of software that passes all your data from your computer to your attached Bluetooth device. For instance, if you are trying to communicate wirelessly from your PC (the host) and you have a Bluetooth device (the controller) attached to your USB port, then you'll need a layer that can understand the USB calls and send that information to the upper layers of the stack. Everything (voice and data) passes though the Host Controller Interface.

Logical Link Control and Adaptation Protocol (L2CAP)

The Logical Link Control and Adaptation Protocol is the core layer of the stack through which all data must pass. L2CAP boasts some powerful features like packet segmentation and reassembling of data, as well as protocol multiplexing. If you are trying to pass a very large packet of data, L2CAP breaks up the packet and sends smaller ones. Conversely, L2CAP also reassembles segmented packets when accepting data. With protocol multiplexing, L2CAP can accept data from more than one upper protocol at the same time (like SDP and RFCOMM). Only data passes through the L2CAP layer; audio links have direct access to the Host Controller Interface.

Service Discovery Protocol (SDP)

A Bluetooth device uses Service Discovery Protocol in order to discover services. What's a Bluetooth service? A good example would be a Bluetooth printer. A Bluetooth printer will publish itself with a message such as, "I am a printer, how can I help you?" If you have a document, and you want to print it, then you would use the Service Discovery Protocol to find a printer that offers a printer service in your range.

RFCOMM

RFCOMM is commonly known as the wireless serial port, or the cable replacement protocol. The name is derived from the fact that your serial ports are called COMM1, COMM2, etc. RFCOMM simulates the functionality of a standard serial port. For instance, a Bluetooth-enabled PDA would use the RFCOMM layer to synchronize its data to a Bluetooth-enabled PC as if they were physically connected by a cable.

Telephony Control Protocol Specification (TCS, TCS Binary, TCS-BIN)

Telephony Control Protocol Specification (TCS, TCS Binary, TCS-BIN) is used to send control signals to devices that want to employ the audio capabilities within Bluetooth. For example, a Bluetooth cordless phone would use this layer of the protocol to send signals to the base station indicating that the user has requested to hang up the current call, or to use call waiting, or to place a three-way call, etc.

Wireless Access Protocol (WAP)

If you've used an Internet-enabled wireless phone before, then you've used WAP. In Bluetooth, this is an adopted protocol, so the Bluetooth SIG has incorporated the existing WAP protocol into the Bluetooth protocol to fit Bluetooth's needs. WAP requires that PPP, IP, and UDP be present in the stack.

Object Exchange (OBEX)

OBEX is a communication protocol initially defined by the Infrared Data Association (IrDA). Unless you've worked with infrared, you've probably haven't heard of OBEX. Just like WAP, OBEX was defined by another group, but it was adopted by the Bluetooth SIG. OBEX is pretty useful when you want to transfer objects like files between Bluetooth devices. OBEX does not require that TCP and IP be present in the stack, but the manufacturer is free to implement OBEX over TCP/IP.

NOTE *A Bluetooth vendor does not need to implement all the Bluetooth protocol layers into its product in order to be Bluetooth compliant. For instance, a Bluetooth cordless phone may very well only have HCI, SDP, L2CAP, and TCS implemented into its stack. That's perfectly fine because a cordless phone may not need any extra functionality.*

Bluetooth Network Encapsulation Protocol (BNEP)

The Bluetooth Network Encapsulation Protocol is a layer in the Bluetooth stack that allows other networking protocols to be transmitted over Bluetooth, namely Ethernet. A Bluetooth vendor has many options if it wants to implement TCP/IP networking in its Bluetooth device. BNEP is a popular choice because it encapsulates TCP/IP packets in L2CAP packets before handing off the data to the L2CAP layer in the stack.

Human Interface Device Protocol (HID)

The Human Interface Device Protocol is another adopted protocol in the Bluetooth specification. It was originally defined in the USB specification, and it lists the rules and guidelines for transmitting information to and from human interface devices like keyboards, mice, remote controls, and video game controllers.

Table 2-3 is a handy guide that gives a brief description of the layers of the Bluetooth stack and their purpose.

Table 2-3. Layers of the Bluetooth Protocol Stack

SHORT NAME	FULL NAME	DESCRIPTION
HCI	Host Controller Interface	The layer that interfaces the host (i.e., the PC) and the controller (the Bluetooth module)
L2CAP	Logical Link Control and Adaptation Protocol	The layer that handles all data transmissions from upper layers
SDP	Service Discovery Protocol	The layer that discovers services on Bluetooth devices in the area
RFCOMM	RFCOMM	The layer that allows you to create a virtual serial port and to stream data
TCS-BIN	Telephony Control Protocol Specification	The layer that allows you to create control signals for audio applications
WAP	Wireless Access Protocol	The adopted protocol that allows you to view content in Wireless Markup Language (WML)
OBEX	Object Exchange	The adopted protocol that allows you to send and receive objects
BNEP	Bluetooth Network Encapsulation Protocol	The layer that encapsulates other protocol data packets into L2CAP packets
HID	Human Interface Device Protocol	The layer that traffics the controls signals and data for input devices like keyboards and mice

 NOTE *For an exhaustive list of all the new and upcoming Bluetooth protocols, go to the Bluetooth Member site at* `http://www.bluetooth.org`.

Profiles

So, let's say that you own a Bluetooth-enabled PDA and a Bluetooth-enabled wireless phone. Both of the devices have Bluetooth stacks. How can you tell if your devices will interact properly and allow you to synchronize the phone lists between each other? How will you know if you can send a phone number from the PDA to the phone? And most importantly, how can you determine if these devices will allow you to browse the Internet on the PDA using the phone as a wireless modem?

That's why the Bluetooth SIG defined profiles. A Bluetooth *profile* is a designed set of functionality for Bluetooth devices. For instance, using the examples just listed, the phone and the PDA must both support the Synchronization Profile in order to synchronize data between themselves. In order to send object data like a .vcf file from the PDA to the phone, both devices need to have the Object Push Profile implemented. And finally, the PDA and the wireless phone must both support the Dial-Up Networking Profile in order for the PDA to wirelessly browse the Internet from the phone. If you want your Bluetooth-enabled devices to interact, having a Bluetooth stack is not good enough. Those devices also need to implement the same profile.

Now, here's a list of many of the Bluetooth profiles and a description of what they do. For most of them, you can basically guess what they do; the names are not cryptic.

 NOTE   *For an exhaustive list of all the Bluetooth profiles, go to the Bluetooth Member site at* http://www.bluetooth.org.

Generic Access Profile

The Generic Access Profile is the most common Bluetooth profile. All other profiles use this profile for basic connection establishment. This is the java.lang.Object in the Bluetooth Profile realm; every profile needs to use the functionality of the GAP.

Service Discovery Application Profile

The Service Discovery Application Profile is a profile that directly interacts with the Service Discovery Protocol (SDP) layer in the Bluetooth protocol stack. This profile is used to find services on Bluetooth-enabled devices in the area.

Serial Port Profile

The Serial Port Profile is a profile that interacts directly with the RFCOMM layer in the Bluetooth protocol stack. This profile is used to create a virtual serial port on your Bluetooth-enabled device. For instance, some Bluetooth kits come with a driver that will allow your operating system to communicate over the virtual serial port as if it were an actual serial port. As far as the operating system is concerned, it's just another serial port, as shown in Figure 2-8.

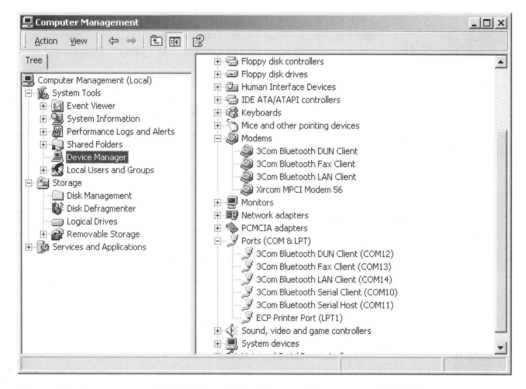

Figure 2-8. As you can see in Windows 2000, the operating system thinks that COMM10 and COMM11 are actual serial ports!

 NOTE *Of course, if you want to connect to another device over the air using your virtual serial port, then you'll need another Bluetooth-enabled device in the area that also supports the Serial Port Profile.*

Dial-Up Networking Profile

If you've used a modem before, then you should be familiar with the concept of dial-up networking. The Dial-Up Networking Profile allows you to mimic the functionality of a modem. Just like the Serial Port Profile, some Bluetooth kits come with a driver that will allow your operating system to communicate over the virtual modem as if it were an actual modem (see Figure 2-8). As far as the operating system is concerned, it's just another modem.

 NOTE *For such an example to work, you'll need another Bluetooth-enabled device in the area that also supports the Dial-Up Networking Profile, like a network access point or a wireless phone.*

FAX Profile

Using the FAX Profile, a Bluetooth-enabled computer can send a fax wirelessly to a Bluetooth-enabled fax machine or to a Bluetooth-enabled wireless phone.

Headset Profile

The Headset Profile is primarily designed for connecting Bluetooth-enabled headsets to Bluetooth-enabled wireless phones.

LAN Access Profile

A Bluetooth-enabled device such as a PC or laptop will use the LAN Access Profile to connect to a network access point connected to a LAN.

Personal Area Networking Profile

The Personal Area Networking Profile is pretty much similar to the LAN Access Profile, except it also has support for devices to form ad-hoc networks among themselves. The PAN Profile also has a requirement that BNEP be present in the underlying protocol stack.

Cordless Telephony Profile

The Cordless Telephony Profile allows you to use a Bluetooth-enabled handset to connect to a Bluetooth-enabled "landline" phone to place calls. For instance, through this profile, you continue to receive calls to your home phone, but you have the convenience of answering that call on your Bluetooth wireless phone, without using the minutes of the calling plan of your wireless phone.

Intercom Profile

If two Bluetooth-enabled devices are within range, and they support the Intercom Profile, then they can function just like regular intercoms.

Generic Object Exchange Profile

The Generic Object Exchange Profile is the generic profile that all profiles use if they want to employ the functionality of the OBEX protocol in the Bluetooth stack.

Object Push Profile

The Object Push Profile provides the functionality for a device to push and pull an object. Using this profile, though, you are limited to a certain class of objects like vCards.

File Transfer Profile

The File Transfer Profile is a more robust profile for transferring objects. You can use the File Transfer Profile to transfer files and folders from one Bluetooth-enabled device to another.

Synchronization Profile

You use the Synchronization Profile to synchronize data between two Bluetooth-enabled devices. The most common applications for this profile would be to synchronize data between a PDA and a PC.

Basic Printing Profile

The Basic Printing Profile allows a Bluetooth-enabled device to send plain text to a Bluetooth-enabled printer for printing.

Hard Copy Cable Replacement Profile

The Hard Copy Cable Replacement Profile is what we call the "Advanced Printing Profile." With this profile, you can print any printable document to a Bluetooth-enabled printer. If you don't already have the driver for that printer, that's okay; the printer will give it to you.

Basic Imaging Profile

The Basic Imaging Profile is intended to be used by imaging devices like cameras for remote control, image transfers, and downloading.

Hands Free Profile

The Bluetooth-enabled hands-free kits in automobiles use the Hands Free Profile to allow the driver to place and receive calls from a Bluetooth-enabled phone.

Human Interface Device Profile

As you might have guessed, the Human Interface Device Profile has a requirement that the HID Protocol must exist in the underlying Bluetooth stack. This profile defines the case scenarios for using Bluetooth-enabled human interface devices like keyboards and mice. One of the goals of this profile is that a Bluetooth-enabled device that conforms to the HID Profile should run for three months on three AAA alkaline batteries.

Profile Interdependencies

The profiles are heavily dependent upon each other, and you should already know that every profile depends upon the Generic Access Profile. The Bluetooth profiles were designed to be building blocks, where a higher level profile is dependent upon the functionality of the lower profiles to exist. Take a look at Figure 2-9 and see how the Bluetooth profiles are dependent upon each other for functionality.

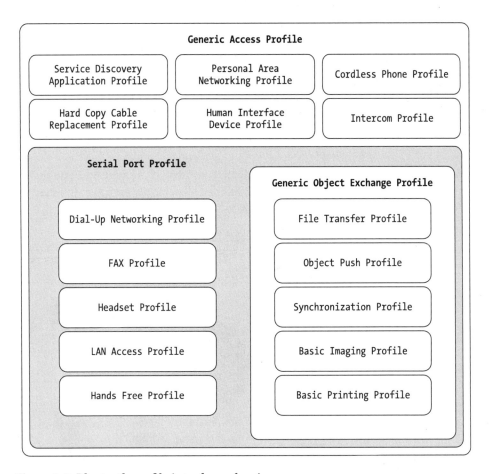

Figure 2-9. Bluetooth profile interdependencies

For example, in order for a PDA vendor to say that it supports the Synchronization Profile for its new Bluetooth-enabled BJL 200 PDA, it also must support the Generic Object Exchange Profile, Serial Port Profile, and Generic Access Profile because the Synchronization Profile cannot function without them. If a phone manufacturer claims that its new Bluetooth-enabled TLJ 50 headset supports the Headset Profile, then it must also include the Serial Port Profile and the Generic Access Profile.

Bluetooth Profiles vs. J2ME Profiles

Do not get Bluetooth profiles confused with J2ME profiles. J2ME profiles are a set of Java classes that extend the functionality of a J2ME Configuration. For instance, the PDA and MID Profiles are both a set of Java classes that extend the functionality of the Connected Limited Device Configuration. On the other hand, a Bluetooth profile can be implemented in any language and on any platform, because it refers to a defined set of functionality for a Bluetooth-enabled device. So, the Object Push Profile can be implemented on a Palm OS PDA in C++, and it can also be implemented on a Bluetooth-enabled printer in Assembler; it's just a defined set of functionality.

Personal Area Networks: Piconets and Scatternets

When two or more Bluetooth-enabled devices come within range and establish a connection, a *personal area network* is formed. A personal area network can either be a piconet or a scatternet. Figure 2-10 shows Bluetooth devices in a piconet.

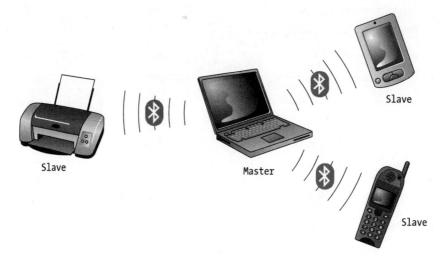

Figure 2-10. In a piconet, the slaves can only communicate to the master.

A Bluetooth *piconet* has a single master and up to seven slaves. No matter what kind of Bluetooth devices are involved (they can be phones, access points, PDAs, laptops, headsets, etc.), the master of the piconet is the one that initiates the connection. The device that accepts the connection automatically becomes the slave. Master/slave roles are not predefined, so if a piconet exists between a laptop and a PDA, either device could be the master or the slave.

NOTE *In certain conditions, a role switch between the master and slave is allowed. These conditions are explained in the Bluetooth specification.*

So what happens to the piconet if a new Bluetooth device wants to join the piconet after the master has acquired seven slaves? Does it shut down? Will older members of the piconet get kicked off? No, actually, the master of the piconet will not invite new members to join until at least one the old members leaves (or goes into an inactive state). Now, on the other hand, if one of the slaves in the Bluetooth piconet also happens to be multipoint-capable, then the newcomer can create a piconet with that slave, thereby creating a *scatternet* (as shown in Figure 2-11). A scatternet will also be created if the master of the existing piconet becomes a slave to the newcomer.

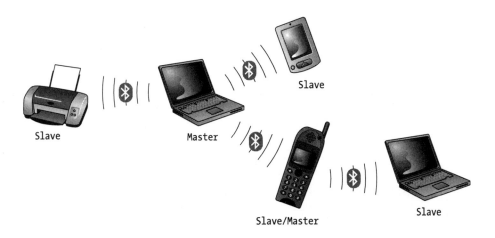

Figure 2.11. A scatternet is formed when a slave in one piconet is the master in another piconet.

The Bluetooth Qualification Process

Okay, so what does it take to turn a product that uses Bluetooth technology into an official Bluetooth-certified product? Well, you first need to join the Bluetooth SIG. How do you join? Just go to http://www.bluetooth.org and fill out the membership form. After becoming a member, you need to submit your product for testing by a Bluetooth Qualification Body. The Qualification Body will test your device against the current Bluetooth specification as well as interoperability with other devices that use your Bluetooth profiles.

> **NOTE** *Java developers really don't need to join the Bluetooth SIG or undergo the qualification process if pre-qualified Bluetooth materials (i.e., stacks and radios) are used in their products. However, if you want to use that really cool-looking Bluetooth logo on your products, then you need to join the SIG.*

Once testing has been completed, and if your device passes the tests, it will be listed on the Bluetooth Qualification Web site (`http://qualweb.bluetoothsig.org`). Most companies will postpone announcing their new Bluetooth-enabled product until it has been certified, so check that site often to see "who's doing what" in Bluetooth.

Summary

In this chapter you learned all about Bluetooth devices, and you found out what they look like. By now, you should also know about the role of the Bluetooth protocol stack and how it interacts with your Bluetooth hardware. You should take away from this chapter a finite knowledge of Bluetooth profiles, and you should know the purpose that they serve. Finally, you should be aware of the difference between piconets and scatternets, and you should know what it takes to get a Bluetooth device certified.

Great! You now should have a good understanding of how the Bluetooth protocol works. In the next chapter, we'll see what happens when we throw in Java.

CHAPTER 3

Before You Get Started

Okay, now that you know the ins and outs of Bluetooth, you're probably eager to find out how to integrate Bluetooth with Java. Well, this chapter is all about doing just that. But wait! Before you learn about how to use Bluetooth and Java, you need to know when it is not a good idea to use the two technologies together.

When NOT to Use Bluetooth and Java

You should not use Bluetooth with Java for the following purposes:

- Signal strength indicator

- Voice applications

- Distance measuring

The next few sections explain why to avoid those scenarios.

Signal Strength Indicator

Let's say that you have two Bluetooth units, and you want to know what the signal strength is between them. A good example is when you want to use the services of a network access point. A signal strength indicator would let you know if you were within range. Well, Java is not the ideal language for that sort of application because that kind of information is not exposed to the level where a JVM would have access to it. The JVM will let you know if you are within range or not within range; there is no middle ground. In this scenario, you're better off using a native language for your device such as C or C++.

Voice Applications

Now, you've already read Chapter 2, and you realize that Bluetooth is a really great technology because you have the ability to transmit voice and data information wirelessly to other Bluetooth devices. Suddenly, you get ideas bubbling in your head about how great it would be to create a speech-to-text application on your Bluetooth-enabled phone. Unfortunately, Java (especially J2ME) is not well suited to this arena just yet. Performance is a key factor in voice-based applications, and once again, in this case, you're better off using a native language such as C. However, this application may be feasible to do in Java if the Java Real-Time Technology can be incorporated.

Distance Measuring

The best wireless technology for accurately measuring distance is light waves and not radio signals. Light waves are direct, and the calculations can be pretty simple because the speed of light (in various mediums) is pretty well documented. Using radio signals to measure distance can be quite tricky, and one of the best ways to do that is to use triangulation, like GPS transceivers do. Whether you are using Java or C, Bluetooth might be a viable technology for triangulation, but definitely not for calculating or measuring accurate distances.

NOTE *The key word here is accurate. You can definitely use Bluetooth for proximity measurement (i.e., where in the building is Bruce Hopkins?). In fact, the Ericsson BlipNet does exactly that! See Chapter 11 for more information on the Ericsson BlipNet.*

So, to put it succinctly, you can only do what is possible using the constraints of the Bluetooth technology and what the JVM exposes to you. If the JVM only gives you access to the RFCOMM layer for communication, then you're stuck with it. If the OBEX layer is not exposed to the JVM, then don't expect to be able to send objects. To increase application portability, your Java Bluetooth vendor should implement the Java Bluetooth specification created through the JCP.

Understanding the JCP

The JCP is the Java Community Process, and it is the formal procedure to get an idea from a simple concept incorporated into the Java standard. This process allows developers and industry experts to shape the future of the Java standard. Popular APIs like Java USB, Java Real-Time, Java Printing, Java New I/O, J2ME MIDP 1.0, J2ME MIDP 2.0, JDBC 3.0, EJB 2.0, and even JDK 1.4 all went through the Java Community Process. If you want to add some new functionality to the Java language, or if you want to suggest a new API, or if you think that some new classes should have a package name of java.* or javax.*, then you need to go through the JCP.

The Role of the JSR-82

A JSR is a Java Specification Request in the Java Community Process. The JSR-82 is the formal JCP name for the Java APIs for Bluetooth. When a proposed JSR is approved, an Expert Group is formed by the specification lead. The specification lead for the JSR-82 was Motorola, and together with the JSR-82 Expert Group, they created the official Java Bluetooth APIs. The following companies participated in the JSR-82 Expert Group:

- Extended Systems

- IBM

- Mitsubishi

- Newbury Networks

- Nokia

- Parthus Technologies

- Research in Motion (RIM)

- Rococo Software

- Sharp Electronics

- Sony Ericsson

- Smart Fusion

- Smart Network Devices

- Sun Microsystems

- Symbian

- Telecordia

- Vaultus

- Zucotto

The JSR-82 Expert Group also had three individual experts: Peter Dawson, Steven Knudsen, and Brad Threatt.

What Is the RI and TCK?

According to the Java Community process, the specification lead company is responsible for creating a Reference Implementation (RI) and also a Technology Compatibility Kit (TCK). The Reference Implementation is basically a proof of concept to prove that the specification can be implemented. Other companies are free to implement the JSR-82, and in order to certify that their vendor kit is compliant to the JSR-82 standard, that vendor's product must pass the TCK.

The JSR-82 specification actually has two Reference Implementations and Technology Compatibility Kits. Why did they do this? Recall in Chapter 2 that the Bluetooth SIG has adopted some preexisting protocols in the Bluetooth specification, namely OBEX. The OBEX protocol was used with infrared technology for object transmissions long before Bluetooth was even invented. The designers of the Java Bluetooth specification decided not to tie OBEX to Bluetooth when creating the Java Bluetooth standard. Therefore, the JSR-82 actually consists of two independent packages:

- `javax.bluetooth` (the 13 classes and interfaces that are needed to perform wireless communication with the Bluetooth protocol)

- `javax.obex` (the 8 classes that are needed to send objects between devices, independent of the transport mechanism between them)

So, to answer your next question, yes, you can use OBEX without Bluetooth. Bluetooth is simply one of many transports with which OBEX can operate.

The classes and interfaces that comprise the Java Bluetooth specification are briefly described in Tables 3-1 and 3-2. These classes and their methods are covered as needed in the following chapters, and their APIs are listed in detail in Appendix A and Appendix B.

Table 3-1. Classes in the javax.bluetooth Package

CLASS NAME	DESCRIPTION
DiscoveryListener	The DiscoveryListener interface allows an application to receive device discovery and service discovery events.
L2CAPConnection	The L2CAPConnection interface represents a connection-oriented L2CAP channel.
L2CAPConnectionNotifier	The L2CAPConnectionNotifier interface provides an L2CAP connection notifier.
ServiceRecord	The ServiceRecord interface describes characteristics of a Bluetooth service.
DataElement	The DataElement class defines the various data types that a Bluetooth service attribute value may have.
DeviceClass	The DeviceClass class represents the class of device (CoD) record as defined by the Bluetooth specification.
DiscoveryAgent	The DiscoveryAgent class provides methods to perform device and service discovery.
LocalDevice	The LocalDevice class represents the local Bluetooth device.
RemoteDevice	The RemoteDevice class represents a remote Bluetooth device.
UUID	The UUID class defines universally unique identifiers.
BluetoothConnectionException	This BluetoothConnectionException is thrown when a Bluetooth connection (L2CAP, RFCOMM, or OBEX) cannot be established successfully.
BluetoothStateException	The BluetoothStateException is thrown when a request is made to the Bluetooth system that the system cannot support in its present state.
ServiceRegistrationException	The ServiceRegistrationException is thrown when there is a failure to add a service record to the local Service Discovery Database (SDDB) or to modify an existing service record in the SDDB.

Table 3-2. Classes in the javax.obex Package

CLASS NAME	DESCRIPTION
Authenticator	This interface provides a way to respond to authentication challenge and authentication response headers.
ClientSession	The ClientSession interface provides methods for OBEX requests.
HeaderSet	The HeaderSet interface defines the methods that set and get the values of OBEX headers.
Operation	The Operation interface provides ways to manipulate a single OBEX PUT or GET operation.
SessionNotifier	The SessionNotifier interface defines a connection notifier for server-side OBEX connections.
PasswordAuthentication	This class holds user name and password combinations.
ResponseCodes	The ResponseCodes class contains the list of valid response codes a server may send to a client.
ServerRequestHandler	The ServerRequestHandler class defines an event listener that will respond to OBEX requests made to the server.

The Benefits of the Java Bluetooth API

There are two key advantages to using the official Java Bluetooth API versus a C-based (or native) API:

- API is independent of the stack and radio

- Standardized Bluetooth API

API Is Independent of Stack and Radio

So what makes the official Java Bluetooth API better than a C/C++ Bluetooth API? One of the principle reasons is that the JSR-82 API is independent of the stack and the Bluetooth hardware. That gives you the ability to write applications without any knowledge of the underlying Bluetooth hardware or stack. And that's essentially what Java gives you today. If you write standard Java code (without any native methods), you can run your code on basically any hardware platform and on any OS with little or no modification. Whether it's an appli-cation, applet, midlet, servlet, or EJB, you can code your application on one platform and deploy to another platform.

The Only Standardized Bluetooth API

If you have a C/C++-based Bluetooth SDK, then you are basically at the mercy of the vendor. There is no standard for a C/C++-based Bluetooth SDK, so each vendor is free to name functions and methods to whatever they choose. Vendor A may have five profiles in its SDK, and Vendor B may only have three. If you want to change Bluetooth hardware or stack libraries, then you'll need to rewrite your Bluetooth application and/or change its functionality. Because the JSR-82 is the official Java API for Bluetooth, all vendors who implement the standard must include a core set of layers and profiles in their Bluetooth SDK.

A JSR-82–compliant Bluetooth stack must include the following layers:

- Host Controller Interface (HCI)

- Logical Link Control and Adaptation Protocol (L2CAP)

- Service Discovery Protocol (SDP)

- RFCOMM

These profiles are also required:

- Generic Access Profile

- Service Discovery Application Profile

- Serial Port Profile

- Generic Object Exchange Profile

CROSS-REFERENCE *See "The Bluetooth Protocol Stack" and "Profiles" in Chapter 2 for details on the Bluetooth protocol stack and profiles just in case you forgot.*

The first thing that may come to your mind is, "Hey, wait a minute, doesn't the Bluetooth specification contain more profiles than that? Why did they implement only a few profiles in Java?" Well, here are two major reasons:

First of all, the JSR-82 team wanted to get the Java Bluetooth specification in the hands of developers as quickly as possible. Recall in Chapter 2 that Bluetooth profiles are designed to be functional enough where higher profiles extend the functionality of the lower, or base, profiles. Refer to Figure 2-9, which shows a diagram of the relationship of the profiles of the Bluetooth specification.

Secondly, by implementing the base profiles (Generic Access Profile, Service Discovery Application Profile, Serial Port Profile, and Generic Object Exchange Profile), the SDK vendor or the application developer is free to implement the higher profiles of the Bluetooth specification.

What You Need to Get Started

We know that this question has been on your mind for a while. Well, here's a list of what you'll need:

- Bluetooth devices (at least two)

- Bluetooth host (at least one)

- Bluetooth stack

- Java Bluetooth API

Now let's cover all these components in detail and describe how they all work together.

Bluetooth Devices

Bluetooth devices were covered in Chapter 2, but just in case you forgot, take another look at Figures 2-1, 2-2, and 2-3. Remember, Bluetooth devices are simply radios, so getting a single device is just like getting a single walkie talkie; it's pretty useless. If your Bluetooth device is point-to-point capable, then that means it can only talk to a single Bluetooth device at a time. If it is multipoint capable, then it can talk to up to seven devices at a time. The Bluetooth device is also known as the *controller*.

Bluetooth Host

The Bluetooth *host* is the computer that is physically connected to the Bluetooth device. For the most part, this is your desktop PC, laptop, PDA, or smart phone. Usually, the connection is USB, RS-232, or UART.

Now, you are definitely going to need two Bluetooth devices, but you can get away with having only one Bluetooth host. How does this work? Well, if you have a PC that has two serial ports or two USB ports (or both), then you can connect both of your Bluetooth devices to your PC's ports. In order for this to work, you need to start two instances of your JVM; each JVM will have its own Bluetooth device.

The Bluetooth host must meet the minimum requirements for the CLDC, so you need at least 512k total memory for the JVM.

Bluetooth Stack

A Bluetooth stack is required in order for a Bluetooth host (the PC) to properly communicate to the Bluetooth device (the controller). If you go back to Figure 2-6, which shows a diagram of the Bluetooth stack, the bottom layer of the stack is the Host Controller Interface! See, it does make sense. The Host Controller Interface is literally the software required to interface the Bluetooth host and the Bluetooth device (the controller).

Since this book is all about Java and Bluetooth, you might think that the Bluetooth stack needs to be written completely in the Java language. Well, not exactly. Some Bluetooth vendors have implemented a completely all-Java stack, while others have implemented a Java interface (i.e., JNI or other means) to a native stack. Either way, you need to access the stack through Java code, whether or not the stack is in Java.

Java Bluetooth API

Finally, you're going to need a set of libraries to interface with your stack. For the most part, a company will sell you a Java Bluetooth API and Bluetooth stack together in a kit. Just be sure to ask them what Bluetooth devices their kit supports.

Another question to ask your Java Bluetooth kit vendor is if their product is JSR-82 compliant. Currently, JSR-82 can only be implemented on the J2ME platform. JSR-82 cannot be implemented on the J2SE platform because the J2SE does not support the Generic Connection Framework. Hopefully, the Generic Connection Framework will be implemented by JDK 1.5.

NOTE *The official JSR to implement the GCF in the JDK is JSR-197.*

Does this mean that it is impossible to do Java and Bluetooth development on the J2SE platform? No, it simply means that whatever Java Bluetooth kit that you obtain for J2SE will not be compliant with JSR-82 until the Generic Connection Framework is implemented in J2SE. The major ramification of this problem is that your J2ME and J2SE code may be drastically different from each other, even if you are doing the same thing.

Java Bluetooth Vendor SDKs

So, who's offering Java Bluetooth SDKs, and which are JSR-82 compliant? Fortunately, there is a plethora of Java Bluetooth SDKs to fit the needs that your application requires. Vendor support is available for Java Bluetooth development on a wide range of operating systems and JVM platforms. Table 3-3 displays various attributes of many Java Bluetooth SDKs.

Table 3-3. Java Bluetooth SDK Vendors*

COMPANY NAME	JSR-82 JAVAX.BLUETOOTH SUPPORT	JSR-82 JAVAX.OBEX SUPPORT	SUPPORTED JAVA PLATFORMS	SUPPORTED OPERATING SYSTEMS
Atinav	Yes	Yes	J2ME, J2SE	Win-32, Linux, Pocket PC
BlueGiga	No	No	Waba JVM	uClinux
Ericsson	No	No	J2SE	Win-32, Linux
Esmertec	Yes	No	J2ME	Win-32, Palm OS, Pocket PC, many others
Harald	No	No	J2SE	Win-32, Linux, others
Possio	Yes	Yes	J2ME	Win-32, Linux
Rococo	Yes	Yes	J2ME, J2SE	Win-32, Linux, Palm OS, Pocket PC
Smart Network Devices	Yes	No	J2ME	HyNetOS
SuperWaba	No	No	Waba JVM	Palm OS
Zucotto	No	No	J2ME, J2SE	Win-32

* The information in this table is subject to change, so check the companion Web site
http://www.javabluetooth.com for up-to-date information. Palm OS is a registered trademark of Palm, Inc.

Summary

This chapter has only skimmed the surface of how to integrate Java Bluetooth. You learned about the advantages of using Java versus C for application development. You also learned about JSR-82 as well as what it takes to get things up and running.

In the next chapter, we'll focus more on integrating Java and Bluetooth, as well as introduce some example code.

CHAPTER 4

Understanding the Java Bluetooth API

THIS CHAPTER WILL BE your formal introduction to the Java Bluetooth API. We'll cover a vast majority of the classes in the javax.bluetooth package and examine how to use them in your applications. Rather than looking at every class and interface individually, we'll take a different approach by first looking at the basic components of a typical Bluetooth application (Java or otherwise). After we have identified these components, we'll explain how to use the Java Bluetooth API in order to create wireless applications.

The Basic Components of a Bluetooth Application

The basic components of any Bluetooth application consist of the following items:

- Stack initialization

- Device management

- Device discovery

- Service discovery

- Service registration

- Communication

The Java Bluetooth specification adds a special component to the mix called the *Bluetooth Control Center* (BCC). We'll talk about the BCC in the next section because in some vendor implementations, stack initialization is handled through the BCC.

The Bluetooth Control Center

The Bluetooth Control Center is an awkward beast due to its ambiguity. It is required to exist in a JSR-82 compliant implementation, but there are no guidelines in the official Java Bluetooth specification about how it should be implemented. One vendor could implement the BCC as a set of Java classes, and another vendor could implement it as a native application on the Bluetooth host. But no matter how it is implemented, it is an integral part of your security architecture because the BCC defines device-wide security settings for your Bluetooth device.

Now, for the most part, if you are working with a JSR-82–compliant Java Bluetooth development kit within your development environment, then the BCC will probably be implemented as one or more Java classes. But because the BCC is vendor specific, the classes that form the BCC will not have a javax.bluetooth package name; they will be in the form of something like com.vendor.bluetooth.bcc. Now, if you're working with a device that comes with the Java Bluetooth standard (like a mobile phone or a PDA), then there is a high probability that the BCC would be implemented as a native application on that device.

According to the Java Bluetooth specification, these are the requirements of the BCC:

- Include base security settings of the device.

- Provide a list of Bluetooth devices that are already known. The devices do not need to be within range.

- Provide a list of Bluetooth devices that are already trusted. The devices do not need to be within range.

- Provide a mechanism to pair two devices trying to connect for the first time.

- Provide a mechanism to provide for authorization of connection requests.

- Information contained in the BCC must not be modified or altered other than by the BCC itself.

Depending upon the JSR-82 implementation that you're using, the BCC may need to be packaged and deployed with your application code.

Stack Initialization

Now before you can do anything, your stack needs to be initialized. Remember, a Bluetooth stack has direct access to the underlying Bluetooth device. Stack initialization can consist of a number of things, but its main purpose is to get the Bluetooth device ready to start wireless communication. Stack initialization sequences can vary, and it's heavily dependent upon the underlying OS and Bluetooth radio. In some cases (in particular, with the Rococo Palm DK) no code is needed at all to initialize your stack. In other cases, you'll need to write a bit of code to get your stack initialized because you need to specify baud rates for your RS-232 interface.

For instance, Listing 4-1 shows the snippet of code that you would need in order to initialize your stack if you were using the Atinav SDK with a RS-232–based Bluetooth device.

Listing 4-1. Stack Initialization Code for the Atinav SDK

```
import com.atinav.bcc.*;
...
BCC.setPortName("COM1");
BCC.setBaudRate(57600);
BCC.setConnectable(true);
BCC.setDiscoverable(DiscoveryAgent.GIAC);
...
```

Esmertec takes a different approach for stack initialization. Their JSR-82 implementation and stack tends to be used mostly by wireless device OEMs. Listings 4-2 and 4-3 show the Java classes that would be part of a startup sequence to initialize the stack for the entire device. After the device has started (which consequently means that the stack is also initialized), other Java applications that reside on the device no longer need to include code to initialize the stack.

Listing 4-2. BluetoothSetup1.java

```
import com.jbed.bluetooth.*;
import java.io.IOException;

public class BluetoothSetup1 {

    private static int device;
    private static BCC myBCC;
```

```
        static {
            device = DeviceProperties.DEVICE_1;
            try {
                myBCC = BCC.getInstance();
                myBCC.startUp(device);

                myBCC.initDriver();
                System.out.println("Bluetooth Started");
            } catch (IOException exc) {
                System.out.println("IOException: " + exc.getMessage());
                exc.printStackTrace();
                System.out.println("Bluetooth Probably NOT Started   ");
            }
        }
    }
}
```

Listing 4-3. DeviceProperties.java

```
import com.jbed.bluetooth.*;
import com.jbed.bluetooth.HciTransport;
import java.util.Hashtable;

public final class DeviceProperties {

    public static final int DEFAULT = 0;
    public static final int ERICSSON = 1;
    public static final int CSR = 2;
    public static final int SILICONWAVE = 3;
    public static final int NON_SECURE_MODE_1 = 1;
    public static final int SERVICE_LEVEL_MODE_2 = 2;
    public static final int LINK_LEVEL_MODE_3 = 3;
    public static final int TRUSTED_DEVICE = 0;
    public static final int UNTRUSTED_DEVICE = 1;
    public static final int UNKNOWN_DEVICE = 2;
    public static final int AUTHORISATION_REQUIRED = 0x1;
    public static final int AUTHENTICATION_REQUIRED = 0x2;
    public static final int ENCRYPTION_REQUIRED = 0x4;
    static int SERVICE_TABLE_SIZE = 32;
    static int DEVICE_TABLE_SIZE = 8;
    public static final int DEVICE_1 = 0;
    public static final int DEVICE_2 = 1;
    static int NAP_GN_MODE = DEVICE_2;
    static int PANU_MODE = DEVICE_1;
```

```java
static int DATA_MTU = 1691;
static int HEADER_LENGTH = 14;
public static int maximumServiceRecordCount = 0xffff;
public static int maximumAttributeByteCount = 0xffff;
static int SDP_SERVER_THREADS = 4;
static int SDP_CLIENT_THREADS = 4;
static int BNEP_CHANNELS = 4;
static int MAX_IN_L2CAP_BUFFERS = 32;
static int SDP_THREAD_TIMEOUT = 120000;
static int BLUETOOTH_EVENT_TIMEOUT = 180000;
public static String DEVICE1_NAME = "Little Device1";
public static String DEVICE2_NAME = "Little Device2";
static int DEVICE1_IP = 0x0a110101; // 10.17.01.01
static int DEVICE2_IP =  0x0a110102; // 10.17.01.02
static int NETMASK =    0xFFFFFF00; // 255.255.255.0
static int BROADCAST = 0x0a1101FF; // 10.17.01.255
static int DST_UUID = Sdp.UUID_PANU;
static int SRC_UUID = Sdp.UUID_GN;

Hashtable ht;
private ExternalSecurityControlEntity myEsce;
String pin = "123";
HciTransport hciTransport;

String device1SerialPort = "COM1";
String device2SerialPort =  "COM1";
int device1BaudRate = 19200; // 38400; //57600; //9600; //115200;
int device2BaudRate = 19200; // 57600; //38400; //9600; //115200;
int roleSwitch = HciConnectionTable.REFUSE_ROLE_SWITCH;
int securityMode = SERVICE_LEVEL_MODE_2;

DeviceProperties(int device) {
    ht = new Hashtable();
    myEsce = new ESCESample(pin);

    // SerialIFHciTransport is a simple UART connection
    if (device == DEVICE_1) {
        hciTransport = new SerialIFHciTransport(device1SerialPort,
                    device1BaudRate);
        // Human readable form of the device name
        ht.put("bluetooth.device.name", DEVICE1_NAME);
    } else {
        hciTransport = new SerialIFHciTransport(device2SerialPort,
```

```
                          device2BaudRate);
            // Human readable form of the device name
            ht.put("bluetooth.device.name", DEVICE2_NAME);
        }

        ht.put("bluetooth.api.version", "1.0a");
        ht.put("bluetooth.security.mode", Integer.toString(securityMode));
        ht.put("bluetooth.l2cap.receiveMTU.max", Integer.toString(DATA_MTU));
        ht.put("bluetooth.connected.devices.max", "7");
        ht.put("bluetooth.connected.inquiry", "true");
        ht.put("bluetooth.connected.page", "true");
        ht.put("bluetooth.connected.inquiry.scan", "true");
        ht.put("bluetooth.connected.page.scan", "true");
        ht.put("bluetooth.master.switch", "true");
        ht.put("bluetooth.sd.trans.max", Integer.toString(SDP_CLIENT_THREADS));
        ht.put("bluetooth.sd.attr.retrievable.max", "64");

        testProperties();
    }


    ExternalSecurityControlEntity getEsce() {
        return myEsce;
    }


    private void testProperties() {
        int i;

        if (hciTransport == null) {
            throw new Error("No connection to Host Controller defined");
        }

        i = getInt("bluetooth.security.mode");

        if (i < NON_SECURE_MODE_1 || i > LINK_LEVEL_MODE_3)
            throw new Error("bluetooth.security.mode must be NON_SECURE_MODE_1,
                        SERVICE_LEVEL_MODE_2, or LINK_LEVEL_MODE_3");
        if (getInt("bluetooth.l2cap.receiveMTU.max") < 48)
            throw new Error("bluetooth.l2cap.receiveMTU.max must be at least" +
                        " 48 bytes, default value is 672");


    }
```

```
    private int getInt(String prop) {
        return Integer.parseInt((String) ht.get(prop));
    }
}
```

So, as we stated earlier, stack initialization must occur before you can do any real work in your Bluetooth application (whether you invoke it directly in your code or not).

Device Management

LocalDevice, RemoteDevice, and DeviceClass are the classes in the Java Bluetooth specification that form the Generic Access Profile and allow you to perform device management. These classes allow you to query some statistical information about your own Bluetooth device (LocalDevice) and also some information on the devices in the area (RemoteDevice). The DeviceClass object gives you information about the official class of device (CoD) as defined in the Bluetooth specification.

javax.bluetooth.LocalDevice

There is a famous quote that says, "Know thyself." Well, this class allows you to do exactly that. The LocalDevice class is the class that gives you information about yourself, the local Bluetooth device. Being a singleton object, you can only have a single instance of this object in your JVM at a time. Its constructor is private, so you can instantiate it by using the static getLocalDevice() method:

```
LocalDevice localdevice = localDevice.getLocalDevice();
```

public String getBluetoothAddress()

Bluetooth devices have unique addresses, which are quite similar to MAC addresses for network cards on your PC. This class allows you to find out what your Bluetooth address is with the getBluetoothAddress() method. It returns a 12-character String in the form of something like 00FE3467B092. In most cases, your Bluetooth radio shows what your address is somewhere externally, but it's nice to have a way to access it programmatically.

public boolean setDiscoverable(int mode)

In order to allow remote Bluetooth devices to find your device, you need to set
the discovery mode of your Bluetooth device. Table 4-1 contains a list of valid
modes and descriptions for the Bluetooth discovery modes.

Table 4-1. Bluetooth Discovery Modes

ACCESS MODE	FULL NAME	DESCRIPTION	VALUE
NOT_DISCOVERABLE	Not Discoverable	Don't allow any devices to discover your device.	0
GIAC	General/Unlimited Inquiry Access Code	Allow all devices to discover your device.	10390323
LIAC	Limited Inquiry Access Code	A temporary access mode that will revert back to a previous state after 1 minute.	10390272

One question that might be on your mind is why the values for the access
modes are 0, 10390272, and 10390323. Wouldn't it be simpler for the values to be
something like 0, 1, and 2? Well, the codes for NOT_DISCOVERABLE, LIAC, and GIAC
are all defined in the Bluetooth Assigned Numbers document from
http://www.bluetooth.org. Each entry in the document (which has more than
just codes for Bluetooth discovery modes) has a unique code in hexadecimal format. The actual codes for LIAC and GIAC as described in the Bluetooth Assigned
Numbers document are 0x9E8B00 (for LIAC) and 0x9E8B33 (for GIAC). For your
convenience, these values are available to you as public constants in the
DiscoveryAgent class:

```
// javax.bluetooth.DiscoveryAgent.java
...
public static final int NOT_DISCOVERABLE = 0;
public static final int LIAC = 0x9E8B00  // 10390272
public static final int GIAC = 0x9E8B33  // 10390323;
...
```

public int getDiscoverable()

Call this method if you want to know the current discovery mode of your Bluetooth device. This will (obviously) return an int that's either NOT_DISCOVERABLE, LIAC, or GIAC.

`javax.bluetooth.RemoteDevice`

The RemoteDevice class gives you access to a single remote Bluetooth device in the area. The most common way to obtain a reference to a RemoteDevice is through device discovery, which is covered in the next section. Here are two useful methods that pertain to device management.

public final String getBluetoothAddress()

As you probably have already assumed, this method returns to you the 12-character Bluetooth address of the remote device.

public String getFriendlyName(boolean alwaysAsk)

Knowing the Bluetooth address of the RemoteDevice is fine, but it is even better to know the "friendly name" of that device. The friendly name of a Bluetooth device is something like "Andrew's PDA", "Home Office Printer", or "Ranjith's MP3 Player".

`javax.bluetooth.DeviceClass`

This class represents the class of device in the Bluetooth specification. A device class is simply a classification of Bluetooth devices. Why is this class useful? Well, by simply calling the methods of this class, you can determine what kind of devices are in the area, like computers, laptops, phones, PDAs, access points, etc. The methods provided to accomplish this task are getMinorDeviceClass() and getMajorDeviceClass(), both of which return an int. Table 4-2 shows some common major and minor device classes.

Table 4-2. Bluetooth Major and Minor Device Classes*

MAJOR CLASS	MINOR CLASS	MAJOR CLASS DESCRIPTION	MINOR CLASS DESCRIPTION
0		Misc. major device	
256	0	Computer	Unassigned, misc.
256	4	Computer	Desktop
256	8	Computer	Server
256	12	Computer	Laptop
256	16	Computer	Sub-laptop
256	20	Computer	PDA
256	24	Computer	Watch size
512	0	Phone	Unassigned, misc.
512	4	Phone	Cellular
512	8	Phone	Household cordless
512	12	Phone	Smart phone
512	16	Phone modem	
768	0	LAN/network access point	Fully available
768	32	LAN/network access point	1–17% utilized
768	64	LAN/network access point	17–33% utilized
768	96	LAN/network access point	33–50% utilized
768	128	LAN/network access point	50–76% utilized
768	160	LAN/network access point	67–83% utilized
768	192	LAN/network access point	83–99% utilized
768	224	LAN/network access point	100% utilized, no service available
1024	0	Audio/video device	Unassigned, misc.
1024	4	Audio/video device	Headset (must conform to the Headset Profile)
1024	8	Audio/video device	Hands-free device
1024	16	Audio/video device	Microphone
1024	44	Audio/video device	VCR

(continued)

Table 4-2. Bluetooth Major and Minor Device Classes*(continued)

MAJOR CLASS	MINOR CLASS	MAJOR CLASS DESCRIPTION	MINOR CLASS DESCRIPTION
1024	72	Audio/video device	Video game system
1280	64	Computer peripheral	Keyboard
1280	128	Computer peripheral	Mouse, trackball, etc.
1280	12	Computer peripheral	Remote control
1536	16	Imaging device	Display device
1536	32	Imaging device	Camera
1536	64	Imaging device	Scanner
1536	128	Imaging device	Printer
7936		Unclassified major device	

* This table has a majority of the major and minor device classes listed in the Bluetooth Assigned Numbers document on the Bluetooth Web site: http://www.bluetooth.org.

So, that's about all it takes to perform device management with the Java Bluetooth APIs. Now, let's take a look at the concept in Bluetooth that allows you to discover other Bluetooth devices: device discovery.

Device Discovery

Your Bluetooth device has no idea of what other Bluetooth devices are in the area. Perhaps there are laptops, desktops, printers, mobile phones, or PDAs in the area. Who knows? The possibilities are endless. In order to find out, your Bluetooth device will use the device discovery classes that are provided in the Java Bluetooth API to see what's out there.

Which Bluetooth devices should use device discovery? Well, if you are planning to use a peer-to-peer application in Bluetooth, like two PDAs in a chat session, then either device would use device discovery to find the other device. If you are planning to use a client-server type application, like printing from a laptop to a printer, then the client is most likely to perform device discovery. It doesn't make sense for the printer to constantly look for devices that want to print something.

Now, let's take a look at the two classes needed in order for your Bluetooth device to discover remote Bluetooth devices in the area: DiscoveryAgent and DiscoveryListener.

javax.bluetooth.DiscoveryAgent

After getting a LocalDevice object, the most logical next step for device discovery is to instantiate the DiscoveryAgent object. You accomplish this task by calling LocalDevice.getDiscoveryAgent().

```
LocalDevice localdevice = LocalDevice.getLocalDevice();
DiscoveryAgent discoveryagent = localdevice.getDiscoveryAgent();
```

When you want to discover other Bluetooth devices in the area, DiscoveryAgent gives you two methods to work with: startInquiry() and retrieveDevices().

public boolean startInquiry(int accessCode, DiscoveryListener listener)

After you have instantiated your DiscoveryAgent, you use this method to make your Bluetooth device search for other devices in the area. The length of the inquiry is totally dependent upon the implementation of the Java Bluetooth specification. The accessCode can be one of the following DiscoveryAgent constants: NOT_DISCOVERABLE, LIAC, or GIAC. You must also pass a reference to a class that implements the DiscoveryListener interface. When new devices are discovered, event callbacks are passed back to this object. This method will return true if the device successfully went into discovery mode. The startInquiry() method is the only way to perform device discovery without blocking the current thread.

public RemoteDevice[] retrieveDevices(int option)

Use the retrieveDevices() method to get a list of RemoteDevice objects that were found by previous inquiries. The option field has either the value of 0 for CACHED or 1 for PREKNOWN. For your convenience, CACHED and PREKNOWN are also defined as constants in the DiscoveryAgent class. Unlike the startInquiry() method, this method blocks the calling thread until it returns. CACHED and PREKNOWN devices are determined by the BCC.

 NOTE *For the most part, a* CACHED *device is simply a Bluetooth device that was found from a* recent *inquiry. Of course, the definition of "recent" is implementation dependent. A* PREKNOWN *device is a level above a* CACHED *device and is one that you frequently communicate with.*

For example, let's say that you own a Bluetooth-enabled PDA. If you have exchanged business cards with another PDA within an hour, an implementation may classify that PDA as CACHED. However, if you own a printer at home, and you print to it often from the PDA, then an implementation may classify the printer as PREKNOWN.

Please note that the retrieveDevices() method does not perform a true inquiry for Bluetooth devices, and subsequently, devices found from this method may not be in the area. However, this really isn't a problem, because the purpose of this method is to quickly give you the references to the devices that you want to connect to. The startInquiry() method will guarantee that the device is in the area, but it may take a considerable amount of time in order to find the device that you want.

javax.bluetooth.DiscoveryListener

If you've worked with event handling in Java, then the concept of listeners is not new to you. Like all listeners, DiscoveryListener is an interface that has a method that is called by the JVM when the desired event occurs. If you want to be informed when a Bluetooth device is found by DiscoveryAgent.startInquiry(), then your class needs to implement the DiscoveryListener interface. Whenever a Bluetooth device is found, the method deviceDiscovered() is called.

public void deviceDiscovered(RemoteDevice btDevice, DeviceClass cod)

As stated in the preceding section, this method is called by the JVM when a remote Bluetooth device is found from an inquiry. The RemoteDevice object is a reference to the Bluetooth device found from the inquiry. The DeviceClass object (which tells you if the remote device is a phone, a PC, a PDA, etc.) is also provided when this method is called. See Table 4-2 for common device classes and their numbers.

 NOTE *The* deviceDiscovered() *method may be called more than once for the same Bluetooth device in the vicinity.*

Now that you know all the semantics about discovering devices, let's discuss how to find what services (if any) that these devices offer.

Service Discovery

After you have located devices in the area, it would be really nice to see what services those devices offer. Of course, you can always inspect the DeviceClass object, but that may only reveal half the picture. Let's say that you want to print a text file. Obviously, if the DeviceClass indicates that the major device class of the RemoteDevice is a printer, then you're all set. But what if the major device class is a computer? Would it come to mind that you can also print to a computer that is acting as a print server?

CROSS-REFERENCE   *This is actually a good segue for Chapter 6. In Chapter 6, you'll learn how to convert your desktop computer into a wireless print server.*

The service discovery–related classes in the Java Bluetooth specification implement the Service Discovery Application Profile. The Service Discovery Application Profile, in turn, uses the Service Discovery Protocol (SDP) layer in your Bluetooth stack to find services on remote Bluetooth devices.

CROSS-REFERENCE   *See Chapter 2 for detailed descriptions of profiles and layers in Bluetooth.*

The following classes are provided in the Java Bluetooth specification for service discovery: DiscoveryAgent, DiscoveryListener, ServiceRecord, DataElement, and UUID. You'll also interact (indirectly) with the SDDB whenever you want to discover services on a remote Bluetooth device.

The Service Discovery Database

The Service Discovery Database (SDDB) is the central repository for all service records, but it's not a database in the sense of Oracle 9i, Sybase, or even MS Access. It's simply a *collection* of service records (and no, we don't mean a Java Collections object). The JSR-82 implementation is free to implement the SDDB in any form, so when a ServiceRecord object is stored in the SDDB, it doesn't necessarily mean that the JVM serialized the ServiceRecord object and stored it in a data store. If a particular JSR-82 implementation does not store service records in the SDDB as Java objects, then it must convert them into ServiceRecord objects when a client performs a search for services and a match is found.

Figures 4-1 through 4-4 present graphical depictions of the SDDB, ServiceRecord, DataElement, and UUID objects in regard to how they all work together for service discovery.

As you can see in Figure 4-1, a service record is an individual entry in the SDDB (Service Discovery Database).

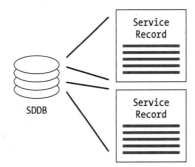

Figure 4-1. Service records in the SDDB

Entries in service records are called *attributes*. Attributes consist of an ID and value. See Figure 4-2 for an illustration.

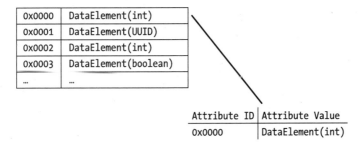

Figure 4-2. An individual attribute of a service record

Attribute IDs are 16-bit unsigned integers (0x000–0xFFFF). In a ServiceRecord object, attribute values are stored as DataElement objects as shown in Figure 4-3.

Attributes

Attribute ID	Attribute Value
0x0000	DataElement(int)

Figure 4-3. An illustration of a service record attribute

DataElements can be created from the following Java types: `int`, `boolean`, `UUID`, and `Enumeration` (see Figure 4-4).

DataElements

```
DataElement(int)
DataElement(UUID)
DataElement(int)
DataElement(boolean)
```

Figure 4-4. DataElements

Figure 4-5 wraps it all up by showing the process of service discovery for a PDA that wants to use the services of a Bluetooth keyboard. A successful service discovery will occur only if there is a match in the UUID of a service record in the SDDB of the `RemoteDevice`.

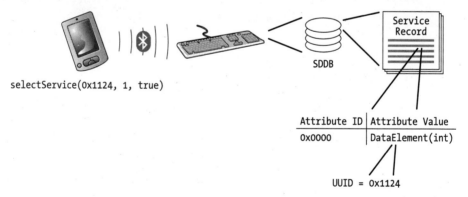

selectService(0x1124, 1, true)

SDDB

Service Record

Attribute ID	Attribute Value
0x0000	DataElement(int)

UUID = 0x1124

Figure 4-5. The service discovery process for a PDA that wants to use the services of a Bluetooth keyboard

Now, let's look at the service discovery–related classes in detail.

javax.bluetooth.UUID

The UUID class is simply a class that uniquely identifies services in the Bluetooth protocol (UUID stands for Universal Unique Identifier). Let's say that you have a Bluetooth client device that supports L2CAP connections. If you want to send a message to a Bluetooth server device, just perform service discovery with the UUID of 0x0100, which is the UUID for L2CAP. If you have a Bluetooth-enabled PDA, and you want to send your business card (.vcf) to other Bluetooth-enabled devices, then you'll perform service discovery with a UUID of 0x1105, which is the UUID for the OBEX Object Push Profile. Table 4-3 lists a sample of UUIDs for Bluetooth protocol layers and Table 4-4 lists UUIDs for Bluetooth services and their corresponding Bluetooth profile. For instance, Headset and HeadsetAudioGateway are both distinct services that are a part of the Headset Profile. Therefore, each service has its own UUID, 0x1108 and 0x1112, respectively. Some profiles, like the FAX Profile, only have one service: FAX (which has a UUID of 0x1111). A more exhaustive list of UUID values for protocols and profile services can be seen in the Bluetooth Assigned Numbers document.

Table 4-3. Common UUID Values for Bluetooth Protocol Layers

PROTOCOL	UUID (DECIMAL)	UUID (HEXADECIMAL)
SDP	1	0x0001
RFCOMM	3	0x0003
L2CAP	256	0x0100
HTTP	12	0x000C
FTP	10	0x000A
TCP	4	0x0004
IP	9	0x0009
UDP	2	0x0002
BNEP	15	0x000F
OBEX	8	0x0008
TCS-BIN	5	0x0005

Table 4-4. Common UUID Values for Bluetooth Profiles

PROFILE	SERVICE NAME	UUID (DECIMAL)	UUID (HEXADECIMAL)
Serial Port	SerialPort	4353	0x1101
Dial-up Networking	LANAccessUsingPPP	4354	0x1102
Dial-up Networking	DialupNetworking	4355	0x1103
Object Push	OBEXObjectPush	4357	0x1105
Object Push	OBEXFileTransfer	4358	0x1106
Cordless Telephony	CordlessTelephony	4361	0x1109
Audio/Video Control Profile	A/V_RemoteControl	4366	0x110E
Intercom	Intercom	4368	0x1110
Fax	Fax	4369	0x1111
Generic Access	Headset	4360	0x1108
Generic Access	HeadsetAudioGateway	4370	0x1112
Handsfree	Handsfree	4382	0x111E
Handsfree	HandsfreeAudioGateway	4383	0x111F
Basic Printing	BasicPrinting	4386	0x1122
Basic Printing	PrintingStatus	4387	0x1123
Hard Copy Cable Replacement	HardCopyCableReplacement	4389	0x1125
Hard Copy Cable Replacement	HCR_Print	4390	0x1126
Hard Copy Cable Replacement	HCR_Scan	4391	0x1127
Human Interface Device	HumanInterfaceDeviceService	4388	0x1124
Generic Networking	n/a	4609	0x1201

Now, let's take a look at the constructors for UUID.

public UUID(long uuidValue)

This is pretty cut and dry—it constructs a UUID object from a long.

public UUID(String uuidValue, boolean shortUUID)

This method allows you to construct a UUID from a `String` representation of a UUID. If `shortUUID` is set to `true`, then a short UUID is returned (one that is made up of 16 bits instead of 128 bits).

 NOTE *When using this method, be sure not to include the "0x" prefix in front of the* `String` *when constructing this object.*

javax.bluetooth.DiscoveryAgent

Hey, wait a minute, didn't we use this class for device discovery? Well, that's why the authors of the Java Bluetooth specification named this class `DiscoveryAgent`, because they intended this class to be used for both device and service discovery. In order to find services on remote devices, you'll use either `selectService()` or `searchServices()`.

public int searchServices(int[] attrSet, UUID[] uuidSet, RemoteDevice btDev, DiscoveryListener discListener)

This method allows you to search for a list of services on a single remote Bluetooth device. The `attrSet[]` parameter must be populated with an array of integers that correspond to attributes that you want to see when the services match the UUIDs. The `UUID[]` parameter is the list of UUIDs of services that you want to look for. `RemoteDevice` is the reference to the remote device that you want to search for services. You must also provide an object that will implement the `DiscoveryListener` interface in order to receive event callbacks when services that match your UUID criteria are discovered. This method returns an `int` that is the transaction ID. You can later use the transaction ID to cancel this search if you need to.

public String selectService(UUID uuid, int security, boolean master)

This method also allows you to search for services, but it has a slight twist that makes it different from `searchServices()`. This method accepts neither a `DiscoveryListener` nor a `RemoteDevice` object. By using this method, you can perform a search for a particular UUID that is available on ANY device in the area. If there is a match, then this method returns a `String` that will be used in the

`Connector.open()` method in order to establish a connection to that device. Be sure to notice that this method only allows you to search on a single UUID and not multiple UUIDs, as in `searchServices()`.

Unfortunately, there is no method available in the JSR-82 specification that will allow you to discover every service offered by remote devices. By using either `searchServices()` or `selectService()`, you need to know the UUID of the service that you're looking for before you attempt to perform a search.

NOTE *You may be able to discover every service on a remote device if that device has all of its services categorized with a* `BrowseGroupList` *attribute in the service record. If not, then you're out of luck. See the Bluetooth specification for more details on how to browse for services.*

javax.bluetooth.DiscoveryListener

Our good ol' buddy `DiscoveryListener`, which helped us to discover devices, comes back to help us discover services on remote Bluetooth devices.

public void servicesDiscovered(int transID, ServiceRecord[] servRecord)

If you use the `DiscoveryAgent.searchServices()` method (which accepts a `DiscoveryListener`), then this method is called by the JVM when services are discovered on the remote device. The transaction ID and an array of `ServiceRecord` objects are provided to this method. With a `ServiceRecord` in hand, you can do plenty of things, but you would most likely want to connect to the `RemoteDevice` where this `ServiceRecord` originated:

```
String connectionURL = servRecord[i].getConnectionURL(0, false);
```

javax.bluetooth.ServiceRecord

`ServiceRecord` objects are representations of individual entries in the SDDB. As you may remember, the SDDB is the central repository of service records for a Bluetooth device.

javax.bluetooth.DataElement

As we continue to break down the anatomy of service discovery, let's now examine the DataElement object. Each ServiceRecord object in the SDDB is made up of attributes. All attributes are stored as DataElement objects. A DataElement object can be from any of the following:

- Integers

- Booleans

- Strings

- UUIDs

- Sequences of the preceding values

Be sure to take another look at Figures 4-1 through 4-4 if you're still in the dark about the relationship between the SDDB, ServiceRecord, DataElement, and UUID objects.

Service Registration

Before a Bluetooth client device can use service discovery on a Bluetooth server device, the server needs to register its services internally. That process is called *service registration*. This section discusses what's involved in service registration for a Bluetooth device, and we'll also give you a rundown of the classes needed to accomplish this.

 NOTE *In a peer-to-peer application, like a file transfer or chat application, be sure to remember that any device can act as the client or the server, so you'll need to incorporate that functionality into your code in order to handle both scenarios of service discovery and service registration.*

Here's a scenario of what's involved in getting your service registered and stored in the SDDB:

1. Call `Connector.open()` and cast the resulting connection to a `StreamConnectionNotifier` object. `Connector.open()` creates a new `ServiceRecord` and sets some attributes.

2. Use the `LocalDevice` object and the `StreamConnectionNotifier` to obtain the `ServiceRecord` that was created by the system.

3. Add or modify the attributes in the `ServiceRecord` (optional).

4. Use the `StreamConnectionNotifier` to call `acceptAndOpen()` and wait for Bluetooth clients to discover this service and connect.

5. The system creates a service record in the SDDB. Wait until a client connects. When the server is ready to exit, call `close()` on the `StreamConnectionNotifier`.

6. The system removes the service record from the SDDB.

`StreamConnectionNotifier` and `Connector` both come from the `javax.microedition.io` package of the J2ME platform. Listing 4-4 is a snippet of code that achieves the service registration process.

Listing 4-4. The Service Registration Process

```
...
// let's name our variables
StreamConnectionNotifier notifier = null;
StreamConnection sconn = null;
LocalDevice localdevice = null;
ServiceRecord servicerecord = null;

// step #1
// the String url will already be defined with the correct url parameters
notifier = (StreamConnectionNotifier)Connector.open(url);

// step #2
// we will get the LocalDevice if not already done
localdevice = LocalDevice.getLocalDevice();
servicerecord = localdevice.getRecord(notifier);
```

```
// step #3 is optional

// step #4
// this step will block the current thread until a client responds
notifier.acceptAndOpen();
// the service record is now in the SDDB

// step #5
// just wait...
// assume the client has connected and you are ready to exit

//slep #6
// this causes the service record to be removed from the SDDB
notifier.close();
```

And that's all that you need to do service registration in Bluetooth. The next step is communication.

Communication

Okay, Bluetooth is a communication protocol, so how do you communicate with it? Well, the official Java Bluetooth API gives you three ways to send and receive data, but for right now we'll cover only two of them: RFCOMM and L2CAP.

RFCOMM Connections

As you may remember from Figure 2-9, the most common Bluetooth profiles use the Serial Port Profile as a foundational layer.

 NOTE *RFCOMM is the protocol layer that the Serial Port Profile uses in order to communicate, but these two items are almost always used synonymously.*

Sessions and Connections

Before we continue, there's a little more terminology to introduce here: *sessions* and *connections.* You can only have a single session between two Bluetooth devices. This limitation isn't a big deal, per se, because the definition of a session is simply one or more connections shared between two devices. You can also relate a Bluetooth session in the same way that sessions are created and used on the Web. When a Web server is communicating to a Web client, there is only one session, although there are numerous connections. Now, a Bluetooth device can have multiple sessions only if each session is linked to a different device. This also applies on the Web; powerful application servers have the capability to create multiple sessions and keep them in memory, but each session is linked to a different client.

Server Connections with the Serial Port Profile

Listing 4-5 demonstrates what is needed to open connections on a Bluetooth device that will act as a server.

Listing 4-5. Opening Connections on a Bluetooth Server

```
...
// let's name our variables

StreamConnectionNotifier notifier = null;
StreamConnection con = null;
LocalDevice localdevice = null;
ServiceRecord servicerecord = null;
InputStream input;
OutputStream output;

// let's create a URL that contains a UUID that
// has a very low chance of conflicting with anything
String url = "btspp://localhost:00112233445566778899AABBCCDDEEFF;name=serialconn";
// let's open the connection with the URL and cast it into
a StreamConnectionNotifier
notifier = (StreamConnectionNotifier)Connector.open(url);

// block the current thread until a client responds
con = notifier.acceptAndOpen();
```

```
// the client has responded, so open some streams
input = con.openInputStream();
output = con.openOutputStream();

// now that the streams are open, send and receive some data
```

For the most part, this is just about the same code used in service registration, and in fact, it is; service registration and server communication are both accomplished using the same lines of code. Here are a few items that need to be pointed out. The String url begins with btspp://localhost:, which is required if you're going to use the Bluetooth Serial Port Profile. Next comes the UUID part of the URL, which is 00112233445566778899AABBCCDDEEFF. This is simply a custom UUID that was made up for this service; any string that's 128 bits long could have been used. Finally, we have name=serialconn in the URL String. We could have left this part off, but we want our custom service to have a name, so the actual service record in the SDDB has the following entry:

```
ServiceName = serialconn
```

The implementation has also assigned a channel identifier to this service. The client must provide the channel number along with other parameters in order to connect to a server.

Client Connections with the Serial Port Profile

Establishing a connection with the Serial Port Profile for a J2ME client is simple because the paradigm hasn't changed. You simply call Connector.open().

```
StreamConnection con = (StreamConnection)Connector.open(url);
```

You obtain the url String that is needed to connect to the device from the ServiceRecord object that you get from service discovery. Here's a bit more code that will show you how a Serial Port Profile client makes a connection to a Serial Port Profile server:

```
String connectionURL = serviceRecord.getConnectionURL(0, false);
StreamConnection con = (StreamConnection)Connector.open(connectionURL);
```

What does a Serial Port Profile client connection URL look like? If the address of the server is 0001234567AB, then the String that the SPP client would use would look something like this:

```
btspp://0001234567AB:3
```

The 3 at the end of the URL String is the channel number that the server assigned to this service when this service was added to the SDDB.

L2CAP Connections

Unlike RFCOMM connections, which are stream oriented, L2CAP connections are packet oriented. Before we cover how to create L2CAP connections, we'll briefly cover a new concept called *Maximum Transmission Unit* (MTU). We'll also cover the classes needed in order to create L2CAP connections: L2CAPConnection and L2CAPConnectionNotifier.

Maximum Transmission Unit

Because of the fact that the L2CAP layer sends data in packets, the official Java Bluetooth API gives you the flexibility to control how large the packets can be. The default MTU is 672 bytes, but you can attempt to negotiate a larger MTU in your connection URL strings. Here's why we say "attempt": If the client indicates that it can receive data in packet sizes of 10MB, and the server is only capable of sending data at 1kB, then there's no real problem; the client'll get its data in 1kB packets. Now on the other hand, if the server indicates that it's sending data in 10MB-size packets, and the client is only capable of handling 1kB packets, then the transmission will fail horribly.

In order to find out the largest packet size that you can receive from a L2CAP connection, just run the following piece of code:

```
LocalDevice local = LocalDevice.getLocalDevice();
String receiveMTUmax = local.getProperty("bluetooth.l2cap.receiveMTU.max");
```

L2CAP Server Connections

Following is the code that a L2CAP server uses to open a connection to a client:

```
L2CAPConnectionNotifier notifier = (L2CAPConnectionNotifier).Connector.open(url);
L2CAPConnection con = (L2CAPConnection)notifier.acceptAndOpen();
```

As you can see, it is not much different from the standard StreamConnectionNotifier and Connection used for RFCOMM server connections.

L2CAP Client Connections

Now here's the code that a client would use in order to establish an L2CAP connection with a server:

```
L2CAPConnection = (L2CAPConnection)Connector.open(url);
```

Once again, it's pretty straightforward.

More on MTUs

Now, let's look at MTUs one more time, in conjunction with opening connections. For instance, if the server code looked like this:

```
String url =
"btl2cap://localhost:00112233445566778899AABBCCDDEEFF;ReceiveMTU=1024;TransmitMTU
=1024";
```

The connection `String` for the client, on the other hand, would look something like this:

```
String url = "btl2cap://2E345BB78902:1055;ReceiveMTU=4096;TransmitMTU=512";
```

As you can see, the server is proposing to send data in packet sizes of 1024 bytes. Since the client is able to receive data packets four times that size, the negotiated connection will have a packet data size of the lowest common denominator: 1024. On the other hand, the client wants to send its data in packets of 512 bytes. The server is able to handle that packet size with no problem at all, and the negotiated connection will be 512 byte packets.

Now, let's take a brief look at the two classes used in order to create L2CAP connections and some of their methods.

javax.bluetooth.L2CAPConnection

This interface is just a subclass of the `Connection` interface, and you use it in the same manner. The following methods are found in `L2CAPConnection` that are not found in `Connection`:

- `public int getReceiveMTU()`: This method gets the negotiated ReceiveMTU value from the connection.

- `public int getTransmitMTU()`: This method gets the negotiated TransmitMTU value from the connection.

- `public boolean ready()`: This method will return true if there is any data ready to be read. If this method returns true, then a call to `receive()` will not block the main thread.

- `public int receive(byte[] inBuf)`: Regardless of the `ReceiveMTU` between your device and the remote device, you can set the size of `inBuf` to be whatever you want it to be. If the size of `inBuf` is greater than or equal to the `ReceiveMTU`, then you won't lose any data during a transmission. If the size of `inBuf[]` is smaller than the size of `ReceiveMTU`, then `inBuf[]` will be filled with data for the incoming packet, but the remainder of the data will be lost.

- `public void send(byte[] data)`: Use this method to send data to a remote Bluetooth device via the L2CAP protocol. You're free to send any size packet that you want, but if you exceed the `TransmitMTU` size, then the excess data will be discarded.

L2CAP vs. RFCOMM

So now that you know how to send data between Bluetooth clients and servers using both L2CAP and RFCOMM, we bet you're wondering about typical usage scenarios for these connections. In other words, why would anyone use RFCOMM instead of L2CAP to send data or vice versa? Well, RFCOMM is also known as the virtual serial port communication protocol. An ideal way to use RFCOMM is in situations when you would replace a serial cable. For instance, if you were a developer for a GPS manufacturer, and your duty was to make one of their units Bluetooth enabled, then RFCOMM would be a likely choice in this scenario. Why? The GPS unit will always have a constant stream of information that needs to be processed, rendered, calculated, etc. So, collect the data from your stream and plot those coordinates on the screen.

On the other hand, L2CAP is great for handling packet data. L2CAP can easily be used (and actually is) as a data multiplexer. You can read data from the connection, and based upon a header in the packet, you can route that data to different methods, threads, and classes in your application.

Summary

This chapter gave you a formal introduction to the official Java Bluetooth APIs. You should be aware of all the basic components of a Bluetooth application, as well as how to implement them using the classes and interfaces of the official Java Bluetooth API. This chapter also discussed the importance and the roles that the Bluetooth Control Center (BCC) plays in your wireless applications.

Essentially, this chapter showed you how a Bluetooth application works by its components. In the next chapter, we'll look at a full working example of a Java Bluetooth application using the Atinav Java Bluetooth SDK.

CHAPTER 5

Bluetooth with J2ME MIDP

Now that we've covered a lot of the foundational material, let's start creating some Java Bluetooth applications. This chapter will give you your first full example of a Java Bluetooth application, but before we dive right in, we're going to give a brief primer on J2ME and the Mobile Information Device Profile (MIDP). Afterwards, we're going to examine two sample applications: Stealth Mode and the Piconet Browser.

NOTE *If you've already developed a MIDlet, or if you have a working knowledge of J2ME, then feel free to skip down to the example code in the sections "Stealth Mode Example" and "Piconet Browser Example."*

J2ME Overview

Under the general term of J2ME, there are two configurations that correspond to two classes of devices. The connected device configuration (CDC) is a classification for devices that have a network connection, but have less processing power than a typical desktop computer. Set-top boxes, appliances, smart phones, and high-end PDAs fit into this category. The connected limited device configuration (CLDC) classifies many mobile devices; they are capable of making a network connection, but it isn't robust or dedicated. CLDC devices typically don't have a lot of processing power, and many mobile phones, two-way pagers, and some PDAs fit into this category.

A J2ME *Profile* is a software layer that is built on top of a configuration (not to be confused with a Bluetooth profile). Configurations typically encompass a broad classification of devices, and profiles help to narrow the scope, while providing more functionality to the configuration. Figure 5-1 shows the J2ME world, and the relationship between configurations and profiles.

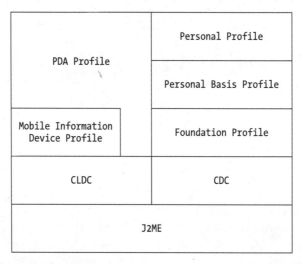

Figure 5-1. J2ME Profiles and configurations

The Mobile Information Device Profile

Now, let's take a look at what is (by far) the most widely used J2ME Profile: Mobile Information Device Profile (MIDP). If you have a Java-enabled mobile phone, then it's most likely a MIDP device. As stated earlier, the J2ME Profiles extend the functionality of a configuration. The CLDC provides the following packages for the developer in order to create Java applications for small devices:

- java.lang (basic core language classes)

- java.io (networking classes)

- java.util (utility classes)

- javax.microedition.io (more networking classes)

NOTE *These are not the full J2SE versions of* java.lang, java.io, *and* java.util *APIs. The CLDC contains a subset of these packages that's optimized for micro devices.*

The MIDP adds these additional packages for mobile devices:

- `javax.microedition.lcdui` (user interface classes)

- `javax.microedition.midlet` (core MIDlet classes)

- `javax.microedition.rms` (data persistence classes)

According to the MIDP specification, these are the qualifications for a MIDP 1.0 device:

- A minimum screen resolution of 96 × 54 pixels.

- A minimum of 128kB nonvolatile memory for the MIDP implementation.

- A minimum of 32kB volatile memory for JVM heap space.

- A minimum of 8kB nonvolatile memory for applications to store persistent data.

- Some type of input mechanism.

- Support for network connectivity.

- The OS must provide minimal scheduling, exception handling, and interrupt processing.

- The OS must support writing of bitmapped graphics to display.

- The OS must be able to accept the input and pass it on to the JVM.

The MIDP 2.0 specification raises the bar by requiring at least 256kB of nonvolatile memory, and 128kB of memory for the Java heap space. However, the MIDP 2.0 specification also brings along more functionality for wireless applications, including the following:

- Secure networking with HTTPS

- Push applications with the `javax.microedition.io.PushRegistry` class

- Standardized serial port communications

- Wireless application deployment with Over-the-Air provisioning (OTA)

- Better gaming applications with the `javax.microedition.lcdui.game` package

Developing MIDlets

What is a MIDlet? A *MIDlet* is a Java application that runs on a mobile device and uses the Mobile Information Device Profile. MIDlets can be created by extending the `javax.microedition.midlet.MIDlet` class. A MIDlet has three states in its life cycle: active, paused, and destroyed. Those three states correspond to three methods: `startApp()`, `pauseApp()`, and `destroyApp()`. One or more MIDlets packaged together in a JAR file constitute a *MIDlet suite*. Software on the mobile device (called the *application manager*) is responsible for loading, running, and destroying the MIDlet.

The skeletal structure of a typical MIDlet looks like this:

```
import javax.microedition.midlet.MIDlet;
public class MyApplcation extends MIDlet
{
        public MyApplication()
        {
        }
        public void startApp()
        {
        }
        public void pauseApp()
        {
        }
        public void destroyApp(boolean unconditional)
        {
        }
}
```

NOTE *Sun has created a very handy tool for MIDlet develop-ment called the* J2ME Wireless Toolkit. *The tool comes bundled with an emulator and can package, compile, pre-verify, and run CLDC and MIDP applications. The examples in this chapter use this tool, and it is available free from the Wireless Java Web site (*`http://wireless.java.sun.com/`*).*

Using the MIDP User Interface Components

The MIDP UI is logically composed of two APIs: high-level and low-level. The *high-level* API is primarily designed for business applications, and it gives you objects like `List`, `TextBox`, `ChoiceGroup`, and `DateField`. This API includes a high level of abstraction because you can't define the visual appearance (i.e., shape, color, font, etc.) of those components. When using the high-level UI components, you won't have direct control of the navigation or scrolling, or have direct access to the input device (you can process input, but you won't have direct access to it). All of these items are handled by the MIDP implementation and are device dependent. This abstraction allows the same MIDlet to run on a Blackberry pager as well as on a Palm PDA.

The *low-level* API, on the other hand, is designed for applications that need precise placement and control of graphic elements, as well as access to low-level input events. The low-level API is well suited for gaming or entertainment-based applications.

Using the RMS for Persistent Storage

So, how do you store persistent data on a micro device? If you think about it, a mobile phone probably wouldn't have a file system in order to store its data. It's really overkill for such a small device that keeps names and phones numbers to have a file system just for data storage. Being aware of this, the J2ME architects have developed a viable alternative to storing data persistently called the *Record Management System* (RMS). The `javax.microedition.rms` package contains all the functionality that will enable your classes to read, write, and sort data in the RMS.

The RMS is a record-oriented database stored in the nonvolatile memory of the mobile device. Since it is record oriented, the RMS is also referred to as a *flat file system*, where the data is stored in a series of rows in a table, much like the data stored in a conventional database. Each row will have a unique identifier. A logical representation of a record store is illustrated in Figure 5-2.

1	Byte Array
2	Byte Array
3	Byte Array

Figure 5-2. A logical representation of an RMS record store

The main class in the RMS is javax.microedition.rms.RecordStore. This class contains the methods for creating, updating, deleting, and querying a record store. A few interfaces are also provided is this package, and they help you whenever you need to enumerate, compare, and filter the data stored inside the record store. The RMS also includes a listener interface called javax.microedition.rms.RecordListener. When you associate this listener with a record store, the interface reports events that correspond to inserts, updates, and deletes of data that are in the record store.

Performing I/O with the GCF

In order for J2ME applications to perform any networking or I/O, they must use the java.io and javax.microedition.io packages. These packages together form the Generic Connection Framework (GFC).

The general philosophy behind the GCF is to create a framework to abstract the communication process through a single class called Connector. You can then use Connector to create any connection like file I/O streams, TCP/IP socket connections, HTTP connections, etc. In order to open a connection, just use the open method:

```
Connector.open("protocol:address:parameters");
```

If a user wants to open an HTTP connection, the connection URL will look like this:

```
Connector.open("http://mydomain.com");
```

Working with the Example Code

Before you try out any of the examples in this book, it is recommended that you first get your JSR-82 implementation on your development environment installed and configured. If you don't have your development environment set up, then here's a checklist of the things that you need to do:

- Select a JSR-82 implementation that supports your OS. You can find an updated listing of JSR-82 implementations at the companion Web site for this book: http://www.javabluetooth.com.

- Select the Bluetooth hardware that is supported by your JSR-82 implementation.

- Install and configure your development environment.

- Try out the demo programs that are included with your JSR-82 implementation.

- Determine what stack initialization code (if any) is used in the demo programs.

The documentation for your JSR-82 implementation really should point out what you need to do in order to initialize your stack. But just in case they don't, a dead ringer would be a class that you need to import that's not part of the javax.bluetooth or javax.obex packages (see Appendices A and B for an exhaustive list). In some cases, your stack initialization code will also be setting the baud rate for your Bluetooth device.

Stealth Mode Example

The Stealth Mode example is a simple program that illustrates the concepts of stack initialization, device management, and device discovery. When the program starts, it looks for remote Bluetooth devices as shown in Figure 5-3.

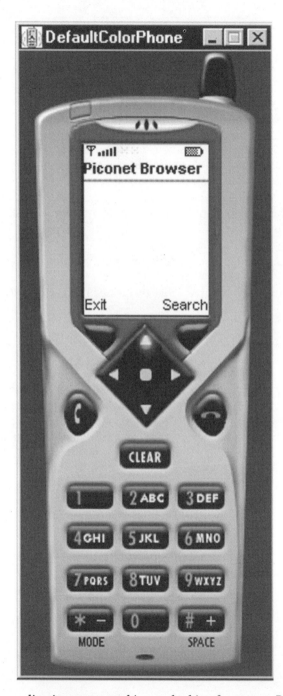

Figure 5-3. The application starts, and is now looking for remote Bluetooth devices.

Once it finds another device, it goes into nondiscoverable mode, as shown in Figure 5-4.

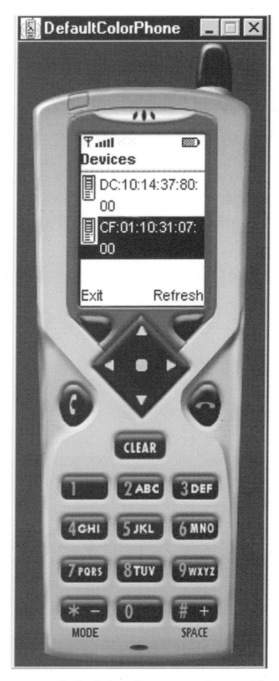

Figure 5-4. After a remote device is found, we now go into stealth mode (i.e., nondiscoverable).

In this example, we're using the J2ME Wireless Toolkit configured with the Atinav Bluetooth SDK. The Bluetooth device that we're using is a TDK USB module, as shown in Figure 5-5.

Figure 5-5. The TDK USB Bluetooth device using a CSR Bluetooth radio

The code for this example is shown in Listings 5-1 and 5-2.

Listing 5-1. Stealth.java

```java
import javax.microedition.midlet.*;
import javax.microedition.lcdui.*;
import javax.bluetooth.*;
import java.io.*;
import java.util.*;
import javax.microedition.io.*;
import com.atinav.bcc.*;


/* The Timer and the BeamTsk class is used to create the beam of
 * 3 concentric circles blinking. It has no purpose except visual enhancement.
 */
public class Stealth extends MIDlet {
    private Display display;
    private GUI canvas;
    private Timer tm;
    private BeamTsk tsk;
    private String dev;
    private RemoteDevice device[];

    public Stealth()
    {
        display=Display.getDisplay(this);
        canvas=new GUI(this);
        tm=new Timer();
        tsk=new BeamTsk(canvas);
        tm.schedule(tsk,1000,1000);


    }
```

```
        protected void startApp()
        {
            display.setCurrent(canvas);
        }

        protected void pauseApp()
        {
        }

        public void destroyApp(boolean unconditional) {
        }

        public void exitStealth()
        {
            destroyApp(true);
            notifyDestroyed();
        }
        public void exitTimer(){
            tm.cancel();
            tsk.cancel() ;
        }
}

class GUI extends Canvas implements CommandListener{
    private Command exitCommand;
    private Image img=null;
    private Image imgArc=null;
    private Stealth midlet;
    public int i=0; // used for creating the beam
    public int count=0; // used to create the blinking
    public boolean cancel=false;
    int x=30;
    int y=30;
    int wd=5;
    int ht=10;
    public GUI(Stealth midlet){
        this.midlet=midlet;
        exitCommand=new Command("Exit",Command.EXIT,1);
        addCommand(exitCommand);
        setCommandListener(this);

        try {
            img=Image.createImage("/phone.png");
```

```
        }
     catch (java.io.IOException e){
         System.err.println("Unnable to locate or read image (.png) file");
     }
     try{
         BCC.setPortName("COM1");
         BCC.setBaudRate(57600);
         BCC.setConnectable(false);
         LocalDevice localDevice = LocalDevice.getLocalDevice();
         discoveryAgent = localDevice.getDiscoveryAgent();
         device = new RemoteDevice[10];
         discoveryAgent.startInquiry(DiscoveryAgent.GIAC,this);
      }catch(BluetoothStateException btstateex)
      {
         btstateex.printStackTrace();
      }


}
  public void deviceDiscovered(RemoteDevice btDevice, DeviceClass cod)
     {
        /* The method is fired every time a device is discovered.
            * The inquiry is cancelled after the first device is discovered.
            */
         BCC.setDiscoverable(DiscoveryAgent.NOT_DISCOVERABLE);
         cancelInquiry(discoveryAgent);
     }
   public void inquiryCompleted(int discType)
 {
     cancel=true;
      this.notify();
 }

/**
 * paint
 */
public void paint(Graphics g) {

 if (i==0){
         // Used to clear the portion of the screen
         g.setColor(255,255,255);
         g.fillRect(25,10,50,70);
     }
 else {
     // draw the image of phone at given
```

```
          // coordinates at the top left of the screen
          g.drawImage(img,10,30,Graphics.LEFT|Graphics.TOP);
          // draw a string at the bottom left
          g.drawString("Me",10,45+img.getHeight(),Graphics.LEFT|
                                      Graphics.BOTTOM);
          if (!cancel){
              // draw an arc at given coordinates
              g.drawArc(x,y,wd,ht,270,180);
          }
          else{

              g.drawImage(img,90,30,Graphics.RIGHT|Graphics.TOP);
              g.drawString("I am in Stealth Mode",2,100,Graphics.LEFT|
                                          Graphics.BOTTOM);
              try {
              img=Image.createImage("/phonegray.png");
              }catch (Exception e){e.printStackTrace();}
              g.drawImage(img,10,30,Graphics.LEFT|Graphics.TOP);

              midlet.exitTimer() ;
          }

      }
    }

    public void commandAction(Command c, Displayable s) {

        if (c == exitCommand)
            midlet.exitStealth();
    }

}
```

Listing 5-2. BeamTsk.java

```
import java.util.*;
public class BeamTsk extends TimerTask {

    private GUI canvas;
    /** Creates a new instance of BeamTsk */
    public BeamTsk(GUI canvas) {
        this.canvas=canvas;
    }
```

```java
public void run() {
    //if (canvas.count>5)
    //      canvas.cancel=true;
    if (canvas.i<3)
        canvas.i=canvas.i+1;
    else
        canvas.i=0;

    switch (canvas.i){
    case 1:{
        canvas.x=30;
        canvas.y=30;
        canvas.ht=10;
        break;
    }
        case 2 :{
        canvas.x=canvas.x+5;
        canvas.y=canvas.y-3;
        canvas.ht=canvas.ht+6;
        break;
        }
    case 3:{
        canvas.x=canvas.x+5;
        canvas.y=canvas.y-3;
        canvas.ht=canvas.ht+6;
        canvas.count=canvas.count+1;
        break;
    }
    }
    canvas.repaint();
    }
}
```

Piconet Browser Example

The Piconet Browser is a handy utility that demonstrates all the concepts presented in the last example and also includes the functionality of service discovery. It's really something that you would want to keep with you at all times, so after you get this example working, be sure to load it on your mobile phone or PDA. Using the Piconet Browser, you can see what Bluetooth devices are in the vicinity. After the list is displayed, you can select a particular Bluetooth device to see what services it offers.

The algorithm for this example is pretty simple. First, the MIDlet creates a form and displays it with buttons labeled Search and Exit (see Figure 5-6).

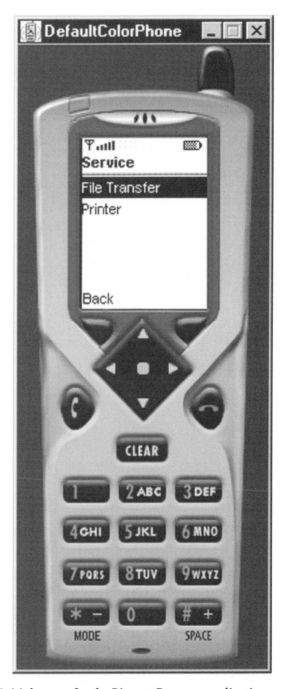

Figure 5-6. The initial screen for the Piconet Browser application

After pressing the Search button, the application performs a device discovery, and displays the search results (see Figure 5-7).

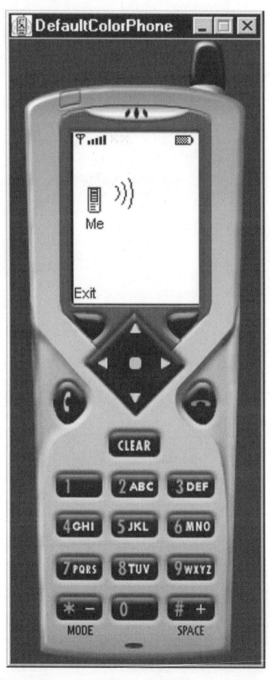

Figure 5-7. The Piconet Browser displays a list of Bluetooth devices in the area.

After you select a Bluetooth device, the application will display the services
that it offers (see Figure 5-8).

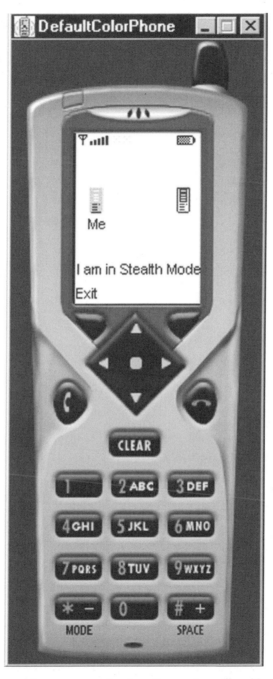

*Figure 5-8. The Piconet Browser now displays the services offered by the remote
device.*

Listing 5-3 shows the code for the Piconet Browser.

Listing 5-3. PiconetMIDlet.java.

```java
import javax.microedition.midlet.*;
import javax.microedition.lcdui.*;
import javax.bluetooth.*;
import java.io.*;
import javax.microedition.io.*;
import com.atinav.bcc.*;

public class PiconetMIDlet extends javax.microedition.midlet.MIDlet implements
                        CommandListener,DiscoveryListener{
    private LocalDevice localDevice=null;
    private RemoteDevice device=null;
    private DiscoveryAgent discoveryAgent = null;
    private Command exitCommand; // The exit command
    private Command srchCommand; //The search command
    private Command backCommand;

    private Display display;     // The display for this MIDlet
    private Form frm;
    private List deviceLst;
    private List ServiceLst;

    int count = 0;

    private String[] dev = null;
    private Image img[] =null;
    private String[] services=null;

    public void startApp() {

        display = Display.getDisplay(this);
        exitCommand = new Command("Exit", Command.EXIT, 1);
        srchCommand=new Command("Search",Command.SCREEN,1);
        backCommand= new Command("Back",Command.BACK,1);
        frm=new Form("Piconet Browser");
        frm.addCommand(srchCommand);
        frm.addCommand(exitCommand);
        frm.setCommandListener(this);
        display.setCurrent(frm);
```

```
}

public void pauseApp() {
}

public void destroyApp(boolean unconditional) {
}
public void commandAction(Command c, Displayable s) {

    if (c == exitCommand) {
        destroyApp(false);
        notifyDestroyed();
    }
    if (c == srchCommand) {
        try{
        BCC.setPortName("COM1");
        BCC.setBaudRate(57600);
        BCC.setConnectable(false);
        BCC.setDiscoverable(DiscoveryAgent.NOT_DISCOVERABLE);
        LocalDevice localDevice = LocalDevice.getLocalDevice();
        //device = new RemoteDevice[10];
        discoveryAgent = localDevice.getDiscoveryAgent();
        discoveryAgent.startInquiry(DiscoveryAgent.GIAC,this);
    }catch(BluetoothStateException btstateex)
    {
        btstateex.printStackTrace();
    }

    try{

        deviceLst=new List("Devices",List.IMPLICIT,dev,img);
        deviceLst.addCommand(exitCommand);
        srchCommand=null;
        srchCommand=new Command("Refresh",Command.SCREEN,1);
        deviceLst.addCommand(srchCommand);
        deviceLst.setCommandListener(this);
        display.setCurrent(deviceLst);
        System.out.println(deviceLst.getSelectedIndex());
    }catch (Exception e){e.printStackTrace();}
    }
    if (c==List.SELECT_COMMAND){
        int index=deviceLst.getSelectedIndex();
```

```
                    //do service search for device[index]
                    int[] attrSet = {100};
                    UUID[] uuids = new UUID[1];
                    uuids[0] = new UUID("9856",true);
                    services=null;
                    int transId=discoveryAgent.searchServices(attrSet,uuids,
                                          device[i],PiconetMIDlet);

                    ServiceLst=new List("Service",List.IMPLICIT);
                    for (int k=0;k<services.length;k++)
                        ServiceLst.append(services[k],null);
                    ServiceLst.addCommand(backCommand);
                    ServiceLst.setCommandListener(this);
                    display.setCurrent(ServiceLst);
                }
                    if (c == backCommand) {
                        display.setCurrent(deviceLst);
                    }
            }


        public void deviceDiscovered(RemoteDevice btDevice, DeviceClass cod)
        {
            /* Store the device address in the array which will be
             * used to create the device list.
             * the getBluetoothAddress() returns the Bluetooth address as a string.
             */
            device[count]=btDevice;
            //Check the type of device so that the appropriate image can be selected
            try{
            if (cod.getMinorDeviceClass()==0x04)
                img[count]=Image.createImage("/phone.png");
            else if (cod.getMinorDeviceClass()==0x0C)
                img[count]={Image.createImage("/laptop.png")};
            else img[count]={Image.createImage("/misc.png")};

            } catch (Exception e){e.printStackTrace();}
          count++;
        }

    public void servicesDiscovered(int transID,ServiceRecord[] servRecords)
    {
```

```
        for(int i=0;i<servRecords.length;i++)
          services[i]=servRecords[i].getAttributeValue(0x0100);
          synchronized(this){
          this.notify();
      }
  }


public void serviceSearchCompleted(int transID, int respCode)
{if(respCode==SERVICE_SEARCH_ERROR){
        System.out.println("\nSERVICE_SEARCH_ERROR\n");
  }
  if(respCode==SERVICE_SEARCH_COMPLETED){
    // System.out.println("\nSERVICE_SEARCH_COMPLETED\n");

  }
  if(respCode==SERVICE_SEARCH_TERMINATED){
        System.out.println("\n SERVICE_SEARCH_TERMINATED\n");
  }
  if(respCode == SERVICE_SEARCH_NO_RECORDS){
        services[0]="None";
      synchronized(this){
                    this.notify();
          }
      System.out.println("\n SERVICE_SEARCH_NO_RECORDS\n");
  }
   if(respCode == SERVICE_SEARCH_DEVICE_NOT_REACHABLE)
      System.out.println("\n SERVICE_SEARCH_DEVICE_NOT_REACHABLE\n");
}

public void inquiryCompleted(int discType)
{
              this.notify();
}

}
```

In order to port these examples to another JSR-82 SDK, just remove the import statement:

```
import com.atinav.bcc.*;
```

and the stack initialization code:

```
BCC.setPortName("COM1");
BCC.setBaudRate(57600);
BCC.setConnectable(false);
BCC.setDiscoverable(DiscoveryAgent.NOT_DISCOVERABLE);
```

Your code is now 100 percent JSR-82 compatible. The next step is to follow the instructions of your JSR-82 implementation on how to initialize your stack. In some cases, as with the Rococo implementation, no additional code is needed at all.

Summary

This chapter gave you your first fully working example of a wireless application using Java and Bluetooth. We gave you two examples, and together they demonstrated stack initialization, device management, device discovery, and service discovery. The Piconet Browser is a good utility program that you'll probably want to keep with you at all times.

If any concepts are unclear to you, right now would be a good time to review them, because in the next chapter we'll demonstrate communication by printing, and we'll also take a look at the JPS API.

CHAPTER 6

Creating a Bluetooth Print Server with JPS API

IN THE YEARS TO COME, many (if not all) printers will include a Bluetooth interface. You'll be able to walk up to any printer, download its drivers, and print to it using the Hardcopy Cable Replacement Profile. Unfortunately, that's not the case today. A large majority of the printers on the market today do not have a Bluetooth interface, and in order to make them Bluetooth enabled, you need to add a Bluetooth printer adapter, like the one shown in Figure 6-1.

Figure 6-1. You can use the 3Com Wireless Bluetooth Printer Adapter in order to make a traditional (i.e., non-Bluetooth) printer Bluetooth enabled.

Let's say that you have a mobile Bluetooth device that is capable of printing (for instance, a laptop or PDA). Whether you're a business user or a home user, you most likely would want to print to the printers that you already have connected to your desktop computer. If you're a consumer with one or two printers in your home, then you may need to buy a few printer adapters for the printers that are not Bluetooth enabled (which is somewhat practical, but can get really expensive if you have more printers). On the other hand, if you're a business user, you probably have a whole network of printers available at your disposal. Buying a printer adapter for each and every printer in a corporate environment really doesn't make a lot of sense.

This chapter gives you a handy utility that will turn your desktop computer into a Bluetooth print server using the Java Print Service (JPS) API. If your desktop computer already has the drivers and mappings that are necessary to print to your printers, why not utilize it? Your mobile device can submit print jobs to your desktop computer, and your desktop will automatically print the file to one of your printers using JPS (see Figure 6-2).

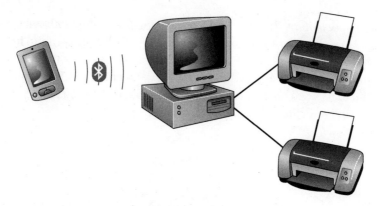

Figure 6-2. Using the handy utility provided in this chapter, you can turn your desktop into a Bluetooth print server.

JPS Overview

The relationship between a printer and its client is pretty simple. The client needs to answer two questions:

- What to print?

- How to print it?

In turn, the printer also needs to answer two questions:

- What's the status of the printer itself?

- What's the status of the print job?

The exchange of information between the printer and its client takes place by means of three entities within the JPS architecture: *documents*, *attributes*, and *events*.

NOTE　*Consequently, the JPS API consists of the following packages:* javax.print, javax.print.attribute, javax.print.attribute.standard, *and* javax.print.event.

Documents

By far, the most important piece of data that will be exchanged between the client and the printer is the document itself. In JPS terminology, the term *document* is used in a generic sense; it only refers to the item to be printed. A document could be an image, a style sheet, an actual text document, or anything that's printable. The classes that will enable you to create a document are included in the javax.print package. This package also has functionality that will allow you to create documents of well-known data formats such as HTML, PostScript, GIF, and JPEG.

Attributes

Of course, you'll have to do more than just give the printer a document; you also need to tell the printer what exactly needs to be done to the document. Print attributes will indicate to the printer things such as the size of the paper required, how many copies to print, the number of pages, and duplexing. The packages javax.print.attribute and javax.print.attribute.standard allow you to create these attributes.

Events

The JPS event model is pretty simple; after you've submitted a print job to the printer, the printer will inform you of its status through events. You can be notified of things like the printer's on/off status, the number of pages printed, and so on. The javax.print.event package deals with creating and handling these events.

A Step-by-Step JPS Application

Let's walk through a simple JPS application. Along the way, we'll identify major classes and interfaces that are a part of the JPS API. Now, in order to create a Java Print Service application, you need to do the following:

1. Identify the format of the data to be printed (i.e., GIF, JPEG, PDF, HTML, etc.).

2. Search for a print service that supports your data format.

3. Create a print job and submit it.

4. Listen for status updates (optional).

....

Printers and Print Services

If you're new to the JPS, you may say to yourself, "I know what a printer is, but what's a *print service*?" In JPS, a javax.print.PrintService object is a logical representation of an actual printer. So instead of printing to a printer, you'll print to a print service.

....

Identifying the Format

The first thing to do is identify the data format. The class that allows you to do this is javax.print.DocFlavor. For instance, if you wanted to tell the print service that you want to print out GIF files, then the code would look something like this:

```
DocFlavor docflavor = DocFlavor.INPUT_STREAM.GIF;
```

The JPS also has the functionality built in to print other popular binary formats like PDF, PostScript, PNG, and JPEG.

Creating a Document

Now that you've specified a document format, the next step is to create a document. All documents in JPS must implement the javax.print.Doc interface. You can implement this interface yourself, or you can use the javax.print.SimpleDoc object to encapsulate your data into a document. Following is a snippet of code that demonstrates how to create a document from a GIF file:

```
DocFlavor flavor = DocFlavor.INPUT_STREAM.GIF;
FileInputStream fInput = new FileInputStream("nicePic.gif");
Doc doc = new SimpleDoc(fInput, flavor, null);
```

Searching for a Print Service

Now it's time to find a suitable printer for your needs. In the JPS, you'll never interact directly with a printer; you will always have to interact with a print service that represents that printer. So, when you are searching for a printer (either connected peripherally to your computer, or somewhere on your network), you are searching for print services.

The code that follows shows you how to search for a print service that can print GIF files. In addition, this example also demonstrates how to specify some print attributes; this print service is capable of printing two copies, double-sided, on A4 size paper.

```
DocFlavor flavor = DocFlavor.INPUT_STREAM.GIF;
PrintRequestAttributeSet attribSet = new HashPrintRequestAttributeSet();
attribSet.add(new Copies(2));
attribSet.add(MediaSizeName.ISO_A4);
attribSet.add(Sides.TWO_SIDED_LONG_EDGE);
PrintService[] services =
PrintServiceLookup.lookupPrintServices(flavor, attribSet);
```

As you can see, the static method `lookupPrintServices()` from the class `javax.print.PrintServiceLookup` returns an array of `PrintService` objects. Each `PrintService` represents a printer that is capable of printing according to the attributes that you specified.

Creating a Print Job and Printing

After that's done, the next step is to create the print job and submit the job to a print service. Once you have an instance of a `PrintService` object, just call the `createPrintJob()` method, and it will return a `DocPrintJob` object (which is a print job). In order to print, just call the `print()` method on the `DocPrintJob` object and provide it with the document that you want to print as well as the print attributes. The code snippet that follows shows how to create a print job and submit it:

```
DocPrintJob printJob = services[0].createPrintJob();
try{
printJob.print(doc, attribSet);
} catch (PrintException e){
}
```

Listening for Status Updates

Optionally, you can listen to status updates on your print job after you have submitted it. For instance, if you haven't received an update from the printer in a while, you may also want to get a status update on the printer itself (it may be out of paper or something). The classes that enable you to do this are `javax.print.event.PrintServiceAttributeListener`, `javax.print.event.PrintJobAttributeListener`, and `javax.print.event.PrintJobListener`. By implementing these interfaces, you'll receive callbacks from the JVM upon changes in state of the printer or the print job.

A Complete JPS Application: JPSPrint

Listing 6-1 shows the complete source for `JPSPrint.java`, summarizing all the material that we've covered so far. It includes an inner class named `PrintStatus`, which implements the `PrintJobListener` interface. This code will provide the status of a print job by displaying a few text messages at the command line.

 CAUTION   *The JPS API is a part of JDK 1.4, and older versions of the JDK are not capable of running the JPSPrint example.*

Listing 6-1. JPSPrint.java

```java
import java.io.*;
import javax.print.*;
import javax.print.event.*;
import javax.print.attribute.*;
import javax.print.attribute.standard.*;

class PrintStatus implements PrintJobListener {

    public void printDataTransferCompleted(PrintJobEvent pje) {
        System.out.println("Data delivered to printer successfully...");
    }
    public void printJobCanceled(PrintJobEvent pje) {
        System.out.println("The print job has been cancelled...");
    }
    public void printJobCompleted(PrintJobEvent pje) {
        System.out.println("The print job completed successfully...");
    }
    public void printJobFailed(PrintJobEvent pje) {
        System.out.println("The document failed to print ..");
    }
    public void printJobNoMoreEvents(PrintJobEvent pje) {
        System.out.println("No more events to deliver...");
    }
    public void printJobRequiresAttention(PrintJobEvent pje) {
        System.out.println("Something terrible" +
                "happened which requires attention...");
    }
}

public class JPSPrint {

    public static void main(String args[]) throws FileNotFoundException{

    PrintStatus status = new PrintStatus();

    // Create the DocFlavor for GIF
    DocFlavor flavor = DocFlavor.INPUT_STREAM.GIF;

    // Create an attribute set comprising of the print instructions
    PrintRequestAttributeSet attribSet = new HashPrintRequestAttributeSet();
    attribSet.add(new Copies(1));
    attribSet.add(MediaSizeName.ISO_A4);
```

```
   // Locate print services, which can print a GIF in the manner specified
   PrintService[] pservices =
PrintServiceLookup.lookupPrintServices(flavor, attribSet);

   if (pservices.length > 0) {

      DocPrintJob job = pservices[0].createPrintJob();

      // Adding a PrintStatus Listener
      job.addPrintJobListener(status);

      // Create a Doc implementation to pass the print data
      FileInputStream fInput = new FileInputStream("nicePic.gif");
      Doc doc = new SimpleDoc(fInput, flavor, null);

      // Print the doc as specified
      try {
         job.print(doc, attribSet);
      }
      catch (PrintException e) {
         System.err.println(e);
      }
   }
   else
    System.err.println("No suitable printers");
   }
}
```

Integrating JPS and Bluetooth

Now that you have a full working example of a JPS application under your belt,
let's see what it will take in order to turn this ordinary JPS print service into
a Bluetooth-enabled, wireless print server (refer back to Figure 6-2).

   The algorithm for the application is pretty simple. The computer that
functions as the print server will start an L2CAP server and wait for clients to connect. After an incoming file is received by the server, it is printed to a printer
using the JPS API.

NOTE *As you may have already guessed, this application won't work if you use a JSR-82–compliant Java Bluetooth development kit. Why? Well, as we stated in Chapter 3, the official Java Bluetooth API has a dependency on the Generic Connection Framework (GCF) to exist, which unfortunately is not a part of the J2SE JDK 1.4.*

That doesn't mean that Java Bluetooth development kits don't exist for the J2SE. In fact, Atinav, Rococo, and Zucotto all make Java Bluetooth development kits for the J2SE. At the time of this writing, Atinav's and Rococo's J2SE implementation closely matches that of the JSR-82 implementations. The next example uses the Atinav J2SE Bluetooth development kit.

Listing 6-2 is the server code for the wireless print server example, JPSBluetoothPrint.java. As you can see, it is simply the JPSPrint.java example with a little Bluetooth code thrown in. All the wireless functionality is encapsulated in the method connectToClientAndPrint(). When this method is called, the server will wait until a client attempts to connect at an L2CAP channel. After the client connects and sends a file, the server will attempt to print it with its printFile() method.

Listing 6-2. JPSBluetoothPrint.java

```java
import java.io.*;
import javax.print.*;
import javax.print.event.*;
import javax.print.attribute.*;
import javax.print.attribute.standard.*;
import javax.bluetooth.*;
import com.atinav.standardedition.io.*;

class PrintStatus implements PrintJobListener {

    public void printDataTransferCompleted(PrintJobEvent pje) {
        System.out.println("Data delivered to printer successfully...");
    }
    public void printJobCanceled(PrintJobEvent pje) {
        System.out.println("The print job has been cancelled...");
    }
```

```
        public void printJobCompleted(PrintJobEvent pje) {
            System.out.println("The print job completed successfully...");
        }
        public void printJobFailed(PrintJobEvent pje) {
            System.out.println("The document failed to print ..");
        }
        public void printJobNoMoreEvents(PrintJobEvent pje) {
            System.out.println("No more events to deliver...");
        }
        public void printJobRequiresAttention(PrintJobEvent pje) {
            System.out.println("Some thing terrible happened which" +
                                "requires attention...");
        }
    }


public class JPSBluetoothPrint implements Runnable {

    L2CAPConnection l2capConn = null;
    private int maxRecv = -1;

    private boolean printFile(String fileName) throws FileNotFoundException{

        System.out.println("Invoking Common printAPI for printing file : " +
                            fileName);

        PrintStatus status = new PrintStatus();

        // Create the DocFlavor for GIF
        DocFlavor flavor = DocFlavor.INPUT_STREAM.GIF;

        // Create an attribute set comprised of the print instructions
        PrintRequestAttributeSet attribSet = new HashPrintRequestAttributeSet();
        attribSet.add(new Copies(1));
        attribSet.add(MediaSizeName.ISO_A4);

        // Locate print services, which can print a GIF in the manner specified
        PrintService[] pservices = PrintServiceLookup.lookupPrintServices(flavor,
                                        attribSet);

        if (pservices.length > 0) {
```

```java
        DocPrintJob job = pservices[0].createPrintJob();

        // Adding a PrintStatus Listener
        job.addPrintJobListener(status);

        // Create a Doc implementation to pass the print data
        FileInputStream fInput = new FileInputStream(fileName);
        Doc doc = new SimpleDoc(fInput, flavor, null);

        // Print the doc as specified
        try {
            job.print(doc, attribSet);
        }
        catch (PrintException e) {
            System.err.println(e);
        }
    }
    else
        System.err.println("No suitable printers");
    return true;
    }

    public void connectToClientAndPrint() throws Exception {
        System.out.println("Host Device = " +
                        LocalDevice.getLocalDevice().getBluetoothAddress());

        String url = "btl2cap://localhost:" + uuid + ";name=simplePrintServer";
        UUID uuid = new UUID("6666", true);
        L2CAPConnectionNotifier l2capNotifier =
                        (L2CAPConnectionNotifier) Connector.open(url);
        l2capConn = l2capNotifier.acceptAndOpen();
        maxRecv = l2capConn.getReceiveMTU();
        System.out.println("Connected to a client..." +
                        "Receive buffer Size is: " + maxRecv);
        new Thread(this).start();
    }

    public void run() {
        try {
            // packet receive
            byte [] data =     new byte[maxRecv];
```

```
// Reading fileName
// blocks assuming fileName always less than 48 bytes
int dataSize = l2capConn.receive(data);
byte [] fileNameAsBytes = new byte[dataSize];

System.arraycopy(data,0,fileNameAsBytes, 0,dataSize);
String fileName = new String(fileNameAsBytes);
System.out.println("File Name is = " + fileName);

FileOutputStream toFileStrm = new FileOutputStream(new File(fileName));

try {

    System.out.println("Starting to Receive file Body");

    // receive File body
    while(true) {
        if (l2capConn.ready()) {
            dataSize = l2capConn.receive(data);

            // after the whole file, an empty packet is sent from
            // the other end
            if (dataSize == 0) {
                System.out.println("Signal to Stop recieved");
                toFileStrm.close();
                toFileStrm = null;
                printFile(fileName);
                break;
            }
            toFileStrm.write(data, 0, dataSize);
        }
        try {
            Thread.currentThread().sleep(10);
        }catch(Exception genExp) {}
    }
}
finally {
    try {l2capConn.close();}catch(Exception genExp) {}
}
}
catch(Exception genEx) {
}
}
```

```
    public static void main(String [] args) throws Exception {

       JPSBluetoothPrint srv =   new JPSBluetoothPrint();
       srv.connectToClientAndPrint();
    }
}
```

Listing 6-3 has the code that a client would use in order to submit a file to the print server. This code would run on any Bluetooth-enabled J2ME device.

Listing 6-3. JPSBluetoothPrintClient.java

```
import java.io.*;
import java.util.*;
import javax.bluetooth.*;
import javax.obex.*;

public class JPSBluetoothPrintClient implements DiscoveryListener {
    LocalDevice local = null;
    DiscoveryAgent agent = null;
    int[] attrSet = null;
    RemoteDevice btDev = null;
    String serviceURL = null;
    L2CAPConnection l2capConn    = null;

    public JPSBluetoothPrintClient() throws BluetoothStateException {

       local = LocalDevice.getLocalDevice();
       agent = local.getDiscoveryAgent();
       agent.startInquiry(DiscoveryAgent.GIAC, this);
       synchronized(this){ //Waiting for Device Inquiry to be completed
         try{
            this.wait();
         }catch(Exception IntE){
            System.out.println(IntE.getMessage());
         }
       }
    }

    }
```

```java
public void deviceDiscovered(RemoteDevice btDevice,DeviceClass cod){
    if ("011114378000".indexOf(btDevice.getBluetoothAddress())> -1){
        btDev = btDevice;System.out.println("Assigned");
    }
    System.out.println("Device discovered "+btDevice.getBluetoothAddress());

}

public void servicesDiscovered(int transID, ServiceRecord[] servRecord){
    System.out.println("Discovered a service. . . . ");
    for(int i =0; i < servRecord.length; i++){
        serviceURL = servRecord[i].getConnectionURL
            (ServiceRecord.NOAUTHENTICATE_NOENCRYPT,true);
        System.out.println("The service URL is "+serviceURL);
    }
}

public void serviceSearchCompleted(int transID, int respCode){
    System.out.println("Service search completed.......... ");
    synchronized(this){ //Unblocking the wait for Service search complete
        try{
            this.notifyAll();
        }catch(Exception IntE){
            System.out.println(IntE.getMessage());
        }
    }

}

public void inquiryCompleted(int discType){
    System.out.println("Inquiry completed...");
    synchronized(this){ //Unblocking the wait for inquiry complete
        try{
            this.notifyAll();
        }catch(Exception IntE){
            System.out.println(IntE.getMessage());
        }
    }

}

public void getServices(){
```

```
        UUID[] uuids = new UUID[1];
        uuids[0] = new UUID("6666", true);
        try{
            if(btDev == null){
                System.out.println("No device has been discovered, " +
                            "hence not worth proceeding,exiting.... ");
                System.exit(1);
            }
         System.out.println("Now searching for services........ ");
         agent.searchServices(attrSet, uuids, btDev, this);

        }
        catch(BluetoothStateException e) {
            System.out.println(e.getMessage());
            System.out.println("Got an exception, so exiting...");
            System.exit(1);
        }

         synchronized(this){ //Waiting for Service Search to be completed
            try{
                this.wait();
            }catch(Exception IntE){
                 System.out.println(IntE.getMessage());
            }
         }
    }
}


public boolean sendFile(String fileName){
    try {
        l2capConn = (L2CAPConnection)Connector.open(serviceURL);

        InputConnection inConn =
        (InputConnection)Connector.open("file://name="+fileName+";mode=r");
        InputStream fileReader = inConn.openInputStream();

        int maxSendMTU = l2capConn.getTransmitMTU();
        byte [] buffer = new byte[maxSendMTU];

        // sending fileName
        // assuming for the time being that the fileName
        // will not be greater than 48 bytes
```

```
                l2capConn.send(fileName.getBytes());
                System.out.println("Send the file Name = " + fileName);

                // sending fileContent
                // after the whole file gets transferred, an empty packet is sent.
                int actualDataSize = -1;
                byte [] pkt = null;
                while((actualDataSize = fileReader.read(buffer)) != -1) {
                    pkt = new byte[actualDataSize];
                    System.arraycopy(buffer, 0, pkt, 0, actualDataSize);
                    l2capConn.send(pkt);
                }
                System.out.println("Completed sendng body of file = " + fileName);

                //sending empty packet signaling end of file
                l2capConn.send(new byte[0]);

                fileReader.close();
                return true;
            }

            catch(IOException e){
                System.out.println(e.getMessage());
                return false;
            }

            finally {
                System.out.println("Closing connection");
                try {l2capConn.close();}catch(Exception genx) {}
            }
        }

    public static void main(String args[]) throws Exception  {
        JPSBluetoothPrintClient client = new JPSBluetoothPrintClient();
        client.getServices();
        System.out.println(client.sendFile(args[0]));
    }

}
```

Summary

This chapter was probably your first time working with the new Java Print Service APIs. The JPS is a platform-independent printing solution that's new in JDK 1.4. In this chapter, you learned about all the steps that are necessary to create a complete JPS application, such as identifying the data format, searching for print services, specifying attributes, and creating and submitting print jobs. After creating a simple JPS application, you learned how to turn your ordinary print service into a Bluetooth-enabled print server!

This chapter demonstrated communication with Bluetooth using the L2CAP protocol. This is ideal if you want to transfer items between two devices that can be broken into packets and reassembled again (such as files). L2CAP is a layer below RFCOMM in the Bluetooth protocol stack, so if you optimize your MTU, you can achieve significantly faster data transfers between wireless devices. In Chapter 7, we'll examine a more robust Bluetooth protocol for transferring files: OBEX.

Java and OBEX

Whether you like it or not, you're surrounded by objects every day. In fact, part of the role of being a good Java programmer is to find out what is the best way to recognize and create objects when developing business applications (and games, too). As we stated in Chapter 4, the Bluetooth specification gives you three protocols to send and receive data:

- RFCOMM (for stream data)

- L2CAP (for packet data)

- OBEX (for object data)

In this chapter, we'll discuss the mechanics of the OBEX protocol, and how to send objects between Bluetooth devices. We'll cover the APIs in the `javax.obex` package, and finish things up by demonstrating how to send files between two devices using OBEX.

What Is OBEX?

OBEX (which stands for OBject EXchange) is a communication protocol that allows object data to be transferred between two devices (it doesn't matter if those devices are wirelessly or physically connected). OBEX was originally created by the Infrared Data Association (IrDA), but it later became one of the Bluetooth adopted protocols (like WAP). Take a look at Figure 7-1 to see where OBEX fits in the Bluetooth and IrDA protocol stacks.

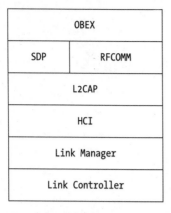 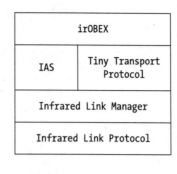

Figure 7-1. OBEX is called IrOBEX in the IrDA protocol stack.

In the Bluetooth specification, OBEX is the underlying protocol that is used to implement the following Bluetooth profiles:

- Generic Object Exchange Profile

- Object Push Profile

- Synchronization Profile

- File Transfer Profile

- Basic Imaging Profile

- Basic Printing Profile

 NOTE   *Did you realize that the official Java OBEX implementation was named* `javax.obex` *and not* `javax.bluetooth.obex`*? It was named* `javax.obex` *because the JSR-82 designers knew that (if structured correctly) the OBEX libraries would be the same regardless of the underlying transmission protocol (also known as the* bearer *or the* transport*). So, you can use the classes in the* `javax.obex` *package to send objects between any device that implements the official Java OBEX API. The JSR-82 provides guidelines on how to use OBEX over Bluetooth, IR, and TCP/IP connections.*

The OBEX protocol has a simple client/server architecture. OBEX clients get objects from and put objects onto OBEX servers. OBEX servers wait around for incoming requests from clients. The OBEX *definition* can be summarized in two parts: the OBEX Object Model and the OBEX Session Protocol. The *Object Model* provides the definition of OBEX objects and information on how to transfer them. The *Session Protocol* defines the handshaking that needs to occur between the client and the server when transferring objects between devices. Let's look at OBEX Object Model and Session Protocol in more detail.

The OBEX Object Model

In the OBEX Object Model, all the details about an object are represented as attributes called *headers*. Each header will contain information about the object (i.e., the name of the object) or the object itself. The Object Model defines headers as one byte for the header ID, and one or more bytes for the header's value. A typical OBEX header is illustrated in Figure 7-2.

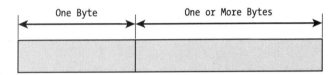

Figure 7-2. An OBEX header

The OBEX Object Model has defined 17 headers for OBEX object attributes. However, the official Java OBEX specification uses only 12 of them as constants in the interface `java.obex.HeaderSet`. These constants are listed in Table 7-1.

Table 7-1. OBEX Headers in the java.obex.HeaderSet Interface

HEADER ID NAME	HEADER ID DECIMAL VALUE	JAVA TYPE	DESCRIPTION
COUNT	192	java.lang.Long	The number of objects to be sent
NAME	1	java.lang.String	The object's name (usually used as the filename)
TYPE	66	java.lang.String	The type of the object, like text/plain
LENGTH	195	java.lang.Long	The length of the object in bytes
TIME_ISO_8601	68	java.util.Calendar	The time in ISO 8601 format
TIME_4_BYTE	196	java.util.Calendar	The time represented as a 4-byte integer
DESCRIPTION	5	java.lang.String	A description of the object
TARGET	70	byte[]	The name of the service that the object is being sent to
HTTP	71	byte[]	The HTTP version 1.x header
WHO	74	byte[]	Refers to the peer OBEX application if peers are involved
OBJECT_CLASS	79	byte[]	The OBEX object class for the object
APPLICATION_PARAMETER	76	byte[]	Data that represents request and response parameters for the OBEX application

You are also free to create your own headers as long as you obey the following guidelines:

- java.lang.String object types should have a header ID decimal value between 48 and 63.

- byte arrays (i.e. byte[]) should have a header ID decimal value between 112 and 127.

- java.lang.Byte object types should have a header ID decimal value between 176 and 191.

- java.lang.Long object types should have a header ID decimal value between 240 and 255.

The OBEX Session Protocol

The OBEX Session Protocol specifies all rules and processes for communication between OBEX clients and servers. The communication scheme is a simple request-response process: The client sends a request, and the server responds. Both requests and responses are sent as packets. Clients communicate to the server via eight simple *operations:*

- CONNECT

- DISCONNECT

- PUT

- GET

- SETPATH

- ABORT

- CREATE-EMPTY

- PUT-DELETE

OBEX servers, in turn, return responses back to the OBEX clients, such as the following:

- SUCCESS

- FAILURE

- CONTINUE

 NOTE *There are a lot more OBEX responses than just these three. All the valid response codes in the* javax.obex *API are contained in the* javax.obex.ResponseCodes *class, which is described later in this chapter.*

Figure 7-3 is an illustration of the message flow that takes place during a simple OBEX session.

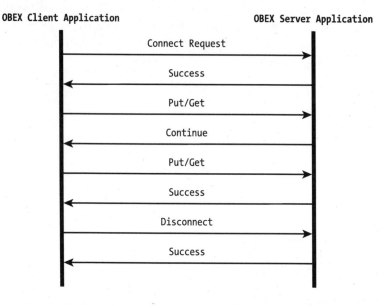

Figure 7-3. A sample message flow between OBEX clients and servers

The client initiates the communication process by sending a request packet with the CONNECT operation. The request packet contains the code for the operation, the length of the packet itself, and the headers. Upon receiving the request, the server responds with a response packet that contains the response code, the response length, and some response data. Under normal circumstances, the server returns a packet with a response code of SUCCESS. If, however, some problem has occurred, then the server returns a FAILURE code.

The PUT operation allows the client to send an object to the server. It's possible that a small object may fit into a single PUT request packet. If not, then the client sends multiple packets, and the server responds with a CONTINUE response code. The server responds to the final PUT packet with a SUCCESS code.

Similarly, clients are able to retrieve objects from the server by sending a GET request packet. If the server accepts the packet, it responds with either a SUCCESS or a CONTINUE response code. If the server responds with a CONTINUE, then the client continues to send a GET request until the server responds with a SUCCESS code.

The client uses the SETPATH operation in conjunction with a PUT or GET operation in order to change the directory on the server. The client can also use the ABORT operation in order to end the session with the server prematurely. The client can create an empty file on the server using the CREATE-EMPTY operation, and it can remove an object from the server using the PUT-DELETE operation.

Now that you have a pretty good understanding of the overall functionality of OBEX, let's take a look at the Java OBEX APIs.

The OBEX APIs in the JSR-82

The following eight classes and interfaces make up the javax.obex package in the JSR-82 API. Some of these classes should look somewhat familiar to you—namely HeaderSet, ResponseCodes, and Operation.

- Authenticator

- ClientSession

- HeaderSet

- Operation

- PasswordAuthenticator

- ResponseCodes

- SessionNotifier

- ServerRequestHandler

Now let's take a look at some of these classes in more detail.

javax.obex.ClientSession

The ClientSession interface is a subclass of the javax.microedition.io.Connection class, and represents an OBEX connection from the client's point of view. You can obtain an instance of this interface by using the following line of code:

```
ClientSession session = (ClientSession)Connector.open(connectURL);
```

This interface provides a way to define headers for OBEX operations. For instance, the methods put() and get() respectively allow you to create PUT and GET operations. Those methods return a javax.obex.Operation object so that you can *complete* the operation.

 NOTE   *See the description of* javax.obex.Operation *later in this section for more information on how to complete* GET *and* PUT *operations.*

The methods connect(), disconnect(), and setPath() complete their respective operations (CONNECT, DISCONNECT, and SETPATH) and return the result in a javax.obex.HeaderSet object.

javax.obex.HeaderSet

The HeaderSet interface can be used to define all OBEX headers (even custom headers). It can be instantiated by calling ClientSession.createHeaderSet(). An example of an OBEX client setting the NAME and TYPE headers is shown here:

```
HeaderSet hdr = clientSession.createHeaderSet();
//Creating a header set  to request Hello.txt file from the server
hdr.setHeader(HeaderSet.TYPE,"text/vCard");
hdr.setHeader(HeaderSet.NAME,"Hello.txt");
```

An OBEX server, in turn, can retrieve the headers sent from the client by calling either getHeader() or getHeaderList().

javax.obex.Operation

The Operation interface provides you with all the methods necessary to complete an OBEX GET or PUT operation. What do we mean by *complete?* As you can see in the following code snippet, an Operation was created using the put() method in ClientSession:

```
ClientSession session = (ClientSession)Connector.open(connectURL);
Operation op = session.put(null);
```

However, the Operation is not complete until you include the object that you want to send (in the case of a PUT) and add some headers. Following is an example of how to complete a PUT operation:

```
ClientSession session = (ClientSession)Connector.open(connectURL);
Operation op = session.put(null);
OutputStream out = op.openOutputStream();
out.write("Test".getBytes());
out.close();
```

Now in order to make a CREATE-EMPTY operation, just open and close the OutputStream without writing any data, as shown here:

```
ClientSession session = (ClientSession)Connector.open(connectURL);
Operation op = session.put(null);
OutputStream out = op.openOutputStream();
out.close();
```

The easiest way to create a PUT-DELETE is to call the delete() method of this class.

javax.obex.ResponseCodes

The ResponseCodes class contains all the valid response codes that an OBEX server can send to its client. Since the OBEX request/response model is very similar to that of HTTP, you will see that the responses are modeled after their HTTP counterparts:

- OBEX_DATABASE_FULL

- OBEX_DATABASE_LOCKED

- OBEX_HTTP_ACCEPTED

- OBEX_HTTP_BAD_GATEWAY

- OBEX_HTTP_BAD_METHOD

- OBEX_HTTP_BAD_REQUEST

- OBEX_HTTP_CONFLICT

- OBEX_HTTP_CREATED

- OBEX_HTTP_ENTITY_TOO_LARGE

- OBEX_HTTP_FORBIDDEN

- OBEX_HTTP_GATEWAY_TIMEOUT

- OBEX_HTTP_GONE

- OBEX_HTTP_INTERNAL_ERROR

- OBEX_HTTP_LENGTH_REQUIRED

- OBEX_HTTP_MOVED_PERM

- OBEX_HTTP_MOVED_TEMP

- OBEX_HTTP_MULT_CHOICE

- OBEX_HTTP_NO_CONTENT

- OBEX_HTTP_NOT_ACCEPTABLE

- OBEX_HTTP_NOT_AUTHORITATIVE

- OBEX_HTTP_NOT_FOUND

- OBEX_HTTP_NOT_IMPLEMENTED

- OBEX_HTTP_NOT_MODIFIED

- OBEX_HTTP_OK

- OBEX_HTTP_PARTIAL

- OBEX_HTTP_PAYMENT_REQUIRED

- OBEX_HTTP_PRECON_FAILED

- OBEX_HTTP_PROXY_AUTH

- OBEX_HTTP_REQ_TOO_LARGE

- OBEX_HTTP_RESET

- OBEX_HTTP_SEE_OTHER

- OBEX_HTTP_TIMEOUT

- OBEX_HTTP_UNAUTHORIZED

- OBEX_HTTP_UNAVAILABLE

- OBEX_HTTP_UNSUPPORTED_TYPE

- OBEX_HTTP_USE_PROXY

- OBEX_HTTP_VERSION

NOTE   *So where are the response codes that we discussed earlier in this chapter like* SUCCESS, FAILURE, *and* CONTINUE*? Good question. Well, the OBEX* SUCCESS *response code is mapped to* OBEX_HTTP_OK *in the* ResponseCodes *class. And rather than simply having a generic response code for* FAILURE, *there are numerous response codes to indicate what kind of failure has occurred. Finally, the* CONTINUE *response will always be handled by your underlying implementation, so you should never see it.*

Here is an example of how to use the ResponseCodes class to determine if your PUT operation was a success:

```
ClientSession session = (ClientSession)Connector.open(connectURL);
Operation op = session.put(null);
OutputStream out = op.openOutputStream();
out.write("Test".getBytes());
out.close();
if(op.getResponseCode() ==
ResponseCodes.OBEX_HTTP_OK)
        System.out.println(" PUT operation is success");
```

javax.obex.ServerRequestHandler

The ServerRequestHandler is a very useful class for OBEX servers. It includes an event listener that responds to specific OBEX requests made to the server.

 NOTE *This is a class and not an interface, so in order to use its functionality, you need to extend this class and not implement it.*

This class has the following methods that will be called when incoming client requests contain the corresponding operation:

- onConnect()

- onSetPath()

- onDelete()

- onGet()

- onPut()

After the callback method has been called by the JVM, you can obtain the headers from the Operation object as shown here:

```
public int onGet(Operation op) {
     try{
          HeaderSet hdr = op.getReceivedHeaders();
     }
```

javax.obex.SessionNotifier

The SessionNotifier interface follows the same pattern as all notifiers in J2ME.
A device that wants to be an OBEX server must implement this interface and call
the acceptAndOpen() method and wait for clients, as shown in the following code:

```
SessionNotifier sn = (SessionNotifier)
Connector.open("btgoep://localhost:1106;name = FTP");
sn.acceptAndOpen(serverRequestHandler);
```

Once the server accepts a connection from a client, it then opens a channel
for the client. The subclass of ServerRequestHandler that you passed to the
acceptAndOpen() method is notified of all subsequent requests from the client.

Now that we've covered many of the classes of the Java OBEX API, let's look at
an example that puts these concepts together.

File Transfer Example

In the file transfer example, we'll examine the code that's needed to send
a file between two Bluetooth devices using the OBEX API of the JSR-82. The
server code is less complex than the client code, so we'll present that first.

File Transfer Server

Before any clients can connect, the server must register the service in the SDDB.
This is accomplished in the main method as shown here:

```
public static void main(String args[]) throws IOException {
    FTServer server = new FTServer();
    LocalDevice localDevice = LocalDevice.getLocalDevice();
    SessionNotifier sn =
    (SessionNotifier)Connector.open("btgoep://localhost:1106;name=FTP");
    System.out.println("Waiting for a client connection. . . . . ");
```

```
        sn.acceptAndOpen(server);
        System.out.println("A Client now connected. . . . ");
    }
```

A service record has now been created and stored in the SDDB of the server device. Now let's take a closer look at the connection URL:

```
btgoep://localhost:1106;name=FTP
```

As you can see, we are using a new protocol for communication: btgoep (which stands for Bluetooth Generic Object Exchange Profile). Because this is a server device, the address will always be localhost. The UUID for this service is 1106, which is the UUID for OBEX file transfers.

CROSS-REFERENCE *See Table 4-4 for UUID values for Bluetooth services and their corresponding profiles.*

We also gave a friendly name for this service, which is FTP. Our file transfer server has extended the ServerRequestHandler class, and has overridden the onConnect() and onGet() methods. Here, the onGet() method will attempt to read the requested file from the local storage and send the file back to the client. Obviously, the onConnect() and onGet() methods are only called if the clients send a CONNECT or GET operation to the server. The code for the file transfer server is shown in Listing 7-1.

Listing 7-1. FTServer.java

```java
import javax.microedition.io.*;
import java.io.*;
import javax.bluetooth.*;
import javax.obex.*;

public class FTServer extends ServerRequestHandler{

    public FTServer() throws BluetoothStateException {

        // initialize the stack, if needed
    }
```

```java
    public int onConnect(HeaderSet request, HeaderSet reply) {
        System.out.println("A OBEX connection has received.... ");
        return ResponseCodes.OBEX_HTTP_OK;
    }


    public int onGet(Operation op) {
        try{
            //The server has received a GET request for client.
            System.out.println("Received a GET request from client.....  ");
            HeaderSet hdr = op.getReceivedHeaders();

          System.out.println("Server has received a request for the file  " +
              (hdr.getHeader(HeaderSet.NAME)).toString());
            String url = "file://name="  +
            (hdr.getHeader(HeaderSet.NAME)).toString() + ";mode=r";
            InputConnection inpcon =
            (InputConnection)Connector.open(url);
            InputStream in = inpcon.openInputStream();
            byte[] fileAsBytes     = new byte[97];
            in.read(fileAsBytes);
            System.out.println("File read fully into the port.... ");
            for(int i =0; i<fileAsBytes.length; i++)
                System.out.print((char)fileAsBytes[i]);
            DataOutputStream out = op.openDataOutputStream();
            out.write(fileAsBytes, 0, fileAsBytes.length);
            System.out.println("\n" + "File written back to client.... ");
            op.close();
            in.close();
        }
        catch(IOException e){
            System.out.println(e.getMessage());
        }
        catch(ArrayIndexOutOfBoundsException e){
            System.out.println(e.getMessage());
        }

    return ResponseCodes.OBEX_HTTP_OK;
    }

    public static void main(String args[]) throws IOException {

        FTServer server = new FTServer();
        LocalDevice localDevice = LocalDevice.getLocalDevice();
```

```
SessionNotifier sn =
(SessionNotifier)Connector.open("btgoep://localhost:1106;name=FTP");
System.out.println("Waiting for a client connection. . . . . ");
sn.acceptAndOpen(server);
System.out.println("A Client now connected. . . . ");


    }

}
```

More on Connection URLs and the SDDB

The Connection URL and the service record attributes in the SDDB are closely related. Although software developers may not care about the inner details of the SDDB, this information will be helpful when searching for services on remote devices. In the File Transfer Server example, the SDDB gets populated with various components of the connection URL:
Connector.open("btgoep://localhost:1106;name=FTP");.

ServiceRecordHandle is a 32-bit unsigned integer that has an attribute ID of 0x0000. This is a unique identifier for each service in the SDDB. The value of ServiceRecordHandle is generated internally and remains unique throughout the database.

ServiceClassIDList is a data sequence of UUIDs with an attribute ID of 0x0001. The underlying Service Discovery Protocol (SDP) implementation generates this list with the first element as the UUID given in the Connection URL. In this example, the first UUID in this list will be 0x1106.

ServiceRecordState is a 32-bit unsigned integer that has an attribute ID of 0x0002. The underlying SDP implementation automatically generates this attribute and changes its value when any modification occurs with this service record.

ProtocolDescriptorList is a data sequence of UUIDs (with optional parameters or protocol-specific values) with an attribute ID of 0x0004. Once again, the SDP implementation automatically generates this attribute based on the protocol described in Connection URL. If the protocol is btl2cap, then ProtocolDescriptorList contains one protocol descriptor for L2CAP in addition to its Protocol Service Multiplexer (PSM) value. If the protocol is btspp, then the ProtocolDescriptorList contains two protocols, L2CAP and RFCOMM (in addition to the RFCOMM server channel). If the protocol is btgoep (as in this example), then the ProtocolDescriptorList contains three protocols: L2CAP, RFCOMM, and GOEP.

ServiceDatabaseState is a 32-bit unsigned integer with an attribute ID of 0x0201. Every modification to the SDDB affects the value of this attribute, and the SDP implementation will automatically take care of this for you.

ServiceName is the friendly name by which the services are known to the devices in the vicinity. In this example, the service name is FTP.

File Transfer Client

Now in order to access the File Transfer server, we must first perform device discovery and service discovery like we always do in Bluetooth applications. In addition to that, in our serviceSearchCompleted() method, we create our Operations and HeaderSets to instruct the OBEX server what we want to do.

The CONNECT Operation

The first OBEX operation that needs to be created and sent to the OBEX server is CONNECT. This is accomplished by the following:

```
con = (ClientSession)Connector.open(serviceURL);
hdr = con.connect(hdr);
```

The connect() method of this ClientSession instance returns a HeaderSet object where we can inspect and determine if our CONNECT operation was a success.

The GET Operation

Now that we have successfully performed our CONNECT operation, we are able to create other operations like GET, PUT, and SETPATH. The code that you would use in order to create and send a GET operation to an OBEX server looks like this:

```
hdr = con.createHeaderSet();
hdr.setHeader(HeaderSet.TYPE,"text/plain");
hdr.setHeader(HeaderSet.NAME,"Hello.txt");
Operation op = con.get(hdr);
```

If the operation was successful, then just open up an InputStream, and read the data:

```
InputStream in = op.openInputStream();
```

Now that you have an InputStream in hand, you can save your file to disk.

The DISCONNECT Operation

Creating and sending a DISCONNECT operation is pretty simple. All you need to do is call the disconnect() method of the ClientSession object:

```
clientSession.disconnect(null);
```

The full code for FTClient is show in Listing 7-2.

Listing 7-2. FTClient.java

```java
import java.io.*;
import java.util.*;
import javax.microedition.io.*;
import javax.bluetooth.*;
import javax.obex.*;

public class FTClient implements DiscoveryListener {
    LocalDevice local = null;
    DiscoveryAgent agent = null;
    int[] attrSet = null;
    RemoteDevice btDev = null;
    String serviceURL = null;
    ClientSession con = null;
    HeaderSet hdr = null;

    public FTClient() throws BluetoothStateException{

        // initialize the stack, if needed
        local = LocalDevice.getLocalDevice();
        agent = local.getDiscoveryAgent();
        agent.startInquiry(DiscoveryAgent.GIAC, this);
    }
    public void deviceDiscovered(RemoteDevice btDevice,DeviceClass cod){
        btDev = btDevice;
        System.out.println("Device discovered " +
        btDevice.getBluetoothAddress());
    }
```

```java
public void servicesDiscovered(int transID, ServiceRecord[] servRecord){
    System.out.println("Discovered a service.... ");
    for(int i =0; i < servRecord.length; i++){
        serviceURL =
        servRecord[i].getConnectionURL(ServiceRecord.NOAUTHENTICATE_NOENCRYPT,
        true);         System.out.println("The service URL is " + serviceURL);
    }
}


public void serviceSearchCompleted(int transID, int respCode){
    System.out.println("Service search completed.......... ");
    System.out.println("Opening a connection with the server.... ");
    try{
        con = (ClientSession)Connector.open(serviceURL);
        hdr = con.connect(hdr);
        System.out.println("Response code of the server after connect..." +
            hdr.getResponseCode());


        //Sending a request to server for file Hello.txt
        hdr = con.createHeaderSet();
        hdr.setHeader(HeaderSet.TYPE,"text/vCard");
        hdr.setHeader(HeaderSet.NAME,"Hello.txt");
        Operation op = con.get(hdr);

        //The server is now sending the file
        InputStream in = op.openInputStream();


        // Writing the file from server to local file system.
StreamConnection filestream =
        (StreamConnection)Connector.open("file://name=HelloFile.txt;mode=w");
OutputStream out = filestream.openOutputStream();

        //read and write the data
        int data = in.read();
        while(data != -1){
            out.write((byte)data);
            data = in.read();
        }
```

```
                // send the DISCONNECT Operation
                con.disconnect();

                // cleanup
         op.close();
                in.close();
                out.close();
          }
          catch(IOException e){
        System.out.println(e.getMessage());
          }
        }
        public void inquiryCompleted(int discType){
          System.out.println("Inquiry completed...");
          UUID[] uuids = new UUID[1];
            uuids[0] = new UUID("1106",true);
            try{
                if(btDev == null){
          System.out.println("No device has been discovered, " +
                    "hence not worth proceeding, exiting. . . . ");
          System.exit(1);
                }
            System.out.println("Now searching for services. . . . . . . . ");
            agent.searchServices(attrSet, uuids, btDev, this);
          }
        catch(BluetoothStateException e) {System.out.println(e.getMessage());}
        }

        public static void main(String args[]) throws IOException {
          FTClient client = new FTClient();
        }
    }
```

More on Operations

Now that we have a full working example of both an OBEX client and an OBEX
server, let's look at what it takes to use other OBEX operations.

The SETPATH Operation

The SETPATH operation allows an OBEX client to make a request to an OBEX server to change its current directory. The server is not required to obey the request, so the server is free to return an error to the client indicating that the request was rejected. The exact syntax for `ClientSession.setPath()` is

```
public HeaderSet setPath(HeaderSet headers, boolean backup, boolean create)
```

To specify the name of the directory that you want to navigate to, you must create a HeaderSet with the name set as a header. If you wanted to set the path to the previous directory (i.e. cd ..) then backup must be set to true. If the directory does not exist, but you want it to be created, then you must set create to be true. The code that follows demonstrates how to create a SETPATH operation:

```
HeaderSet folderHdr = clientSession.createHeaderSet();
folderHdr.setHeader(HeaderSet.NAME, "temp");
HeaderSet resultHdr = clientSession.setPath(folderHdr, false, true);
```

The PUT Operation

After creating and sending a CONNECT operation, creating a PUT operation is very straightforward as shown in the code presented here:

```
hdr = con.createHeaderSet();
String filename = "resume_cv.txt";

// setting values
hdr.setHeader(HeaderSet.NAME, fileName);
hdr.setHeader(HeaderSet.TYPE,"text/plain");

// creating and sending the PUT Operation
Operation op = con.put(hdr);

// sending the BODY
OutputStream writeStrm = op.openOutputStream();
StreamConnection strmCon = (StreamConnection)Connector.open("file://name=" +
fileName + ";mode=r");
InputStream readStrm = strmCon.openInputStream();
byte[] block = new byte[512];
int dataSize = -1;
```

```
while((dataSize = readStrm.read(block))!= -1) {
      writeStrm.write(block, 0, dataSize);
}

readStrm.close();
// setting final bit and
// sending the END-OF-BODY-HEADER
writeStrm.close();
```

Summary

OBEX (which stands for OBject EXchange) is a powerful, transport agnostic, communication protocol that allows the transmission of objects between clients and servers. The OBEX protocol is an adopted protocol in the Bluetooth specification, and originally gets its roots from the IrDA specification. This chapter helped you to get familiar with many of the concepts of the OBEX semantics including headers, operations, and response codes. This chapter gave you an introduction of the classes in the javax.obex API, and also provided a working example on how to send files between wireless devices.

OBEX opens the door to a world of powerful wireless applications by providing Bluetooth developers with the ability to send files between devices. In the next chapter, we'll change gears a bit and discuss how to simulate a Bluetooth network.

CHAPTER 8

Using a Bluetooth Simulator

OKAY, WE HAVE TO ADMIT IT: If you're new to Bluetooth, developing wireless client/server code can (sometimes) be rather inconvenient. After writing the client code and then the server code, you may have to do a lot of debugging to get things working properly. Maybe your logic is incorrect—perhaps you have a problem with one of your Bluetooth modules (maybe both of them). With so many points of failure, it can be a real daunting task to debug even the simplest Bluetooth application. However, with the help of a Bluetooth network simulator, all of the hardware and its underlying complexities are abstracted, and this will enable you to focus more time and effort to debug your application code.

NOTE *A Bluetooth network simulator can also be helpful if you're on a budget or if you're a student. If either case applies to you, you certainly don't have a lot of money to buy a test lab full of Bluetooth devices.*

This chapter is all about how to use a Bluetooth network simulator in your application development process. A Bluetooth network simulator isn't a panacea for all of your development woes, but it can be a very useful tool in many areas of the wireless application development life cycle. We'll start this chapter off by explaining the difference between a simulator and an emulator, just in case you didn't know that there's a difference. Next, we'll take a look at the pros and cons of using a simulator. In the rest of the chapter, we'll get you up to speed on how to use the first and only Bluetooth network simulator in which you can execute your JSR-82–compatible code: the Rococo Impronto Simulator.

NOTE *This chapter is intended to provide a brief overview of the concepts of simulation and the Rococo software. For more detailed information on how to use the Rococo Impronto Simulator, be sure to read the user manual.*

....

Difference Between a Simulator and an Emulator

Is there a difference between a simulator and an emulator? Yes, definitely. An *emulator* is a software program (or sometimes a hardware device) that emulates the functionality of another computer system. Behind the scenes, the emulator translates the instructions of the device being emulated to the machine code of the foreign system. Essentially, only computers can emulate other computers, and due to the translation process, emulation works best when a faster computer emulates a slower computer. Emulators are handy when you want to run a program, but the computing system for which it was originally designed no longer exists or isn't available. For instance, the Multiple Arcade Machine Emulator (MAME) project is a popular emulator that allows you to play classic arcade games on your desktop computer. PalmSource also makes an emulator that allows you to run different versions of the Palm OS on your desktop computer. This can be useful when testing to see if your code is backward compatible with older versions of the Palm OS.

On the other hand, a *simulator* is something (usually software) that represents the functionality of an entire system. A simulator will mimic the interaction and communication process between devices in the system, and try to display the results as if those occurrences actually happened. For instance, an automotive company can create a crash test simulator. Using this simulator, the automotive engineer can simulate what would happen to the car if it collides with another object like a wall, a deer, or even another car. Now, in order for the simulator to be even remotely useful, formulas must exist that describe the interaction of the objects in the system. If such formulas do not exist, then a lot of mapping and modeling of the objects in the system need to be done ahead of time before the simulator is created.

With the use of a Bluetooth network simulator, you can mimic the interaction of multiple Bluetooth devices on your desktop computer as if those occurrences were actually happening between Bluetooth devices.

....

The Pros and Cons of Using a Simulator

A Bluetooth simulator can be a useful and beneficial tool. One of the major benefits of a Bluetooth network simulator is that it allows you to work on your application code without worrying about setting up and administrating your Bluetooth hardware configurations. This enables you to create quick proof of concepts and algorithm verification. In larger development teams, the use of a simulator can greatly reduce the expense of creating a development environment for each developer. Instead of buying Bluetooth hardware for each and every individual (which would be used throughout all the phases of the application development life cycle), fewer Bluetooth devices can be purchased and used for only the final phase of application development: testing.

Now, on the other hand, no matter how good a Bluetooth network simulator may claim to be, it is no substitute for scenarios that require the presence of real Bluetooth hardware. For instance, a Bluetooth network simulator isn't capable of telling you what would happen if you ran your file transfer application code using 3Com or TDK Bluetooth modules. A Bluetooth network simulator is also incapable of telling you how your application would behave in the presence of other devices that operate in the 2.4 GHz range like WLAN devices or microwave ovens. Due to the absence of any Bluetooth hardware, Bluetooth network simulators are also a poor choice for testing the performance of your application (such as I/O throughput).

Impronto Simulator from Rococo

The Rococo Impronto Simulator is a 100 percent Java application that allows you, the developer, to create JSR-82–compliant Bluetooth applications. Using the Impronto Simulator, you can create virtual Bluetooth devices using the environment, and deploy your code to those virtual devices to see how they interact.

> **NOTE** *Using the Rococo Impronto Simulator, you can create Bluetooth applications for both the J2ME and J2SE platforms. Note that J2SE Bluetooth applications will not be JSR-82 compliant until the GCF for J2SE is released.*

Product Features

The following features are supported by the Rococo Impronto Simulator:

- Provides full support for L2CAP, RFCOMM, OBEX, SDP, and HCI protocols

- Provides a management console for tracking and controlling the runtime behavior of simulated devices

- Runs JSR-82 code on simulated Bluetooth devices

- Has full logging capability for Bluetooth events, and can capture events for specific devices with event filtering

Installation Guide

The Impronto Simulator runs on any J2SE environment, including Windows and Linux. You can obtain a free trial of the software from the Rococo Web site http://www.rococosoft.com. In order to install the software on Windows 2000, just execute simulator.exe. When installing the software on UNIX platforms, you need to execute simulator.bin. The Simulator requires at least 64 MB of RAM and 5 MB of free disk space. Figure 8-1 is a screenshot of the installation program.

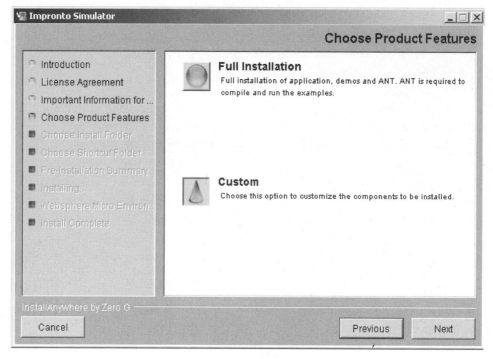

Figure 8-1. The Rococo Impronto Simulator version 1.1 installation screen

In order to verify that your installation went smoothly, you should try to build the example applications that are included with the Impronto Simulator: Echo, Chat, and AirHockey. First, you should open a command prompt and run the setEnvVars script. On Windows platforms, this file is located at

{*simulator_home*}\bin\setEnvVars.bat

On UNIX platforms, the file is located at

{*simulator_home*}/bin/setEnvVars.sh

After the script has executed successfully, navigate to the examples directory and type ant at the command prompt to build the examples.

> **NOTE**   *Just in case you didn't notice, the Apache Ant build utility was installed with the Impronto Simulator.*

The final step is to start up the Simulator Console. All you need to do is go back to the bin directory and execute manager. A screenshot of the Simulator Console is shown in Figure 8-2.

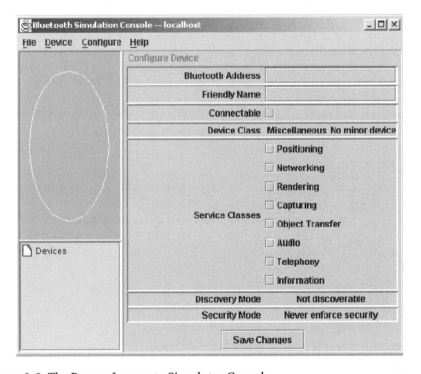

Figure 8-2. The Rococo Impronto Simulator Console

Working with the Simulator Console

The Simulator Console is the control panel to the Impronto Simulator. Using the Simulator Console, you can create and edit simulated Bluetooth devices. The characteristics of each device that you create are stored in an XML file in the config directory. For instance, to create a new Bluetooth device, just go to the File menu and select New Device as shown in Figure 8-3.

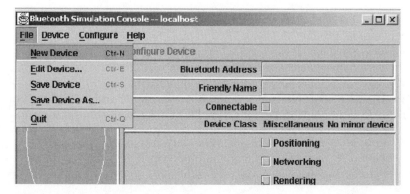

Figure 8-3. Creating a new Bluetooth device in the Simulator Console is pretty simple.

The Impronto Simulator then gives you the option to set other properties for your simulated Bluetooth device such as the address, the connectable mode, the friendly name, and the device class. Figure 8-4 shows a cell phone being configured in the Simulator Console.

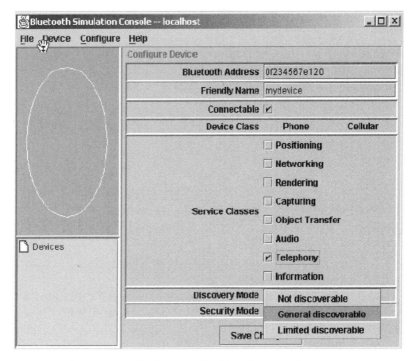

Figure 8-4. Configuring a cell phone in the Simulator environment

Since the friendly name of the device is mydevice, the Console will generate a file named mydevice.xml in the config directory.

The contents of mydevice.xml are shown in Listing 8-1.

Listing 8-1. mydevice.xml

```
<device bluetoothAddress="01234567e012"
    friendlyName="mydevice"
    isConnectable="true"
    deviceClass="Phone/Cellular"
    serviceClasses="Audio,Telephony"
    discoveryMode="Not discoverable"
    securityMode="Never enforce security">
</device>
```

Running an Application in the Simulator

Okay, now that you've set up your environment, let's see what it takes to get your code running within the Impronto Simulator environment. In order to link your application code to the virtual Bluetooth devices that you've created, you need to specify an `improntolocaldevice.friendlyname` property for your application. In the J2SE, you can do this by executing the following line of code at runtime:

```
java -Dimprontolocaldevice.friendlyname=TestPDA RemoteControl
```

That's of course assuming that the name of your application is `RemoteControl` and the friendly name of your virtual device is `TestPDA`. You can also specify this property within your Java class itself before calling any JSR-82 code:

```
System.setProperty("improntolocaldevice.friendlyname", "TestPDA");
```

If you're creating a J2ME MIDP application, you can set this property in your MIDlet's Java Application Descriptor (JAD) file. For example, the JAD file would contain the following line:

```
impronto.localdevice.friendlyname: foo
```

You must also insert the following code into your MIDlet's constructor so that Impronto Simulator can read the JAD file using the `getAppProperty()` method of MIDlet:

```
import com.rococosoft.impronto.configuration.*;
import javax.microedition.midlet.*;
public class SomeMIDlet extends MIDlet
    public SomeMIDlet() {
        Configuration.setConfiguration (new MIDPConfigurationImpl(this));
    }
...
}
```

 NOTE *Any application that uses pure JSR-82 code (i.e., no vendor libraries) can run in the simulator as well. The only downside is that the simulator will create generic "dummy" devices.*

Chat Example

The chat example we present here uses the Serial Port Profile to send text messages from one simulated Bluetooth device to another. In ChatServer.java, the chat server registers its service and waits for a client to connect. After a client connects, the server prints the client's message to the command line and prompts the server to respond. In ChatClient.java, the client searches for the server and creates a Serial Port Profile connection after obtaining the connection URL. Listing 8-2 shows the code for ChatServer.java and Listing 8-3 shows the code for ChatClient.java.

Listing 8-2. ChatServer.java

```java
import java.io.*;
import javax.bluetooth.*;
import com.rococosoft.io.*;

class Server {

    StreamConnection con = null;
    StreamConnectionNotifier service= null;
    InputStream ip  = null;
    OutputStream op = null;
    String serviceURL = "btspp://localhost:1111;name=ChatServer";

public Server() throws  IOException{
//Extends a stream for client to connect
    service = (StreamConnectionNotifier)Connector.open(serviceURL);
//Server waiting for client to connect
    con = service.acceptAndOpen();
//Open streams for two way communication.
    ip = con.openInputStream();
    op = con.openOutputStream();
//Starts a new thread for reading data from inputstream
//while the present thread, goes forward and write data to outputstream
//thus enabling a two way communication with the client
    ReadThread rdthr = new ReadThread(ip);
    rdthr.start();
    writeData();
}
private void writeData() throws IOException{
    int data = 0;
    do{
```

```
        try{
        data = System.in.read();
        op.write(data);
        }catch(IOException e){}
        }while(true);
        }
    }
class ReadThread extends Thread {
    InputStream ip = null;
    public ReadThread(InputStream inp){
    ip = inp;
    }
public void run() {
    char data;
    int i =      0;
    do{
    try{
//Read data from the stream
    data = (char)ip.read();
    System.out.print(data);
//This is a bit sneaky and hard to explain.
//comment out the following line to see the difference in how
//the application behaves.
    if(data == 0x0d)System.out.println();
    }
    catch(IOException e){}
    }while(true);
    }
}


public class ChatServer {
    public static void main(String args[]) throws IOException {
    System.setProperty("improntolocaldevice.friendlyname", "ChatServer");
    Server chatServer = new Server();
    }
}
```

Listing 8-3. ChatClient.java

```
import java.io.*;
import javax.bluetooth.*;
import com.rococosoft.io.*;
```

```
class Client implements DiscoveryListener{

private static LocalDevice localDevice = null;
private DiscoveryAgent discoveryAgent = null;
private String connectionURL = null;
private RemoteDevice[] device = null;
private ServiceRecord[] records = null;
private boolean inquiryCompl = false;
int count = 0;
int maxSearches =  10;
InputStream ip  = null;
OutputStream op = null;
public Client() throws  IOException, InterruptedException{
    localDevice = LocalDevice.getLocalDevice();
    discoveryAgent = localDevice.getDiscoveryAgent();
    device = new RemoteDevice[10]
// Starts inquiry for devices in the proximity and waits till the
//inquiry is completed.
    System.out.println("\nSearching for Devices...\n");
    discoveryAgent.startInquiry(DiscoveryAgent.GIAC,this);
    synchronized(this){
    this.wait();
    }

//Once the Device inquiry is completed it starts searching for the
//required service. Service search is done with the given uuid.
//After starting each search it waits for the result. If the
//connectionURL is null, ie, if No service Records are obtained, then
//it continues search in the next device detected.

    int[] attrSet = {0,3,4,0x100};
    UUID[] uuids = new UUID[1];
    uuids[0] = new UUID("1111",true);
    for(int i = 0; i< count;i++) {
    int transactionid = discoveryAgent.searchServices
                                (attrSet,uuids,device[i],this);
    if(transactionid != -1){
    synchronized(this){
    this.wait();
    }
    }
    if(connectionURL != null)
    break;
```

```
    }// end of forloop
//If the URL returned from SPP Server begins with btspp then
//we call the getConnection method which
//establishes a connection with the SPPServer and returns it. Connection
// returned is of type  StreamConnection.
//A piece of raw data is being sent over RFCOMM.

    if(connectionURL == null)
    System.out.println("No service available......... .");
    else if(connectionURL.startsWith("btspp")){
    StreamConnection connection = getconnection();
    op  = connection.openOutputStream();
    ip  = connection.openInputStream();
    }
    WriteThread wrthr = new WriteThread(op);
    wrthr.start();
    readData();
}
private void readData()throws IOException{
    char data;
    int i =    0;
    do{
    data = (char)ip.read();
    System.out.print(data);
    if(data == 0x0d)System.out.println();
    }while(true);
}


//When a device is discovered it is added to the remote device table.

public synchronized void deviceDiscovered(RemoteDevice btDevice, DeviceClass cod)
{
    System.out.println("New Device discovered : "+btDevice.getBluetoothAddress());
    device[count++] = btDevice;
}



//When a service is discovered in a particular device
// and the connection url is not null //then the thread that
//is waiting in the main is notified.

public synchronized void servicesDiscovered(int transID,
                                        ServiceRecord[] servRecords) {
```

```
    records = new ServiceRecord[servRecords.length];
    records = servRecords;
    for(int i=0;i<servRecords.length;i++) {
    int[] atrids = servRecords[i].getAttributeIDs();
    String servName = (String)((DataElement)
servRecords[i].getAttributeValue(0x100)).getValue();
    System.out.println("Service Name : "+servName);
    connectionURL = servRecords[i].getConnectionURL
(ServiceRecord.NOAUTHENTICATE_NOENCRYPT,true);
    System.out.println("Connection url :" + connectionURL);
    if(connectionURL != null) {
    synchronized(this) {
    this.notify();
    }
    break;
    }
    }
}
//This function notifies the Thread waiting in main if a service search is
// terminated, i.e., if the responsecode is SERVICE_SEARCH_COMPLETED or
//SERVICE_SEARCH_NO_RECORDS

public synchronized void serviceSearchCompleted(int transID, int respCode)    {

    if(respCode==SERVICE_SEARCH_ERROR)
    System.out.println("\nSERVICE_SEARCH_ERROR\n");
    if(respCode==SERVICE_SEARCH_COMPLETED)
    System.out.println("\nSERVICE_SEARCH_COMPLETED\n");
    if(respCode==SERVICE_SEARCH_TERMINATED)
    System.out.println("\n SERVICE_SEARCH_TERMINATED\n");
    if(respCode == SERVICE_SEARCH_NO_RECORDS){
    synchronized(this) {
    this.notify();
    }
    System.out.println("\n SERVICE_SEARCH_NO_RECORDS\n");
    }
    if(respCode == SERVICE_SEARCH_DEVICE_NOT_REACHABLE)
    System.out.println("\n SERVICE_SEARCH_DEVICE_NOT_REACHABLE\n");
}
//Once the device inquiry is completed it notifies the Thread that waits in the Main.
    public synchronized void inquiryCompleted(int discType)        {
    this.notify();
```

```
        }
        StreamConnection getconnection() throws IOException {
        return (StreamConnection)Connector.open(connectionURL);
        }
    }



class WriteThread extends Thread {
    OutputStream op = null;
    public WriteThread(OutputStream oup){
    op = oup;
    }
    public void run() {
    int data = 0;
    int i =    0;
    do{
    try{
    data = System.in.read();
    op.write(data);
    }catch(IOException e){}
    }while(true);
    }
}
public class ChatClient {
    public static void main(String args[]) throws IOException,InterruptedException
  {
    System.setProperty("improntolocaldevice.friendlyname", "ChatClient");
    Client chatClient = new Client();
    }
}
```

In order to test the application, you need to set the system properties for each class. Figure 8-5 shows the Impronto Simulator after we ran the ChatServer application.

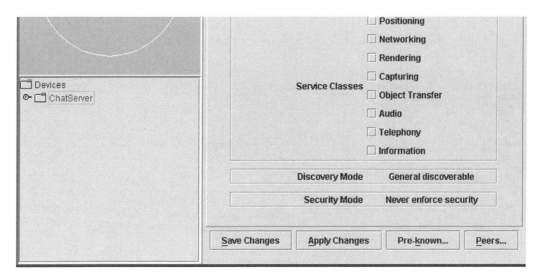

Figure 8-5. The ChatServer Bluetooth device in the Impronto Simulator device list

Now that the server is running, let's open a new command window and run the chat client. Figure 8-6 shows the Impronto Simulator with ChatClient making a connection to ChatServer.

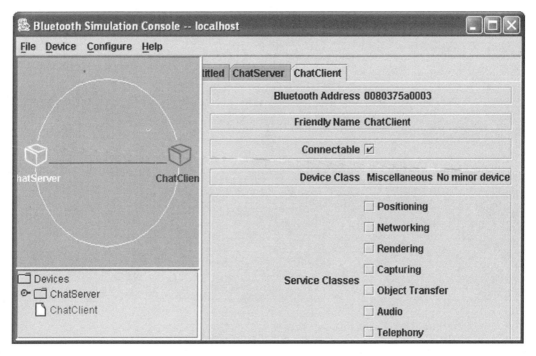

Figure 8-6. The ChatServer interacting with the ChatClient in the Impronto Simulator environment

And that's it! You now have a complete simulated JSR-82 application. Figures 8-7 and 8-8 show the conversation between the client and the server.

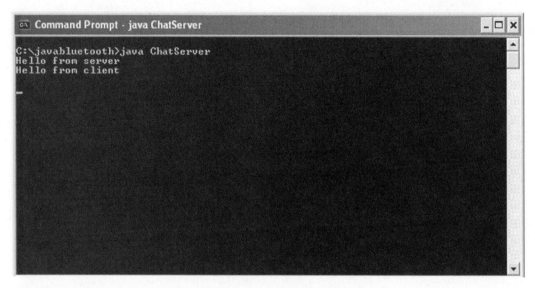

Figure 8-7. The server has sent a message and the client responds.

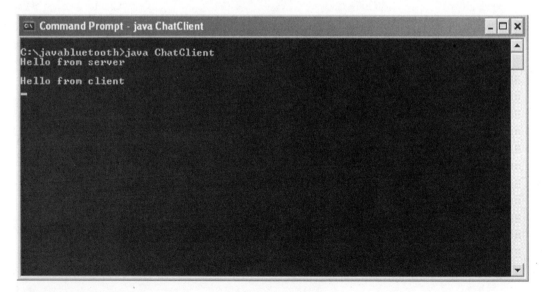

Figure 8-8. The client receives a message and sends a reply.

Summary

This chapter gave you an introduction to the Rococo Impronto Simulator, the first and only development environment that allows you to create JSR-82–compliant applications using simulated Bluetooth devices. Bluetooth simulators are very useful tools in the application development process because they allow you to avoid configuring or debugging Bluetooth devices in your test environment.

In Chapter 9, we're going to discuss the security measures that are provided by the Bluetooth specification and the JSR-82 in order to make your applications more secure.

CHAPTER 9

Bluetooth Security

SO FAR, WE'VE DISCUSSED THE benefits and the advantages of using Java and Bluetooth, but we haven't addressed (in any detail) the security implications of using this technology. What prevents other people from using your Bluetooth devices? What prevents a hacker from intercepting your transmission if you're transmitting sensitive information like financial, personal, or medical data? In this chapter, we'll take a look at the security measures built into the Bluetooth specification and the JSR-82 API in order to make your wireless applications more secure. We'll wrap things up with a demonstration of how to use the Mobiwave Bluetooth Protocol Analyzer in order to see "what's in the air" when you're transmitting data between Bluetooth devices.

Bluetooth Security Measures

Data security is an important aspect of any networked application. All data that is in transit is vulnerable to an attack from an eavesdropper (it doesn't matter if the connections are physical or wireless). Developers must realize that there is no way to completely ensure that information transmitted wirelessly will *only* reach the intended destination.

 NOTE *Well, except for infrared...but of course, you already knew that!*

For application developers, the Bluetooth specification addresses security in three ways: authentication, authorization, and encryption. Let's look at these in more detail.

Authentication

Authentication with Bluetooth consists of a simple challenge/response mechanism. The Bluetooth specification does not provide any means to authenticate users; you can only authenticate devices. So, the challenge/response does not involve a user name and password as typical authentication schemes. Authentication with Bluetooth only involves a personal identification number (PIN).

During the authentication process, the PIN code is never transmitted from the client to the server. In order to authenticate, the client creates a 128-bit *shared link key*, which is derived from the PIN. If the PIN codes on the client and the server do not match, then the authentication process fails.

A practical example for the usage of Bluetooth authentication would be a Bluetooth-enabled hotel business center. A hotel that's oriented to business travelers could enable authentication on all of its Bluetooth-enabled devices (like printers and scanners) in the business center. Upon check-in, a registered guest of the hotel will be given the PIN code in order to access the services in the business center, and this would prevent non–hotel customers from simply walking up and using the services that are reserved for hotel guests.

Server Authentication

Bluetooth servers can request authentication by adding the `authenticate` parameter to the connection URL `String`. The code that follows shows a server using the Serial Port Profile, and requesting authentication:

```
String url = "btspp://localhost:00112233445566778899AABBCCDDEEFF;authenticate=true"
```

If the `authenticate` parameter is set to `true`, then the JSR-82 implementation attempts to enforce authentication when devices connect to the server.

NOTE   *The key word here is* attempt.
A `BluetoothConnectionException` *will be thrown if the server does not support authentication, or if there is a conflict with the settings of the BCC. It is ultimately the decision of the BCC to allow authentication or to throw the exception. If the server device has a user interface, then the device may prompt the user to change the device's settings.*

If the authenticate parameter is set to false, then the implementation does not attempt to authenticate the client. If the authenticate parameter is not in the URL String at all, then the implementation treats it as false, unless you set encrypt or authorize to true.

Client Authentication

Bluetooth clients can also require the server to authenticate by setting the authenticate parameter to true as shown here:

```
String url = "btspp://02AB45AC35DF:00112233445566778899AABBCCDDEEFF;authenticate=true"
```

If the authenticate parameter is set to false (or is not in the URL at all), then the client will not require the server to authenticate.

 NOTE *Why would the client request the server to authenticate it (especially if the server didn't require authentication)? Well, since authentication is a requirement for encryption, the client may want to be authenticated to the server in order to send some data securely, even though the server doesn't require it.*

Whether you're a client or a server, you can request authentication even after the connection is established, as shown here:

```
// get an instance of the RemoteDevice if we don't already have it
// assume that we have an active Connection object named "conn"
RemoteDevice remoteDevice = RemoteDevice.getRemoteDevice(conn);
remoteDevice.authenticate();
```

The JSR-82 API also gives you a method to check to see if your Connection to a RemoteDevice is authenticated. Just call the isAuthenticated() method of RemoteDevice.

> **NOTE** *Have you noticed that in both client and server authentication, the PIN is never specified in the URL (or anywhere else)? Assigning and entering the PINs on both the client and server are handled by the BCC.*

Bluetooth Server Authorization

Bluetooth servers can request that only authorized devices connect and use a particular service. These authorized devices are called *trusted* devices.

Servers can require that clients be authorized by setting the `authorize` parameter to `true` in the connection URL, as shown here:

```
String url = "btspp://02AB45AC35DF:00112233445566778899AABBCCDDEEFF;authorize=true"
```

Authorization requires authentication, so the following line of code is more descriptive of what's actually going on:

```
String url =
"btspp://02AB45AC35DF:00112233445566778899AABBCCDDEEFF;
authenticate=true;authorize=true"
```

However, if you explicitly set `authenticate` to `false`, and `authorize` to `true`, then the system will throw a `BluetoothConnectionException`. If authorization was not specified in the connection URL, the server can require the client to be authorized by calling the `authorize()` method of the `RemoteDevice` class as follows:

```
// get an instance of the RemoteDevice if we don't already have it
// assume that we have an active Connection object named "conn"
RemoteDevice remoteDevice = RemoteDevice.getRemoteDevice(conn);
remoteDevice.authorize(conn);
```

Whether the connection is established or not, the server can check to see if the client is a trusted device by calling the `isTrustedDevice()` method of the `RemoteDevice` class.

NOTE *There is no such thing as client authorization. Why? Well, since authorization is not a requirement for encryption, it doesn't make sense for a client to request a server to authorize it, if the server does not require it.*

A good use of the authorization security measure occurs when you're dealing with personal devices. For instance, if you have a Bluetooth-enabled TV and a Bluetooth-enabled remote control, then you want your TV to only obey commands coming from your remote, obviously. Otherwise, you'll be vulnerable to common pranksters coming within range of your house, and changing your channels while you're watching TV—or even worse, turning on your TV at a high volume at 3:00 a.m.!

Encryption

Authentication and authorization are good if you want to prevent unwanted users from accessing the services of your Bluetooth devices. However, neither of those security measures will protect your sensitive data from a hacker who has the right tools to "sniff" your data while it's being transmitted. Encryption, however, is the security measure that you can employ in order to protect your sensitive data transmissions.

Now, in order to encrypt information (whether you're using Bluetooth or not), you need an encryption algorithm, an encryption key, and the information that you want to protect. An encryption algorithm (also called a *cipher*) is simply a procedure that is followed in order to scramble the data. Some well-know encryption algorithms are Blowfish, Twofish, RC4, DES, TripleDES, IDEA, CAST, and Rijndael. The encryption key is simply a code that is used by the algorithm to encrypt the data. In symmetrical encryption, the same key is used to encrypt and decrypt the data. In asymmetrical encryption, however, two keys are used to encrypt and decrypt the data.

NOTE *We won't talk about asymmetrical encryption any further because Bluetooth uses symmetrical encryption to encrypt its data transmissions.*

Now let's look at a quick example. Listing 9-1 shows some information that needs to be cryptographically protected if transmitted from a Bluetooth-enabled cash card.

Listing 9-1. Bank Account Information

```
Bank Name: SDH Bank
Account Name: Bruce Hopkins
Account Number: 123456789
Account Balance: $0.03
```

NOTE   *Of course, we're protecting the bank account number, not the balance!*

When the encryption key, as shown in Listing 9-2, and the CAST algorithm are applied to the data, then sensitive bank account information will get encrypted, as shown in Listing 9-3.

Listing 9-2. A 1024-Bit Encryption Key

```
mQGiBD1ZRx4RBADgiQLiScTmdxd5aMvRIZbcmSsAzwXWtEBwarMO6xR4SDgp/ji0
KaU02yODO8XxMA2k9yvaQXGpKK6JrTeaqMF9vKyy26Sur3eMtjNxbPJok2XWgcZj
hFCYZjG1/wRbx60sf/xtWSeuhHyKENGhp352/rByvTFOKSEMf2txYZLOOQCg/0al
rqcZT0QyhOWufgMlEIQ21dED/A3i5oK+ibyN2t10aJpyxFe/NFL5uwbIjyWAndFN
2rdhOih7fOhNgVVVm6MGuNu/lqD5M576JSEngyQcxaG4G7jCOPElVk79+EJa6eku
ebAaPeq5osCHUAsbUD31vuxSK8qGsMy1xtOgid2gCuS52HDaUAnvIt9ojpMnOPrZ
zrgzBACZAnCz0Z+RNkYP50ch/UWFqbo6oPROZ4Vbi1UFvoZl/B8auxSvYueXjAuC
bo8YEEjBlpygWCtw8hPOjxFG3L/hWe95Qkgu8kNTX+SX6bthPBWnvZ7vTgstYyAQ
yXLwfLJRYuuT9i80uqODw3Kc0u3xTwIE4KIIvlHwadYv5z2G+7QhRWR3aW4gSG9w
a2lucyA8YmhvcGtpbnNAZ2x0Zy5jb20+iQBYBBARAgAYBQI9WUceCAsCAwkIBwEK
AhkBBRsDAAAAAoJEJION/w1q4wQWDAAnAmrZRbJXWARLbowLBwfTrJmMfhwAJ9V
l477oH3TB/W2SLbJoSLY9q1CW7kCDQQ9WUceEAgA9kJXtwh/CBdyorrWqULzBej5
UxE5T7bxbrlLOCDaAadWoxTpjOBV89AHxstDqZSt90xkhkn4DIO9ZekX1KHTUPj1
WV/cdlJPPT2N286Z4VeSWc39uK50T8X8dryDxUcwYc58yWb/Ffm7/ZFexwGqo1ue
jaClcjrUGvC/RgBYK+XOiP1YTknbzSCOneSRBzZrM2w4DUUdD3yIsxx8Wy2O9vPJ
I8BD8KVbGI2Ou1WMuFO4OzT9fBdXQ6MdGGzeMyEstSr/POGxKUAYEY18hKcKctaG
xAMZyAcpesqVDNmWn6vQClCbAkbTCD1mpF1Bn5x8vYlLIhkmuquiXsNV6TILOwAC
Agf+M1E08J4AnzN2oaLhjbO81jrJn5BIVPkHxm6smP5rIHJ4kpmkoLJstXV+P7HD
```

```
rWaQXBqBzxOwEchZL+S7qazRQA6dQ8e2fSeMOABQgo7pDjDEn1rKitTh55O1qFK6
yH+tpEC/C9zkpeLNEODK/v1wKj7X1+d8gEUYxoDALbQ5rZ5e3eTEu+3WFmAIp6AQ
Z14BKmP4RYw8ij21LEHPJ+F6aAZAmzp7U/2HEvQH/7ZrZogzOdmOrAIMpRHgPVsI
uOryEYXSdsG6I3s5xgqY4JRON96hg38GZjV4/22kt5uncXWbupmOXtyyxBW5roxb
W/AS2KMkb6Y5sOsSsfQ63inD8IkATAQYEQIADAUCPVlHHgUbDAAAAAAKCRCSNDf8
NauMECO3AKD1UonZcLkmDxOCGCbJwmp2mOP2jwCgO3KNtDRx6FyyZpZc5QRAWbgP
P4M=
=trVX
```

Listing 9-3. Bank Account Information Encrypted with the CAST Algorithm

```
qANQR1DBwU4DMCkFM4tTfBsQCAC4WJhOUK5Osv3gZJ3ivf5BUb+jm9R6n2vKUijp
KUzu3B1PSS3ignZ9t1Bvp+HSXuX31Bq8KsoMYYSwj3QLSkKgYJz1PkAyvyR9bXed
5agRoFvNdQiGDQEP4GtrIjA8/Y6UFvXskQq4w37vwyUoyvS9ONYxGPOeHEA/YkOb
CjA3i6aFIH81Pksb8pNqr+vOmq5XPFSaYbvLveErCQh6wd63cGzKL8Q23St6JkXi
rBqfFYa7Eu+Vjc78mTe9vVlWIdw6zyhb35bnaybrLEPW7/xp2K6eIsoiiHngL5MK
M4fqruoPp2k7UOnzwOtf1EojEZ8nyOvJCPOZARHhzNAonA6zB/Of2ygNnNtsEaId
10CiIGKohIMmOaO7VTXx7cmXUCToSuorIgF43KNs3wP9nPPvxlV3+MhuG4DHF6Tm
oVcR5jdfbFRbbUjzLHVPntP+QSOnE2LAxLsbfMQ6zEkz2F2iJlGbOFy8cjc+eOXJ
jnfG1+z4TiOMtyvA1T6fd9qJP7TYsBmrQyLLF60PCMVQsnE26+mLH9gn4sgPdPhv
y8ZHjtSfyon5+vgY6tgrY+OSB6GypgN8b2v/RCi9y5WnsNAO10W6Xm/iKowTEQAB
j7YxBkoPqC2eOfKwZnAgMcImunFX1767ewIQkcBTiWvOsQ2jQZImD9Fu1xpywdfk
5GLoVny3yXRXHLrAbxysNU+OylOdRNiPEjvnLG2NpXiCtcWAvuGGw4SID9FIkRiM
Dw/D//p40grachGmhZ2rwn9HPIkHjvxbTwtm1qRxlt99yBtP6mfDEWkI8QibLVYr
2RUElEF+3Ak/hVd2er82XjeNbqerhbfCSOLd9w==
=rZCL
```

As we stated earlier, Bluetooth uses symmetrical encryption, so there's only one key for encrypting and decrypting information. However, the key is never transmitted from the server to the client. The encryption key is derived from several factors that are known to both the client and server (including the PIN). Now let's take a look at how to encrypt your data transmissions using the JSR-82.

Server Encryption

Bluetooth servers can specify that they want their transmissions encrypted by setting the encrypt parameter to true in the connection URL, as follows:

```
String url = "btspp://02AB45AC35DF:00112233445566778899AABBCCDDEEFF;encrypt=true"
```

Encryption requires authentication, so the following line of code is more descriptive of what's actually going on:

```
String url =
"btspp://02AB45AC35DF:00112233445566778899AABBCCDDEEFF;
authenticate=true;encrypt=true"
```

However, if you explicitly set `authenticate` to `false`, and `encrypt` to `true`, then the system will throw a `BluetoothConnectionException`. If encryption was not specified in the connection URL, the server can later encrypt the transmission by calling the `encrypt()` method of the `RemoteDevice` class as shown here:

```
// get an instance of the RemoteDevice if we don't already have it
// assume that we have an active Connection object named "conn"
RemoteDevice remoteDevice = RemoteDevice.getRemoteDevice(conn);
remoteDevice.encrypt(conn, true);
// now that the sensitive information has been
// transmitted, turn off encryption and send the
// rest of the data unencrypted for better performance
remoteDevice.encrypt(conn, false);
```

Client Encryption

Bluetooth clients can also require that their communication with their servers be encrypted by setting the `encrypt` parameter to `true` in the URL as demonstrated here:

```
String url = "btspp://02AB45AC35DF:00112233445566778899AABBCCDDEEFF;encrypt=true"
```

The following line of code is also harmless:

```
String url =
"btspp://02AB45AC35DF:00112233445566778899AABBCCDDEEFF;
authenticate=true;encrypt=true"
```

If the `encrypt` parameter is set to `false` (or is not in the URL at all) then the transmissions between the client and server are not encrypted.

After the connection has been established, both the server and the client can check to see if the transmission is encrypted by calling the `isEncrypted()` method of the `RemoteDevice` class.

If all of this sounds really complex to you, don't worry; the encryption/decryption process is all done behind the scenes by your underlying JSR-82 implementation, so you don't have to worry about ciphers, keys, and other cryptographic elements.

Security Example

Now let's take a look at a practical demonstration of the security measures that are provided to us by Bluetooth and the JSR-82. In this example, the client uses authentication and authorization over an L2CAP connection to send a simple message to the server. Initially, encryption is not enabled so that we can demonstrate how easily a third party can capture your wireless data transmissions if left unprotected. When running the example, we used some of the many features of Mobiwave BPA-D10 Protocol Analyzer. The BPA-D10 is a noninstructive Bluetooth Protocol Analyzer that allows the real-time capturing, logging, decoding, and displaying of the Bluetooth data transmissions. The BPA-D10 is capable of capturing protocol information over the air and relaying the data to a host desktop computer through an Ethernet connection. This allows remote data logging and unlimited storage capability. Figure 9-1 shows a picture of the device.

Figure 9-1. The Mobiwave BPA-D10 Bluetooth Protocol Analyzer

Listing 9-4 presents the server code for our security example.

Listing 9-4. ServerApp.java

```java
import java.io.*;
import javax.bluetooth.*;
import com.atinav.standardedition.io.*;
```

```
public class ServerApp {

    public static void main(String args[]){
        ServerApp a = new ServerApp();
        L2CAPConnection con = null;
        L2CAPConnectionNotifier service = null;
        InputStream in = null;
        OutputStream out = null;
        String serviceURL = "btl2cap://localhost:1111;name=ATINAV;" +
                            "authorize=true;authenticate=true;encrypt=false";
        LocalDevice local = null;

        try {
            local = LocalDevice.getLocalDevice();
            System.out.println("\n Atinav aveLink Bluetooth Server Application \n");
            System.out.println("_____\n");
            System.out.println("My BDAddress: " + local.getBluetoothAddress());
            System.out.println("_____\n");
            service = (L2CAPConnectionNotifier)Connector.open(serviceURL);

            //
            // Add the service record to the SDDB and
            // accept a client Connection
            //

            con = service.acceptAndOpen();
            System.out.println("\nConnection established to the remote device\n");

            byte[] data = new byte[1000];
            while (!con.ready()){
                try{
                    Thread.sleep(1);
                }catch(InterruptedException ie){}
            }
            con.receive(data);
            System.out.println("Data received at the Server Side " +
                            new String(data));

            String strData= "This is the Data From the Server Application to " +

                        " the Client Application";
            byte[]datax = strData.getBytes();
            con.send(datax);
```

```
            //System.out.println("Data sent from the server side." + strData);
            try{
                Thread.sleep(10);
                }catch(Exception e){}
        }catch(Exception e){
                e.printStackTrace();
        }


    }
}
```

Listing 9-5 shows the client code for our security demonstration.

Listing 9-5. ClientApp.java

```
import java.io.*;
import javax.bluetooth.*;
import com.atinav.standardedition.io.*;

public class ClientApp implements DiscoveryListener{

    private static LocalDevice localDevice = null;
    private DiscoveryAgent discoveryAgent = null;
    private String connectionURL = null;
    private RemoteDevice[] device = null;
    private ServiceRecord[] records = null;
    private boolean inquiryCompl = false;
    int count = 0;
    int maxSearches = 10;



    public ClientApp(){
        System.out.println("\n Atinav aveLink Bluetooth Client Application \n");
        System.out.println("_____\n");

        try{
            localDevice = LocalDevice.getLocalDevice();
            discoveryAgent = localDevice.getDiscoveryAgent();
            device = new RemoteDevice[10];
            System.out.println("_____\n");
            System.out.println("My BDAddress: " +
                            localDevice.getBluetoothAddress());
            System.out.println(" _____\n");
```

```
// Starts inquiry for devices in the proximity and waits till the
// inquiry is completed.

System.out.println("\nSearching for Devices...\n");
discoveryAgent.startInquiry(DiscoveryAgent.GIAC,this);

synchronized(this){
    this.wait();
}

// Once the Device inquiry is completed it starts searching for the
// required service. Service search is done with the given uuid. After
// starting each search it waits for the result.

// If the connection URL is null, i.e., if No service Records obtained,
// then it continues search in the next device detected.

int[] attrSet = {0,3,4,0x100};
UUID[] uuids = new UUID[1];
uuids[0] = new UUID("1111",true);
System.out.println("\nSearching for Service...\n");

for(int i = 0; i< count; i++){

    int transactionid =
        discoveryAgent.searchServices(attrSet,uuids,device[i],this);
    if(transactionid != -1){
        synchronized(this){
            this.wait();
        }
    }

    if(connectionURL != null)
        break;
}

}catch(Exception ie){
    ie.printStackTrace();
}
```

```
// If the URL of the device begins with btl2cap, then we call the
// getConnection method which establishes a connection with the L2CAPServer
// and returns it.
// Connection returned is of type L2CAPConnection. A piece of raw data is
// being sent over L2CAP.


if(connectionURL == null)
   System.out.println("No service available.......... .");

else if(connectionURL.startsWith("btl2cap")){
   try{
      L2CAPConnection connection = getconnection();

      System.out.println("\nConnection established to the remote device\n");
      String strData = "This is the Data From Client Application " +
                       "to Server Application";
      byte[] data = strData.getBytes();
      connection.send(data);
      try{
         Thread.sleep(10);
      }catch(Exception e){}

      while(true){
         byte[] datax = new byte[1000];

         while (!connection.ready()){
            try{
               Thread.sleep(1);
            }catch(InterruptedException ie){}
         }
         connection.receive(datax);
         System.out.println("Data received at the Client Side " +
                            new String(datax));
      }
      //   connection.close();

   }catch(Exception ioe){
      ioe.printStackTrace();
   }
```

```
        }// end of else if


    }



    //
    //  When a device is discovered it is added to the remote device table.
    //
    public synchronized void deviceDiscovered(RemoteDevice btDevice,
                                              DeviceClass cod){

        device[count++] = btDevice;
        System.out.println("New Device discovered : " +
                            btDevice.getBluetoothAddress());
    }


    //
    // When a service is discovered in a particular device and the connection URL
    // is not null then the thread that is waiting in the main is notified.
    //
    public synchronized void servicesDiscovered(int transID,
                                                ServiceRecord[] servRecords){
        records = new ServiceRecord[servRecords.length];
        records = servRecords;
        for(int i=0;i<servRecords.length;i++){

            int[] atrids = servRecords[i].getAttributeIDs();
            String servName =
        (String)((DataElement)servRecords[i].getAttributeValue(0x100)).getValue();
            System.out.println("Service Name : "+ servName);
            connectionURL = servRecords[i].getConnectionURL(1,true);
            System.out.println("Connection url :" + connectionURL);
            if(connectionURL != null){
                synchronized(this){
                    this.notify();
                }
            break;
            }
        }
    }
```

```
//
// This function notifies the Thread waiting in main if a service
// search is terminated,ie,ig the responsecode
// is SERVICE_SEARCH_COMPLETED or SERVICE_SEARCH_NO_RECORDS
//
public synchronized void serviceSearchCompleted(int transID, int respCode){

    if(respCode==SERVICE_SEARCH_ERROR)
        System.out.println("\nSERVICE_SEARCH_ERROR\n");


    if(respCode==SERVICE_SEARCH_COMPLETED)
        System.out.println("\nSERVICE_SEARCH_COMPLETED\n");


    if(respCode==SERVICE_SEARCH_TERMINATED)
        System.out.println("\n SERVICE_SEARCH_TERMINATED\n");


    if(respCode == SERVICE_SEARCH_NO_RECORDS){
        synchronized(this){
            this.notify();
        }
        System.out.println("\n SERVICE_SEARCH_NO_RECORDS\n");
    }


    if(respCode == SERVICE_SEARCH_DEVICE_NOT_REACHABLE)
        System.out.println("\n SERVICE_SEARCH_DEVICE_NOT_REACHABLE\n");
}


//
// Once the device inquiry is completed it notifies the Thread
//  that waits in the Main.
//
public synchronized void inquiryCompleted(int discType){
    this.notify();
}



//
//  Opens the connection to the Server.
//
L2CAPConnection getconnection() throws IOException{
    return (L2CAPConnection)Connector.open(connectionURL);
}
```

```
public static void main(String[] args){
    ClientApp client = new ClientApp();
}
}
```

Running the Security Example

Now let's see what happens when we run the example. Figure 9-2 shows our security server waiting for a client to connect.

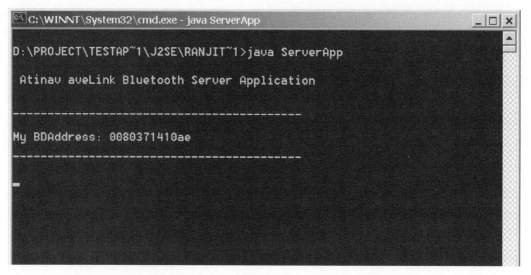

Figure 9-2. The security server is waiting for the client to connect.

Figure 9-3 shows the security client attempting to connect to the server.
The security server requires all clients to authenticate, so the Atinav stack prompts the user to enter a PIN code as shown in Figure 9-4.

```
C:\WINNT\System32\cmd.exe - java ClientApp                    _ □ X

D:\PROJECT\TESTAP~1\J2SE\RANJIT~1>java ClientApp

 Atinav aveLink Bluetooth Client Application


 --------------------------------------------

My BDAddress: 0080371410f3

 --------------------------------------------


Searching for Devices...

New Device discovered : 0080371410ae

Searching for Service...
```

Figure 9-3. The security client is attempting to connect to the server.

Figure 9-4. The security server prompts the user to enter a PIN for the application.

NOTE *This of course, is a part of Atinav's implementation of the BCC for their stack. Other JSR-82 implementations may allow you to enter the PIN for your server prior to runtime.*

Similarly, the client is also prompted to enter a PIN. Of course, if the client enters an incorrect PIN, then the authentication process will fail. Figure 9-5

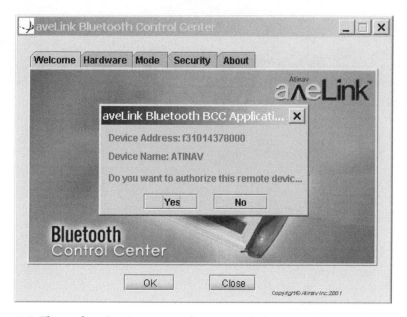

Figure 9-5. The authentication process has succeeded.

shows that the authentication process is a success.

In this example, the encrypt parameter in the connection URL was initially set to false in order to show you how easy it is to capture unencrypted data while in transit. Figure 9-6 shows the Mobiwave BPA-D10 sniffing the data transmission.

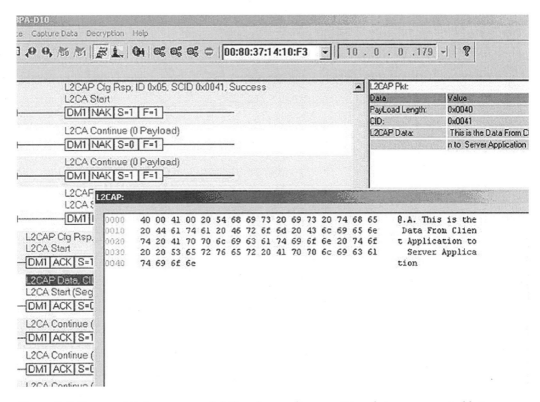

Figure 9-6. You need to be very careful if you're sending sensitive data unencrypted between Bluetooth devices because it can be captured by a third party using a Bluetooth Protocol Analyzer.

Now let's see what happens when we set the encrypt parameter to true in the connection URL. The results are shown in Figure 9-7.

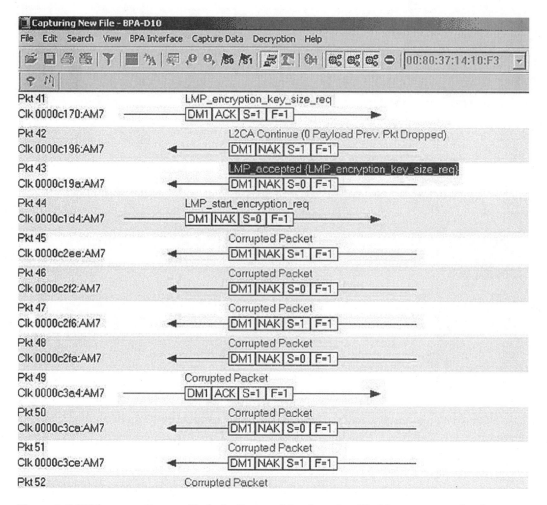

Figure 9-7. With encryption enabled, the Protocol Analyzer is still able to capture the data transmission; however, the data is corrupted.

More on Mobiwave BPA-D10

Given sufficient information, the Mobiwave Protocol Analyzer could decrypt those encrypted packets over the air. The Mobiwave Protocol Analyzer is equipped with a feature called SmartDecrypt. SmartDecrypt was designed to tackle the noisy RF environment so that all the seven client/slave sessions could be decrypted in real time. Here's what you need to do in order to enable SmartDecrypt on the Mobiwave BPA-D10.

The first thing that you need to do is to add the slave devices to the list of known slave devices. From the BPA-D10 main menu, select Decryption and then select Decryption Setup. This brings up the slave list dialog box, shown here:

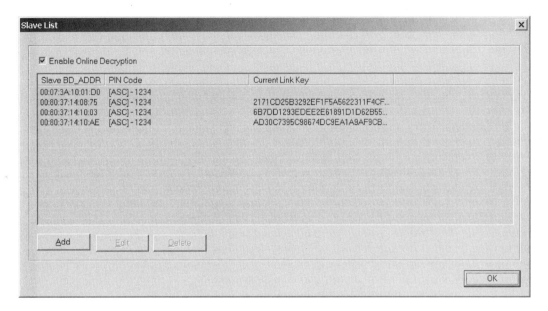

Click Add to bring up the Add New Slave dialog box as shown here:

If the PIN is not available or defined, enter HEX "00" (this is the default PIN). If the current link key is known, you can enter it, else leave this field blank. Click OK when you are done. The current link key, if not specified, will be automatically generated during the capture of a good pairing or bonding session between the two Bluetooth devices.

Now let's run the security sample application again with the encrypt parameter set to true. Remember to set the same PIN code you used to configure your slave device in the BPA-D10. The following figure illustrates how the Mobiwave Protocol Analyzer intelligently decrypted data packets on the fly:

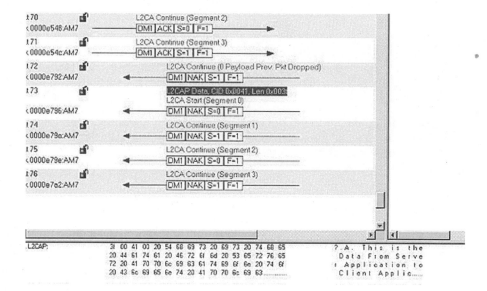

Please note that the SmartDecrypt feature of the BPA-D10 does not illustrate any of the limitations or shortcomings of Bluetooth's wireless encryption capabilities.

Prior to decrypting the Bluetooth-encrypted packets successfully, the following information must be available:

- The slave or client BD address that is involved

- The PIN that is used during the pairing or bonding session

- When the pairing or bonding session is carried out

- Confirmation of a good capture of the pairing or bonding session

If any of this information is missing or incomplete, the decryption will not be successful. Information such as when a pairing or bonding session is made is a rare and random event. Furthermore, during the capturing of a pairing or bonding session, many things could go wrong due to interference over the air or Bluetooth devices being out of range. Bluetooth's encryption mechanism is not easily breached or compromised.

Java developers can further mitigate this risk by creating their own symmetric or asymmetric encryption routines by using the libraries from the JCE (Java Cryptography Extension) or from the Bouncy Castle at `http://www.bouncycastle.org`.

Summary

This chapter introduced you to the security measures that you can employ to make your Bluetooth applications with the JSR-82 more secure. You learned about how to use the APIs in the JSR-82 in order to enable authentication, authorization, and encryption in your Bluetooth applications. This chapter also gave you an introduction to the Mobiwave BPA-D10 Protocol Analyzer.

So far, we have used the JSR-82 in order to make client-server, peer-to-peer, and cable replacement wireless applications. In the next chapter, we'll take a look at the SND Micro BlueTarget in order to make fixed-wireless applications using the JSR-82.

CHAPTER 10

Wireless Embedded Systems with the Micro BlueTarget

So far, this book has taken mainly a software-based approach to things, and rightfully so since the JSR-82 is a software specification about controlling Bluetooth devices with the Java language. In the past, Bluetooth device manufacturers envisioned their devices to be programmed in a native language like assembly or C, and making a Java interface to their devices was pretty much an afterthought. In this chapter, we're going to take a look at a device that was developed with the JSR-82 in mind: the Micro BlueTarget from Smart Network Devices (http://www.smartnd.com).

What Is the Micro BlueTarget?

So what is the Micro BlueTarget and what can it do? The Micro BlueTarget is a fully self-contained computer that includes a Bluetooth radio, a Bluetooth stack, Bluetooth profiles, an operating system, a J2ME VM, and the JSR-82 libraries. Figure 10-1 shows the Micro BlueTarget standard version, and Figure 10-2 shows the Micro BlueTarget Starter Kit.

Figure 10-1. The Micro BlueTarget standard version is a small form factor embedded system with a board outline of just 3.2×5.9 cm! This is a great solution for OEMs that want to make their devices Bluetooth enabled.

Figure 10-2. The Micro BlueTarget Starter Kit uses a standard Micro BlueTarget and adds RS-232 and Ethernet ports, which is ideal for developers who need to create quick prototypes and proofs of concepts.

The Micro BlueTarget has been designed to meet typical requirements of fixed-wireless infrastructure components. What's a *fixed-wireless* device? A fixed-wireless system is typically a large, stationary device that is capable of wireless communication. Consumer-oriented fixed-wireless systems are things like network access points, information kiosks, and vending machines (see Figure 10-3). On the other hand, a typical example of a fixed-wireless system for commercial use would be a large machine in a manufacturing center (see Figure 10-4).

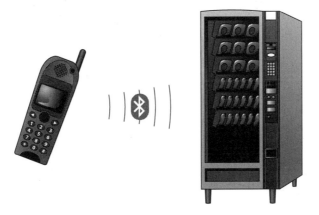

Figure 10-3. A Bluetooth phone utilizing the services of a fixed-wireless consumer system: a Bluetooth-enabled vending machine

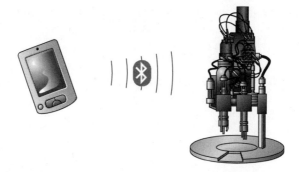

Figure 10-4. A Bluetooth PDA receiving the status from a fixed-wireless commercial system: a Bluetooth-enabled machine in a manufacturing facility

In the rest of this chapter, we'll take a look at the physical aspects of Micro BlueTarget, starting off with its hardware configuration. Next, we'll add a brief discussion about its software configuration by looking at the operating system and its Java implementation. Finally, we'll round up the chapter with some information on how to start the development process with this device by providing some example code.

The Micro BlueTarget Hardware Configuration

Figure 10-5 is a block diagram that describes the interrelationship of the hardware components that comprise the Micro BlueTarget.

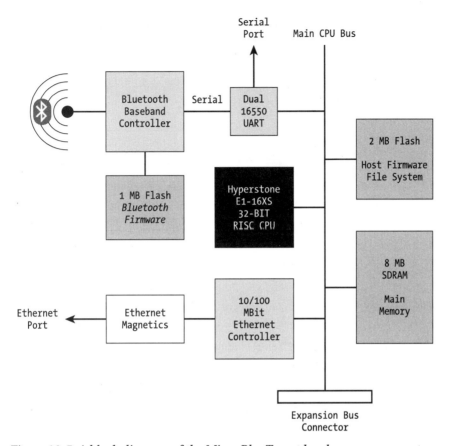

Figure 10-5. A block diagram of the Micro BlueTarget hardware components

The Micro BlueTarget is based upon the 32-bit RISC/DSP embedded microprocessor architecture from Hyperstone AG (http://www.hyperstone.com). Smart Network Devices chose this architecture primarily because of its extremely low gate count (the CPU itself consists of only just 35,000 gates), which equates to its low power consumption. In the future, this opens the door for the possibility of smaller form factor solutions, even System-on-Chip (SoC) architectures.

The Bluetooth baseband controller is a BlueCore 01b from CSR (see Figure 2-2), which is interfaced through a standard 16550-compatible UART device. By using a dual UART module (the 16752 chip) in the device, one UART is still free for external serial communication.

NOTE   *The Micro BlueTarget Starter Kit connects the available UART to the RS-232 port. This allows developers who don't have a lot of hardware experience to quickly utilize the Micro BlueTarget for external serial communication.*

 NOTE   *As an option, the dual UART device can be substituted by one of the many PIC family microcontrollers. This will enable the Micro BlueTarget to externally communicate via other protocols such as SPI, I2C, and GPIO. Some PIC chips will even enable the Micro BlueTarget to have a CAN bus interface or perform A/D conversion.*

Here's a quick synopsis of the hardware details of the Micro BlueTarget:

- 120 MHz, 32-bit RISC/DSP Hyperstone E1-16XS CPU

- 3.3 VDC (@ 250 mA)

- 8MB SDRAM memory

- 2+1MB flash memory

- 10/100 Mb/s Ethernet interface

- Integrated Class 2 Bluetooth radio (10m nominal radio range)

- Available serial communication port (UART with up to 3 Mb/s transfer rate)

- Peripheral I/O bus connector (addresses, 8-bit data, RD/WR, chip selects, interrupts)

The Micro BlueTarget Software Configuration

The Micro BlueTarget board runs the HyNetOS, SND's specialized operating system for the Hyperstone RISC/DSP CPU architecture. The HyNetOS was created for primarily two reasons. The first reason was to have the smallest possible memory footprint in order to match internal memory sizes of future Systems-on-Chip (SoC) architectures. The memory footprints for Embedded Linux and Embedded Windows (also known as Windows CE .NET) were simply too large to even think about SoC. Secondly, by creating their own OS, Smart Network Devices can have a highly efficient network and data communication architecture, which is optimized for the underlying platform. All interprocess communication is event driven and takes place through an internal message system.

The HyNetOS is based upon a highly efficient multitasking real-time kernel (only 16kB in size) and is written entirely in Hyperstone assembler. On top of the kernel is a complete operating environment that consists of following components:

- Device manager

- Protocol manager

- File manager

- Java Virtual Machine

The device manager is simply a layer that abstracts the underlying hardware, and the protocol manager is a layer that implements the TCP/IP and Bluetooth protocol stacks. The multifaceted file manager can handle different file systems, including RAM disk and flash disk, as well as external memory cards (we'll cover the details of the JVM in the next section). Figure 10-6 gives an illustration of the overall structure of the HyNetOS.

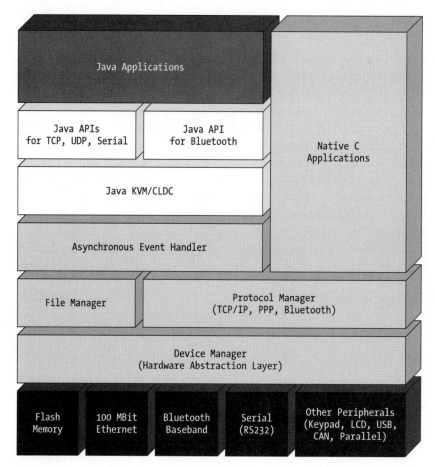

Figure 10-6. A structural overview of the HyNetOS for the Micro BlueTarget

The Java Implementation

The Java Virtual Machine for the Micro BlueTarget is an implementation of the Sun Microsystems Java 2 Micro Edition (J2ME) KVM/CLDC V1.0.3 and has passed the CLDC Technology Compatibility Kit (TCK). In addition to providing the JSR-82 APIs, Smart Network Devices has provided additional libraries for Micro BlueTarget development, such as

- UDP (datagram) socket communication

- TCP (stream) socket communication

- HTTP 1.1 libraries

- RS-232 serial communication (you can address ports COM1–COM5)

- Graphics library for monochrome LCD (128×64 pixel)

- Java interface to ITU-style keypad (keys: 0–9,*,#)

- File I/O library

For performance reasons and memory footprint size, the TCP/IP and the Bluetooth stacks were written in C and were implemented as asynchronous native processes. The Java VM, which exists as a native HyNetOS executable, has its own internal thread scheduler. A second process, called the *asynchronous event handler*, interfaces the asynchronous protocol software to the synchronous Java VM task. So what does all this mean? Once a Java thread makes a blocking I/O call (while waiting to receive data), not only will all other native OS tasks be scheduled on the CPU, but all other Java threads as well. This approach ensures the best possible match of synchronous and asynchronous computing architectures in order to achieve the best optimum system performance.

The Bluetooth Implementation

On the Bluetooth side of things, the CSR baseband controller handles all low-level Bluetooth protocols up to the HCI interface. The corresponding firmware is located in a separate flash memory (refer back to Figure 10-5), which can be updated dynamically through the HyNetOS host system. An HCI driver, L2CAP, RFCOMM, SDP, and some of the basic profiles like General Access Profile, Serial Port Profile, LAN Access Profile, and Service Discovery Application Profile comprise the Bluetooth portion of the HyNetOS protocol manager.

Now that you have a general overview of the underlying hardware implementation of the Micro BlueTarget, let's take a look at the OS and included software for this device.

Application Development on the Micro BlueTarget Platform

The core HyNetOS system is contained in a single file, named PROJECT.HEX. Figure 10-7 is a diagram of the memory map of the Micro BlueTarget's 2MB flash memory module.

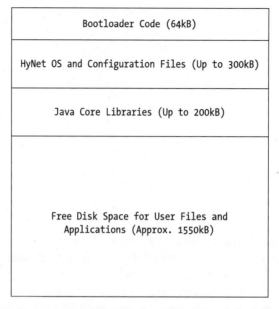

┌───┐
│   Bootloader Code (64kB)   │
├───┤
│   │
│ HyNet OS and Configuration Files (Up to 300kB) │
│   │
├───┤
│   │
│   Java Core Libraries (Up to 200kB)   │
│   │
├───┤
│   │
│   │
│   │
│   │
│   Free Disk Space for User Files and   │
│   Applications (Approx. 1550kB)   │
│   │
│   │
│   │
└───┘

Figure 10-7. The memory map of the Micro BlueTarget. End user applications have about 1.5MB of space on the flash disk.

Apart from the bootloader section (also called the *ROM section*), the remaining flash memory space is organized as a large solid-state disk. Since HyNetOS comes built-in with an FTP server, this flash disk can easily be administrated using any FTP client program.

In order to specify device drivers or interfaces that you would like to see started with HyNetOS after a system reset, you need to edit a configuration file named JSTARTUP.INI. This file can also be used to designate the class files that you want be executed at boot time. A typical JSTARTUP.INI would look like this:

```
[devices]
COM1
COM2
ETHSMSC111
LCD12864
KEYPAD
BLUETOOTH

[protocols]
TCP/IP
BLUETOOTH

[applications]
myapp.class
```

Operating System Tools

Several tools are provided to the user in order to perform common sysadmin tasks on the Micro BlueTarget. You can do things like load a new OS, reboot the system, format the flash disk, and trace the application code. All these tools are Java desktop applications (J2SE), and can be executed on any Java-enabled platform.

HYFLASH

HYFLASH is an administration tool for the Micro BlueTarget's flash memory (the flash disk). It can check and update the ROM section, format the flash disk, and upload content from any directory on your PC to the target system.

HYLOAD

HYLOAD is the dynamic OS loader. If the HyNetOS is already stored on the flash disk, the bootloader will automatically boot the system after a system reset. At runtime, however, an OS restart can always be triggered using HYLOAD while dynamically uploading a newer version of the OS.

HYMON

HYMON is the Micro BlueTarget's system monitor console. On the PC, this text-based monitor can be used to check the file system, display directories, and set network settings (such as the IP address, netmask, gateway, etc.). The HYMON utility can also be used to start Java applications on the device. At the system prompt, simply type

```
kvm myapp
```

to start up `myapp.class` on the device.

HYTRACE

HYTRACE is the Micro BlueTarget's system trace window. Stacktrace messages and output from your `System.out.println()` statements in your Java code will appear here.

Programming the Micro BlueTarget

In order to start developing wireless applications for the Micro BlueTarget, you first need to set up your development environment. Here are the steps that are involved:

1. Connect your Micro BlueTarget board to your PC using a crossover Ethernet cable.

2. Configure your Micro BlueTarget's IP network parameters using the HYMON utility.

3. Format the Micro BlueTarget's flash disk using the HYFLASH utility.

4. Create the necessary configuration files and transfer them to the Micro BlueTarget's flash disk.

These steps are all explained in detail in the Micro BlueTarget Starter Kit documentation. After you compile and preverify your code, just FTP the corresponding class files for your application to the Micro BlueTarget and hit the reset button. If your app is specified in the `JSTARTUP.INI` file, then it will automatically start up; otherwise, just start your application manually using the HYMON utility.

NOTE *The HyNetOS is a multilanguage, multitasking embedded operating system that can run native C applications and Java apps at the same time. In order to resolve conflicting requests between native and Java applications that want to utilize the Bluetooth stack and radio, Smart Network Devices created a centralized entity called the* Bluetooth Service. *The Bluetooth Service in JSR-82 vernacular is called the* Bluetooth Control Center *(BCC). As mentioned in Chapter 4, the Bluetooth Control Center doesn't necessarily have to be a Java application, and in the case of the Micro BlueTarget, the Bluetooth Control Center is a native application. For the Micro BlueTarget, you can initialize and control the Bluetooth Control Center via configuration files.*

The Wireless Network Access Point

Let's say that you have a Bluetooth-enabled device like a PDA or laptop, and want to use it to access the Internet via a traditional LAN access point (refer to Figure 10-8). With the Micro BlueTarget, you're already halfway there, and no Java coding is needed!

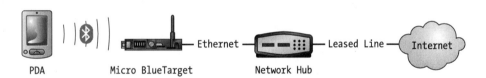

Figure 10-8. Using the built-in functionality of the Micro BlueTarget, you can have any Bluetooth device with the LAN Access Profile access the Internet (or any other Ethernet-based network).

So, in order to accomplish this with the HyNetOS, all you need to do is to edit the parameters in a configuration named BTAUTOLAN.CFG. The contents of the file would look something like this:

```
[BT LAN ACCESS]
MODE=automatic
IP-ASSIGNMENT=automatic
INQUIRY-CYCLE=15            ; in seconds

[PPP]
USER-ID=myName
PASSWORD=myPassword
AUTHENTICATION=PAP,CHAP     ; preferred methods
```

The Micro BlueTarget would then constantly search (in this case, every 15 seconds) for appropriate devices and provide them with network access.

NOTE *Now, it's nice to know that the Micro BlueTarget has the built-in capability to function as a wireless network access point, but what type of effort would be involved if you wanted to develop that functionality yourself? First of all, since the JSR-82 doesn't provide any foundational classes to write apps according to the LAN Access Profile, then you'll need to implement it on your own. According to the LAN Access Profile portion of the Bluetooth specification, data terminals (i.e., phones, PDAs, etc.) are supposed to authenticate with the LAN access point using the PPP protocol. After that, the data terminal will be assigned a dynamic IP address, an IP gateway, and a DNS server for Internet name resolution. You're not out of the woods yet, but that's where a majority of the effort should exist.*

L2CAPEcho Example

L2CAPEcho is a very simple example that will demonstrate communication between two Micro BlueTarget devices. This is the first example involving two Micro BlueTarget devices, and this is the kind of example that you want to run just to make sure you can get two devices talking to each other. If this example doesn't work, then you need to troubleshoot your setup and configuration.

So how does it work? Well, as shown in Figure 10-9, one board is offering an "echo service" to the public. The other board is the client that is using that service and is sending messages to the server.

Micro BlueTarget
1 (Client)

Micro BlueTarget
2 (Server)

Figure 10-9. The L2CAPEcho Service

Since this example contains most of the foundational elements that were described previously in this book, we won't go into further explanation other than the fact that the client sends a message once per second to the server. The server reads the message from the InputStream and writes it back to the OutputStream, and the client gets the message back as an echo. Listing 10-1 shows the code for the L2CAPEchoServer.

Listing 10-1. L2CAPEchoServer.java

```java
import java.lang.*;
import java.io.*;
import javax.microedition.io.*;
import javax.bluetooth.*;

public class L2CAPEchoServer
{
    static ClientProcess Client = null;

    public static void main(String[] args)
    {
        L2CAPConnectionNotifier Server = null;

        try
        {
            LocalDevice local = LocalDevice.getLocalDevice();
            local.setDiscoverable( DiscoveryAgent.GIAC );
        }
        catch (BluetoothStateException e)
        {
            System.err.println( "Failed to start service" );
```

```
        System.err.println( "BluetoothStateException: " + e.getMessage() );
        return;
}


try


{
    // start the echo server (with a fictional UUID)
    String url = "btl2cap://localhost:00112233445566778899AABBCCDDEEFF";
    Server = (L2CAPConnectionNotifier)Connector.open(url);
}
catch (IOException e)
{
    System.err.println( "Failed to start service" );
    System.err.println( "IOException: " + e.getMessage() );
    return;
}

System.out.println( "Starting L2CAP Echo Server" );

// This server actually runs forever. However, it can be stopped
// by terminating the KVM from the command line
// The server can terminate client connections by
// setting the client connections public variable "end" to "true"
// like: L2CAPEchoServer.Client.end = true;
while( true )
{
    L2CAPConnection conn = null;

    try
    {
        // wait for incoming client connections (blocking method)
        conn = Server.acceptAndOpen();

        // here we've got one, start it in a separate thread
        L2CAPEchoServer.Client = new ClientProcess( conn );
        L2CAPEchoServer.Client.start();
    }
    catch (IOException e)
    {
        System.out.println("IOException: " + e.getMessage());
    }
}
```

```
    }
}

class ClientProcess extends Thread
{
    static L2CAPConnection clientconn;
    public boolean         end;

    // the constructor
    ClientProcess( L2CAPConnection conn )
    {
        this.clientconn = conn;
        this.end = false;
    }

    // start the communication with the client
    public void run()
    {
        byte[] data = null;
        int length;

        System.out.println( "Client is connected" );

        while( !end )
        {
            try
            {
                // prepare a receive buffer
                length = clientconn.getReceiveMTU();
                data = new byte[length];


                // read in the data sent by the client (method blocks!)
                length = clientconn.receive(data);
                System.out.println( "Received " + length + " bytes from client" );

                // and immediately send it back on the same connection (echo)
                clientconn.send(data);
            }
            catch( IOException e )
            {
                System.out.println("IOException: " + e.getMessage());
            }
```

```
        }
        try
        {
            clientconn.close();
        }
        catch( IOException e )
        {
            System.out.println("IOException: " + e.getMessage());
        }
    }
}
```

Listing 10-2 shows the code for the L2CAPEchoClient.

Listing 10-2. L2CAPEchoClient.java

```java
import java.lang.*;
import java.io.*;
import java.util.*;
import javax.microedition.io.*;
import javax.bluetooth.*;

public class L2CAPEchoClient implements DiscoveryListener
{
    // The DiscoveryAgent for the local Bluetooth device.
    private DiscoveryAgent agent;

    // The max number of service searches that can occur at any one time.
    private int maxServiceSearches = 0;

    // The number of service searches that are presently in progress.
    private int serviceSearchCount;

    // Keeps track of the transaction IDs returned from searchServices.
    private int transactionID[];

    // The service record to an echo server that can reply to the message
    // provided at the command line.
    private ServiceRecord record;

    // Keeps track of the devices found during an inquiry.
    private Vector deviceList;
```

```java
    // The constructor: creates an L2CAPEchoClient object and prepares the
object
    // for device discovery and service searching.
    public L2CAPEchoClient() throws BluetoothStateException
    {
        // Retrieve the local Bluetooth device object.
        LocalDevice local = LocalDevice.getLocalDevice();

        // Retrieve the DiscoveryAgent object that allows us to perform device
        // and service discovery.
        agent = local.getDiscoveryAgent();

        // Retrieve the max number of concurrent service searches that can
        // exist at any one time.
        try
        {
            maxServiceSearches =
            Integer.parseInt( LocalDevice.getProperty("bluetooth.sd.trans.max") );
        }
        catch( NumberFormatException e )
        {
            System.out.println( "General Application Error" );
            System.out.println( "NumberFormatException: " + e.getMessage() );
        }

        transactionID = new int[maxServiceSearches];

        // Initialize the transaction list
        for( int i=0; i<maxServiceSearches; i++ )
        {
            transactionID[i] = -1;
        }

        record = null;
        deviceList = new Vector();
    }

    // Adds the transaction table with the transaction ID provided.
    private void addToTransactionTable( int trans )
    {
        for( int i=0; i<transactionID.length; i++ )
        {
            if( transactionID[i] == -1 )
```

```
        {
            transactionID[i] = trans;
            return;
        }
    }
}


// Removes the transaction from the transaction ID table.
private void removeFromTransactionTable( int trans )
{
    for( int i=0; i<transactionID.length; i++ )
    {
        if( transactionID[i] == trans )
        {
            transactionID[i] = -1;
            return;
        }
    }
}


// Completes a service search on each remote device in the list until all
// devices are searched or until an echo server is found that this application
// can send messages to.
private boolean searchServices( RemoteDevice[] devList )
{
    UUID[] searchList = new UUID[2];

    // Add the UUID for L2CAP to make sure that the service record
    // found will support L2CAP.  This value is defined in the
    // Bluetooth Assigned Numbers document.
    searchList[0] = new UUID( 0x0100 );

    // Add the UUID for the echo service that we are going to use to
    // the list of UUIDs to search for. (a fictional echo service UUID)
    searchList[1] = new UUID( "00112233445566778899AABBCCDDEEFF", false );

    // Start a search on as many devices as the system can support.
    for( int i=0; i<devList.length; i++ )
    {
        System.out.println( "Length = " + devList.length );

        // If we found a service record for the echo service, then
        // we can end the search.
```

```
if( record != null )
{
    System.out.println( "Record is not null" );
    return true;
}

try
{
    System.out.println( "Starting Service Search on " +
                        devList[i].getBluetoothAddress() );
    int trans =
        agent.searchServices( null, searchList, devList[i], this );

    System.out.println( "Starting Service Search " + trans );
    addToTransactionTable( trans );
}
catch( BluetoothStateException e )
{
    // Failed to start the search on this device, try another device.
    System.out.println( "BluetoothStateException: " + e.getMessage() );
}

// Determine if another search can be started. If not, wait for
// a service search to end.
synchronized( this )
{
    serviceSearchCount++;
    System.out.println( "maxServiceSearches = " + maxServiceSearches );
    System.out.println( "serviceSearchCount = " + serviceSearchCount );
    if( serviceSearchCount == maxServiceSearches )
    {
        System.out.println( "Waiting" );
        try
        {
            this.wait();
        }
        catch( Exception e ) {}
    }
    System.out.println( "Done Waiting " + serviceSearchCount );
}
```

```
        // Wait until all the service searches have completed.
        while( serviceSearchCount > 0 )
        {
            synchronized (this)
            {
                try
                {
                    this.wait();
                }
                catch (Exception e) {}
            }
        }

        if( record != null )
        {
            System.out.println( "Record is not null" );
            return true;
        }
        else
        {
            System.out.println( "Record is null" );
            return false;
        }
    }

    // Finds the first echo server that is available to send messages to.
    public ServiceRecord findEchoServer()
    {
        // If there are any devices that have been found by a recent inquiry,
        // we don't need to spend the time to complete an inquiry.
        RemoteDevice[] devList = agent.retrieveDevices( DiscoveryAgent.CACHED );
        if( devList != null )
        {
            if( searchServices(devList) )
            {
                return record;
            }
        }

        // Did not find any echo servers from the list of cached devices.
        // Will try to find an echo server in the list of pre-known devices.
        devList = agent.retrieveDevices( DiscoveryAgent.PREKNOWN );
        if( devList != null )
```

```
    {
        if( searchServices(devList) )
        {
            return record;
        }
    }


    // Did not find an echo server in the list of pre-known or cached
    // devices. So start an inquiry to find all devices that could be
    // an echo server and do a search on those devices.
    try
    {
        agent.startInquiry(DiscoveryAgent.GIAC, this);

        // Wait until all the devices are found before trying to start the
        // service search.
        synchronized( this )
        {
            try
            {
                this.wait();
            }
            catch (Exception e) {}
        }
    }
    catch( BluetoothStateException e )
    {
        System.out.println( "Unable to find devices to search" );
    }

    if( deviceList.size() > 0 )
    {
        devList = new RemoteDevice[deviceList.size()];
        deviceList.copyInto( devList );
        if( searchServices(devList) )
        {
            return record;
        }
    }

    return null;
}
```

```java
// This is the main method of this application.
public static void main(String[] args)
{
    L2CAPEchoClient client = null;

    // Validate the proper number of arguments exist when starting this
    // application.
    if( (args == null) || (args.length != 1) )
    {
        System.out.println( "usage: java L2CAPEchoClient <message>" );
        return;
    }

    // Create a new EchoClient object.
    try
    {
        client = new L2CAPEchoClient();
    }
    catch( BluetoothStateException e )
    {
        System.out.println( "Failed to start Bluetooth System" );
        System.out.println( "BluetoothStateException: " + e.getMessage() );
    }

    // Find an Echo Server in the local area
    ServiceRecord echoService = client.findEchoServer();

    if( echoService != null )
    {
        // retrieve the connection URL string
        String conURL =
echoService.getConnectionURL( ServiceRecord.NOAUTHENTICATE_NOENCRYPT, false );

        // create a new client instance
        EchoClient echoClient = new EchoClient( conURL );

        // and send the message give on the command line
        echoClient.sendMessage( args[0] );
    }
    else
    {
```

```
            System.out.println( "No Echo Server was found" );
        }
    }


    // Called when a device was found during an inquiry.  An inquiry
    // searches for devices that are discoverable.  The same device may
    // be returned multiple times.
    public void deviceDiscovered( RemoteDevice btDevice, DeviceClass cod )
    {
        System.out.println( "Found device = " + btDevice.getBluetoothAddress() );
        deviceList.addElement( btDevice );
    }


    // The following method is called when a service search is completed or
    // was terminated because of an error. Legal values include:
    // SERVICE_SEARCH_COMPLETED, SERVICE_SEARCH_TERMINATED,
    // SERVICE_SEARCH_ERROR, SERVICE_SEARCH_DEVICE_NOT_REACHABLE
    // and SERVICE_SEARCH_NO_RECORDS
    public void serviceSearchCompleted( int transID, int respCode )
    {
        System.out.println( "serviceSearchCompleted(" + transID + ", " +
                            respCode + ")" );

        // Removes the transaction ID from the transaction table.
        removeFromTransactionTable( transID );

        serviceSearchCount--;

        synchronized( this )
        {
            this.notifyAll();
        }
    }


    // Called when service(s) are found during a service search.
    // This method provides the array of services that have been found.
    public void servicesDiscovered( int transID, ServiceRecord[] servRecord )
    {
        // If this is the first record found, then store this record
        // and cancel the remaining searches.
        if( record == null )
        {
            System.out.println( "Found a service " + transID );
```

```
                    System.out.println( "Length of array = " + servRecord.length );
                    if( servRecord[0] == null )
                    {
                        System.out.println( "The service record is null" );
                    }
                    record = servRecord[0];
                    if( record == null )
                    {
                        System.out.println( "The second try was null" );
                    }

                    // Cancel all the service searches that are presently
                    // being performed.
                    for( int i=0; i<transactionID.length; i++ )
                    {
                        if( transactionID[i] != -1 )
                        {
                          System.out.println(agent.cancelServiceSearch(transactionID[i]));

                        }
                    }
                }
            }

    // Called when a device discovery transaction is
    // completed. The <code>discType</code> will be
    // INQUIRY_COMPLETED if the device discovery transaction ended normally,
    // INQUIRY_ERROR if the device discovery transaction failed
    // to complete normally,
    // INQUIRY_TERMINATED if the device discovery transaction
    // was canceled by calling
    // DiscoveryAgent.cancelInquiry().
    public void inquiryCompleted( int discType )
    {
        synchronized( this )
        {
            try
            {
                this.notifyAll();
            }
            catch (Exception e) {}
```

```
                }
        }
}


// The EchoClient will make a connection using the connection string
// provided and send a message to the server to print the data sent.
class EchoClient
{
        // Keeps the connection string in case the application would like to make
        // multiple connections to an echo server.
        private String serverConnectionString;

        // The constructor: creates an EchoClient object that will allow an
        // application to send multiple messages to an echo server.
        EchoClient( String server )
        {
                serverConnectionString = server;
        }

        // Sends a message to the server.
        public boolean sendMessage( String msg )
        {
                L2CAPConnection con = null;
                byte[] data = null;
                int index = 0;
                byte[] temp = null;

                try
                {
                        // Create a connection to the server
                        con = (L2CAPConnection)Connector.open( serverConnectionString );

                        // Determine the maximum amount of data I can send to the server.
                        int MaxOutBufSize = con.getTransmitMTU();
                        temp = new byte[MaxOutBufSize];

                        // Send as many packets as are needed to send the data
                        data = msg.getBytes();
```

```
                while( index < data.length )
                {
                    // Determine if this is the last packet to send or if there
                    // will be additional packets
                    if( (data.length - index) < MaxOutBufSize )
                    {
                        temp = new byte[data.length - index];
                        System.arraycopy( data, index, temp, 0, data.length-index );
                    }
                    else
                    {
                        temp = new byte[MaxOutBufSize];
                        System.arraycopy( data, index, temp, 0, MaxOutBufSize );
                    }
                    con.send(temp);
                    index += MaxOutBufSize;
                }

                // Prepare a receive buffer
                int rxlen = con.getReceiveMTU();
                byte[] rxdata = new byte[rxlen];

                // Wait to receive the server's reply (method blocks!)
                rxlen = con.receive( rxdata );

                // Here, we've got it
                String message = new String( rxdata, 0, rxlen );
                System.out.println( "Server replied: " + message );

                // Close the connection to the server
                con.close();
            }
            catch( BluetoothConnectionException e )
            {
                System.out.println( "Failed to send the message" );
                System.out.println( "BluetoothConnectionException: " +
                                    e.getMessage() );
                System.out.println( "Status: " + e.getStatus() );
            }
            catch( IOException e )
            {
                System.out.println( "Failed to send the message" );
                System.out.println( "IOException: " + e.getMessage() );
```

```
        return false;
    }

    return true;
    }
}
```

Wireless System Monitor Example

In the Wireless System Monitor example, we're going to look at an industrial device that is in great need of wireless communication: the Programmable Logic Controller (PLC). PLCs are industrial control devices that programmatically control large machinery. They are widely used with manufacturing facilities to control relays, switches, motors, sensors, test chambers, assembly lines, robotic arms—the list goes on and on.

Now a large manufacturing facility is very likely to have a considerable number of PLCs, each doing a particular task. Now, if you want to monitor the status of a particular PLC, you typically would have to walk over to the machine that you want to inquire about, and hook up a portable computer to the PLC's RS-232 interface. You would then run some program on the computer that would read the data coming from the serial port of the PLC.

This in itself can become a tedious process, especially if you're the guy who has to check the status on the PLCs. Sometimes, the hardest part of the job is trying to hook up the serial cable. We're not kidding here; in some industrial environments, the PLC may be located in a hard to reach area, and the communication ports may be even harder to reach. As you can see, PLCs make good candidates to be converted into fixed-wireless systems.

As shown in Figure 10-10, with the addition of a Micro BlueTarget, a PLC can instantly become a fixed-wireless system. The Micro BlueTarget will read the data from the RS-232 interface and transmit the data wirelessly with the Serial Port Profile. All a status technician needs to do is to come within range of the PLC to gather the data.

PDA   Micro BlueTarget   Serial   Programmable

Figure 10-10. Using the Micro BlueTarget to create a fixed-wireless system

SPP2COMM.java is a dual-purpose application that you could run on a Micro BlueTarget in order to read the data from its serial port and transmit it wirelessly. When the Micro BlueTarget receives data coming in from its COMM port, it will go into "server mode" and create a Serial Port Profile server and pipe the data from the COMM port to its Serial Port Profile "port."

This same code could also be run on a JSR-82–enabled client in order to collect the data from the Micro BlueTarget. Since the client isn't collecting data from its serial port, it will automatically go into "client mode" and create a Serial Port Profile client. When the client receives data, it will try to pipe the data to its native serial port. The code for SPP2COMM.java is shown in Listing 10-3.

Listing 10-3. SPP2COMM.java

```java
import java.lang.*;
import java.io.*;
import java.util.*;
import javax.microedition.io.*;
import javax.bluetooth.*;

public class SPP2COMM implements DiscoveryListener
{
    // The connection to the serial port
    static StreamConnection serialport = null;

    // The Input/Output streams to the local serial port
    static OutputStream ser_out = null;
    static InputStream  ser_in = null;

    // The Bluetooth connection to the peer device
    static StreamConnection bluetoothport = null;

    // The Input/Output streams to the Bluetooth connection
    static OutputStream bt_out = null;
    static InputStream  bt_in = null;

    // The DiscoveryAgent for the local Bluetooth device.
    private DiscoveryAgent agent;

    // The max number of service searches that can occur at any one time.
    private int maxServiceSearches = 0;

    // The number of service searches that are presently in progress.
    private int serviceSearchCount;
```

```java
// Keeps track of the transaction IDs returned from searchServices.
private int transactionID[];

// The service record to a cable replacement service
private ServiceRecord record;

// Keeps track of the devices found during an inquiry.
private Vector deviceList;

// The constructor: creates an SPP2COMM and prepares the object
// for device discovery and service searching.
public SPP2COMM() throws BluetoothStateException
{
    // Retrieve the local Bluetooth device object.
    LocalDevice local = LocalDevice.getLocalDevice();

    // Retrieve the DiscoveryAgent object that allows us to perform device
    // and service discovery.
    agent = local.getDiscoveryAgent();

    // Retrieve the max number of concurrent service searches that can
    // exist at any one time.
    try
    {
        maxServiceSearches =
          Integer.parseInt( LocalDevice.getProperty("bluetooth.sd.trans.max"));

    }
    catch( NumberFormatException e )
    {
        System.out.println( "General Application Error" );
        System.out.println( "NumberFormatException: " + e.getMessage() );
    }

    transactionID = new int[maxServiceSearches];

    // Initialize the transaction list
    for( int i=0; i<maxServiceSearches; i++ )
    {
        transactionID[i] = -1;
    }
```

```
    record = null;
    deviceList = new Vector();
}


// Adds the transaction table with the transaction ID provided.
private void addToTransactionTable( int trans )
{
    for( int i=0; i<transactionID.length; i++ )
    {
        if( transactionID[i] == -1 )
        {
            transactionID[i] = trans;
            return;
        }
    }
}


// Removes the transaction from the transaction ID table.
private void removeFromTransactionTable( int trans )
{
    for( int i=0; i<transactionID.length; i++ )
    {
        if( transactionID[i] == trans )
        {
            transactionID[i] = -1;
            return;
        }
    }
}


// Completes a service search on each remote device in the list until all
// devices are searched or until a cable replacement peer is found that this
// application can connect to.
private boolean searchServices( RemoteDevice[] devList )
{
    UUID[] searchList = new UUID[2];

    // Add the UUID for L2CAP to make sure that the service record
    // found will support L2CAP.  This value is defined in the
    // Bluetooth Assigned Numbers document.
    searchList[0] = new UUID( 0x0100 );
```

```java
    // Add the UUID for the cable replacement service that we are going
    // to use to the list of UUIDs to search for.
    // This is a fictional cable replacement service UUID
    searchList[1] = new UUID( "FFEEDDCCBBAA998877665544332211", false );

    // Start a search on as many devices as the system can support.
    for (int i = 0; i < devList.length; i++)
    {
        System.out.println( "Length = " + devList.length );

        // If we found a service record for the cable replacement service, then
        // we can end the search.
        if (record != null)
        {
            System.out.println( "Record is not null" );
            return true;
        }

        try
        {
            System.out.println( "Starting Service Search on " +
                                devList[i].getBluetoothAddress() );
           int trans = agent.searchServices(null, searchList, devList[i], this );
            System.out.println( "Starting Service Search " + trans );
            addToTransactionTable( trans );
        }
        catch (BluetoothStateException e)
        {
            // Failed to start the search on this device, try another device.
            System.out.println( "BluetoothStateException: " + e.getMessage() );
        }

        // Determine if another search can be started. If not, wait for
        // a service search to end.
        synchronized( this )
        {
            serviceSearchCount++;
            System.out.println( "maxServiceSearches = " + maxServiceSearches );
            System.out.println( "serviceSearchCount = " + serviceSearchCount );
            if( serviceSearchCount == maxServiceSearches )
            {
                System.out.println( "Waiting" );
                try
```

```
                    {
                        this.wait();
                    }
                    catch( Exception e ) {}
                }
                System.out.println( "Done Waiting " + serviceSearchCount );
            }
        }


        // Wait until all the service searches have completed.
        while( serviceSearchCount > 0 )
        {
            synchronized (this)
            {
                try
                {
                    this.wait();
                }
                catch (Exception e) {}
            }
        }

        if( record != null )
        {
            System.out.println( "Record is not null" );
            return true;
        }
        else
        {
            System.out.println( "Record is null" );
            return false;
        }
    }

    // Finds the first cable replacement peer that is available to connect to.
    public ServiceRecord findCableReplacementService()
    {
        // If there are any devices that have been found by a recent inquiry,
        // we don't need to spend the time to complete an inquiry.
        RemoteDevice[] devList = agent.retrieveDevices( DiscoveryAgent.CACHED );
        if( devList != null )
        {
            if( searchServices(devList) )
```

```
        {
            return record;
        }
    }


    // Did not find any cable replacement peer from the list of cached devices.
    // Will try to find a cable replacement peer in the list of
    // pre-known devices.
    devList = agent.retrieveDevices( DiscoveryAgent.PREKNOWN );
    if( devList != null )
    {
        if( searchServices(devList) )
        {
            return record;
        }
    }


    // Did not find a cable replacement peer in the list of pre-known or
    // cached devices. So start an inquiry to find all devices that could be
    // a cable replacement peer and do a search on those devices.
    try
    {
        agent.startInquiry(DiscoveryAgent.GIAC, this);

        // Wait until all the devices are found before trying to start the
        // service search.
        synchronized( this )
        {
            try
            {
                this.wait();
            }
            catch (Exception e) {}
        }
    }
    catch( BluetoothStateException e )
    {
        System.out.println( "Unable to find devices to search" );
    }


    if( deviceList.size() > 0 )
    {
        devList = new RemoteDevice[deviceList.size()];
```

```
                    deviceList.copyInto( devList );
                    if( searchServices(devList) )
                    {
                        return record;
                    }
            }

        return null;
    }

    // This is the main method of this application.
    public static void main(String[] args)
    {
        SPP2COMM client = null;
        SppServerProcess server = null;
        int baudrate;

        // Validate the proper number of arguments exist when starting
        // this application.
        if( (args == null) || (args.length != 1) )
        {
            System.out.println( "usage: java SPP2COMM <baudrate>" );
            return;
        }

        // Create a new SPP2COMM object.
        try
        {
            client = new SPP2COMM();
        }
        catch( BluetoothStateException e )
        {
            System.out.println( "Failed to start Bluetooth System" );
            System.out.println( "BluetoothStateException: " + e.getMessage() );
        }

        // get the baudrate for the serial port from the command line
        baudrate = Integer.parseInt( args[0] );

        // make the connection to the serial port
        try {
            // get the connection
            serialport = (StreamConnection)Connector.open( "comm:1;baudrate=" +
                                        baudrate, Connector.READ_WRITE, true );
```

```
        }
        catch( Exception e )
        {
            System.out.println( "serial port open exception: " + e );
            System.exit( 0 );
        }

        // open the serial port's output stream
        try
        {
            ser_out = serialport.openOutputStream();
        }
        catch( Exception e )
        {
            System.out.println( "serial output stream open exception: " + e );
            System.exit( 0 );
        }

        // open the serial port's input stream
        try
        {
            ser_in = serialport.openInputStream();
        }
        catch( Exception e )
        {
            System.out.println( "serial input stream open exception: " + e );
            System.exit( 0 );
        }

        // Create a new SPP server object.
        try
        {
            server = new SppServerProcess();
            server.start();
        }
        catch( Exception e )
        {
            System.out.println( "Failed to start Spp Server" + e );
            System.exit( 0 );
        }

        // the main loop runs forever. However, it can be stopped
        // by terminating the KVM from the command line
```

```java
while( true )
{
    // Create buffer to receive data from the serial port
    byte[] rxdata = new byte[64];
    int     rxlen=0;
    int     data;

    try
    {
        // read in as many bytes from the serial port
        // as currently available but do not exceed the
        // current buffer length.
        // The read() method blocks but is periodically released
        // by an InterruptedIOException in order to allow other
        // things to happen meanwhile
        while( true )
        {
            data = ser_in.read();
            rxdata[rxlen] = (byte)data;
            rxlen++;
            if( rxlen >= 64 || data == -1 )
                break;
        }
        System.out.println( "data received from serial port, len=" +
                                rxlen );

    }
    catch( InterruptedIOException e )
    {
        System.out.println( "serial port receive timeout: " + e );
    }
    catch( Exception e )
    {
        System.out.println( "serial port receive exception: " + e );
    }

    // Did we get any data from the serial port?
    if( rxlen > 0 )
    {
        // Do we have a Bluetooth connection already?
        if( bluetoothport != null )
        {
```

```
                // Do we have an OutputStream on the BT connection already?
                if( bt_out == null )
                {
                    // no, then create one
                    try
                    {
                        bt_out = bluetoothport.openOutputStream();
                    }
                    catch( Exception e )
                    {
    System.out.println( "Bluetooth output stream open exception: " + e );

                    }
                }
                System.out.println( "send serial data on Bluetooth link" );
                try
                {
                    bt_out.write( rxdata );
                    bt_out.flush();
                }
                catch( Exception e )
                {
    System.out.println( "Bluetooth output stream write exception: " + e );
                }
            }
            else
            {
    System.out.println( "No Bluetooth link: try to establish one..." );

                // Find a cable replacement service in the local area
                ServiceRecord cableReplacementService =
                    client.findCableReplacementService();

                if( cableReplacementService != null )
                {
                    // retrieve the connection URL string
                    String conURL =
                        cableReplacementService.getConnectionURL(
                            ServiceRecord.NOAUTHENTICATE_NOENCRYPT, false );

                    try
                    {
                        // Create a connection to the SPP peer
```

```
                        bluetoothport =
                            (StreamConnection)Connector.open( conURL );
                }
                catch( Exception e )
                {
        System.out.println( "Failed to establish Bluetooth link: " + e );
                }

                if( bluetoothport != null )
                {
                    try
                    {
                        // open an OutputStream on the Bluetooth connection
                        bt_out = bluetoothport.openOutputStream();
                    }
                    catch( Exception e )
                    {
            System.out.println( "Bluetooth output stream open exception: " + e );
                    }

                    // and send the data from the serial port
            System.out.println( "send serial data on Bluetooth link" );
                    try
                    {
                        bt_out.write( rxdata );
                        bt_out.flush();
                    }
                    catch( Exception e )
                    {
        System.out.println( "Bluetooth output stream write exception: " + e );
                    }
                }
            }
            else
            {
                System.out.println( "No SPP peer found" );
            }
        }
    }

    // do we have a Bluetooth connection already?
    if( bluetoothport != null )
    {
```

```
        // do we have an InputStream on the Bluetooth connection already?
        if( bt_in == null )
        {
            // no, then create one
            try
            {
                bt_in = bluetoothport.openInputStream();
            }
            catch( Exception e )
            {
    System.out.println( "Bluetooth output stream open exception: " + e );
            }
        }


        // listen on the bluetooth connection
        rxlen = 0;
        try
        {
            // read in as many bytes from the serial port
            // as currently available but do not exceed the
            // current buffer length.
            // The read() method blocks but is periodically released
            // by an InterruptedIOException in order to allow other
            // things to happen meanwhile
            while( true )
            {
                data = bt_in.read();
                rxdata[rxlen] = (byte)data;
                rxlen++;
                if( rxlen >= 64 || data == -1 )
                    break;
            }
    System.out.println( "data received from bluetooth port, len=" + rxlen );

        }
        catch( InterruptedIOException e )
        {
            System.out.println( "Bluetooth port receive timeout: " + e );
        }
        catch( Exception e )
        {
            System.out.println( "Bluetooth port receive exception: " + e );
        }
```

```
                try
                {
                    System.out.println( "send Bluetooth data on serial link" );
                    ser_out.write( rxdata );
                    ser_out.flush();
                }
                catch( Exception e )
                {
        System.out.println( "Bluetooth output stream write exception: " + e );
                }
            }
        }
    }


    // Called when a device was found during an inquiry.  An inquiry
    // searches for devices that are discoverable.  The same device may
    // be returned multiple times.
    public void deviceDiscovered( RemoteDevice btDevice, DeviceClass cod )
    {
        System.out.println( "Found device = " + btDevice.getBluetoothAddress() );
        deviceList.addElement( btDevice );
    }


    // The following method is called when a service search is completed or
    // was terminated because of an error. Legal values include:
    // SERVICE_SEARCH_COMPLETED, SERVICE_SEARCH_TERMINATED,
    // SERVICE_SEARCH_ERROR, SERVICE_SEARCH_DEVICE_NOT_REACHABLE
    // and SERVICE_SEARCH_NO_RECORDS
    public void serviceSearchCompleted( int transID, int respCode )
    {
System.out.println( "serviceSearchCompleted(" + transID +
                        ", " + respCode + ")" );

        // Removes the transaction ID from the transaction table.
        removeFromTransactionTable( transID );

        serviceSearchCount--;

        synchronized( this )
        {
            this.notifyAll();
        }
    }
```

```
// Called when service(s) are found during a service search.
// This method provides the array of services that have been found.
public void servicesDiscovered( int transID, ServiceRecord[] servRecord )
{
    // If this is the first record found, then store this record
    // and cancel the remaining searches.
    if( record == null )
    {
        System.out.println( "Found a service " + transID );
        System.out.println( "Length of array = " + servRecord.length );
        if( servRecord[0] == null )
        {
            System.out.println( "The service record is null" );
        }
        record = servRecord[0];
        System.out.println( "After this" );
        if( record == null )
        {
            System.out.println( "The Second try was null" );
        }

        // Cancel all the service searches that are presently
        // being performed.
        for( int i=0; i<transactionID.length; i++ )
        {
            if( transactionID[i] != -1 )
            {

System.out.println(agent.cancelServiceSearch(transactionID[i]));
            }
        }
    }
}


// Called when a device discovery transaction is
// completed. The <code>discType</code> will be
// INQUIRY_COMPLETED if the device discovery transactions ended normally,
// INQUIRY_ERROR if the device discovery transaction failed
// to complete normally,
// INQUIRY_TERMINATED if the device discovery transaction was canceled
// by calling DiscoveryAgent.cancelInquiry().
```

```java
    public void inquiryCompleted( int discType )
    {
        synchronized( this )
        {
            try
            {
                this.notifyAll();
            }
            catch (Exception e) {}
        }
    }
}


class SppServerProcess extends Thread
{
    /* the constructor */
    SppServerProcess()
    {
    }

    public void run()
    {
        StreamConnectionNotifier Server = null;

        try
        {
            LocalDevice local = LocalDevice.getLocalDevice();
            local.setDiscoverable( DiscoveryAgent.GIAC );
        }
        catch( BluetoothStateException e )
        {
            System.err.println( "Failed to start service" );
            System.err.println( "BluetoothStateException: " + e.getMessage() );
            return;
        }

        try
        {
            // start the SPP server (with a fictional UUID)
            Server = (StreamConnectionNotifier)Connector.open(
                    "btspp://localhost:FFEEDDCCBBAA99887766554433221100" );
```

```
            }
            catch( IOException e )
            {
                System.err.println( "Failed to start service" );
                System.err.println( "IOException: " + e.getMessage() );
                return;
            }

            System.out.println( "Starting SPP Server" );

            while( true )
            {
                // accept connections only if we are not yet connected
                if( SPP2COMM.bluetoothport == null )
                {
                    try
                    {
                        // wait for incoming client connections (blocking method)
                        SPP2COMM.bluetoothport = Server.acceptAndOpen();
                    }
                    catch( IOException e )
                    {
                        System.out.println("IOException: " + e.getMessage());
                    }
                }
                try
                {
                    Thread.sleep( 1000 );
                }
                catch( Exception e ) { }
            }
        }
    }
}
```

Client Options

Once you get data feeding the Micro BlueTarget and have SPP2COMM running on it,
then you're all set from the server's point of view; you have created a fixed-
wireless system. Now on the client side of things, you have a few options. Let's say
that the vendor of the PLC makes a program to read and interpret the data from
the PLC (when connected serially, of course). You really don't need to use the

SPP2COMM in client mode at all; all you need to do is Bluetooth-enable your laptop and pair it with the Micro BlueTarget. The vendor's program will read the data from the PLC (via the Micro BlueTarget) through COMM7 or COMM8 (which are typical Serial Port Profile ports) instead of COMM1 or COMM2.

Now let's say that all the preceding conditions exist, but for some reason you can't Bluetooth-enable the laptop that will read the data from the PLC. Don't worry, there's hope for you too! All you need to do is attach another Micro BlueTarget to your non–Bluetooth-enabled laptop and run the SPP2COMM program. Since this Micro BlueTarget is not collecting data over its serial port, it will automatically run in client mode and look for a Serial Port Profile server. It will then read the data from the Serial Port Profile server, and pipe that data to its own serial port. Your laptop can then use the vendor program to read and interpret the PLC data (this time via two Micro BlueTargets) through a traditional serial port like COMM1 or COMM2. In this case, you have made a serial-to-wireless bridge.

Now let's say that you're in a very special situation in that the vendor doesn't make a program to read and interpret the data from the PLC. Now, you can be really creative and just make your own! In this case all you need is a JSR-82–enabled client device (like a PDA or laptop), and you have to make a slight modification to SPP2COMM program. For the client mode part of it, instead of sending the data to the COMM port, just interpret, display, or process it.

Summary

In this chapter, you were introduced to one of the first fully functional computing systems that is JSR-82 compliant: the Micro BlueTarget. You should be fully aware of its physical aspects for computational power, data connectivity, and wireless communication. You should also be familiar with HyNetOS, the operating system for the Micro BlueTarget.

Due to its small form factor, low power requirements, and extensibility, the Micro BlueTarget is a great device to create fixed-wireless systems and proofs of concepts for wireless applications. In Chapter 11, we'll explore what it takes to create scalable and robust wireless applications in Bluetooth that can handle more than just seven concurrent users.

Enterprise Bluetooth Applications with the Ericsson BlipNet

As you have seen in the previous chapters of this book, the JSR-82 is a great API for creating Bluetooth applications with the Java language. With any vendor implementation of the JSR-82, you can create hundreds of client-server, peer-to-peer, cable replacement, and fixed-wireless Bluetooth applications. However, this API falls short when you need to create enterprise Bluetooth applications. So what's an enterprise Bluetooth application? Well, here are the major qualifications of an enterprise Bluetooth application:

- Capability to handle more than just seven active connections

- A connection range greater than just 30 or 300 ft

- Centralized communication to the devices (also called *nodes*) that comprise your network

- A means for managing groups of nodes

- A means for session management when clients move between nodes

NOTE   *Of course, Class 1 Bluetooth devices have a range of 300 ft, but you must realize that if the client is a Class 2 or Class 3 device (like most mobile phones and PDAs), then it doesn't matter if the server is a Class 1 device (like some LAN access points).*

The JSR-82 was not created to handle enterprise Bluetooth applications, and doesn't provide any way to address the problems that enterprise Bluetooth applications can solve.

Consider the locations where Bluetooth applications will be widely deployed, like shopping malls, airports, museums, office buildings, and grocery stores. At a mall, for instance, the scaling issue is very important. It's not practical to create a Bluetooth-enabled information kiosk at a mall without being able to scale up to handle more than just seven active connections. In order to accomplish this, your enterprise Bluetooth applications will contain more than a single Bluetooth-enabled node.

Centralized communication is an important feature in enterprise Bluetooth applications because there's no way to implement group management or session management without it. For instance, in a Bluetooth-enabled museum exhibit, there should be a way to activate or deactivate a group of nodes without disturbing the other nodes on the network. Session management comes into play in a Bluetooth-enabled retail location like a grocery store. Without session management, a customer may be offered the same e-coupon multiple times when passing by a different node in a grocery store.

In an office building, providing wireless network access to Bluetooth-enabled clients is a common enterprise Bluetooth application. Session management in this scenario is also important so that clients can freely roam around the building without having to reauthenticate when they go in and out of range of different nodes.

In order to create enterprise Bluetooth applications, you need more than just a single Bluetooth device and an API. Enterprise Bluetooth applications also require an infrastructure to be in place that will allow your system to be scalable and robust.

The Ericsson BlipNet

The Ericsson BlipNet contains the infrastructure, functionality, and scalability that will allow developers to create enterprise Bluetooth applications using the Java language. An architecture diagram of the Ericsson BlipNet is shown in Figure 11-1.

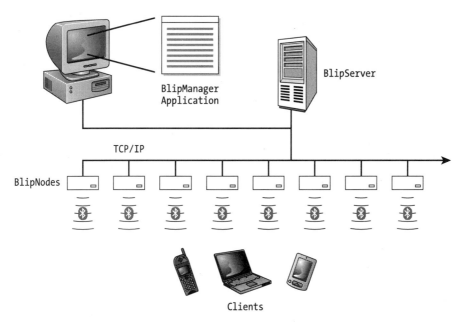

Figure 11-1. An architecture diagram of the Ericsson BlipNet

 NOTE *Although the Ericsson BlipNet allows you to create enterprise Bluetooth applications in Java, it does not support the JSR-82. The JSR-82 is oriented toward creating applications where a single Bluetooth device communicates to other devices in a piconet. The BlipNet API is oriented toward managing a network of Bluetooth-enabled nodes, where each node has the capability to interact with Bluetooth-enabled clients.*

BlipNet Architecture

The core part of the BlipNet system is the BlipServer. The BlipServer itself is not Bluetooth enabled at all. It does, however, have a direct TCP/IP connection to each of the BlipNodes (which are Bluetooth enabled) and controls them via Java RMI. In order to create your enterprise Bluetooth applications, you write J2SE classes that interface with the BlipNet API. Now, since you're writing J2SE code here, you may realize that there's nothing preventing you from accessing external resources on behalf of your Bluetooth-enabled clients. In fact, that's the whole point of it. Using the Ericsson BlipNet, external resources such as databases, LDAP directories, Web servers, and e-mail servers are all available at your client's disposal (as long as you can access them via a Java API). This is reflected in Figure 11-2.

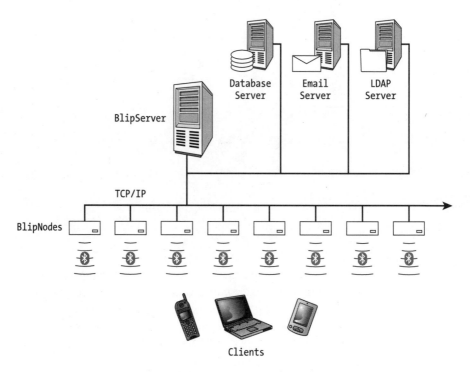

Figure 11-2. You can use the BlipNet API and custom J2SE code to access external resources like databases, directories, and e-mail servers.

BlipServer

The BlipServer does not require any specialized hardware and can run on either Windows or Linux operating systems. The statistics on the BlipServer are pretty impressive: a Pentium 400 MHz computer with 256MB of RAM can manage 200 BlipNodes!

BlipNodes

In an enterprise Bluetooth application, the BlipServer cannot directly communicate to your Bluetooth-enabled clients; it has to interface with the BlipNodes. Each BlipNode is capable of multipoint communication and includes the following profiles to interact with clients:

- Generic Access Profile

- Service Discovery Application Profile

- LAN Access Profile

- Object Push Profile

 NOTE *The BlipNodes also conform to the WAP over Bluetooth interoperability requirements as defined in the Bluetooth specification.*

Your enterprise Bluetooth application will listen for events from the BlipNodes and act accordingly. For instance, let's say that you want to track where employees are in the building (assuming, of course, that they are wearing Bluetooth-enabled ID badges). When users come within range of a BlipNode, your application will listen to device-discovered events via the Generic Access Profile. The BlipNet system is sophisticated enough to let you know which BlipNode detected a user, so all you need to do is store that data in a database, and create another application to view the results.

Now let's say that you're the manager of a hotel, and you want to allow your customers with Bluetooth-enabled devices to send e-mails wirelessly from within the conference rooms. At these "e-mail stations," the BlipNodes will use the Object Push Profile to send clients the custom e-mail application (of course, this works well if the app is a JSR-82 application). Clients compose their e-mail using the custom application, and when they are ready to send the e-mail, they simply come within range of an e-mail station and push the e-mail OBEX object to the BlipNode. On the BlipServer, your enterprise Bluetooth application will be listening for an Object Push event, and will connect to an e-mail server to send the e-mail on behalf of the hotel guest.

NOTE *This might be a perfect time for you to try creating custom headers for your OBEX e-mail object. There's nothing stopping you from defining a custom header for the "to", "from", and "subject" fields for the e-mail.*

As you can see, the wireless e-mail station scenario clearly demonstrates the difference between the programming paradigms of the JSR-82 and the BlipNet. Using the JSR-82, you can create the client app that generates the e-mail OBEX object and pushes it to the server. One of the major drawbacks, however, is that you need to implement the Object Push Profile in your application code (which may be an inconvenience for inexperienced developers). On the other hand, the Object Push Profile is already defined within the BlipNet API, so all you need to do is write the event handling code when your object arrives from your Bluetooth-enabled clients.

BlipNode Installation

Installation of a BlipNode is pretty simple. All you need to do is supply the Ethernet connection and power. The device will then register itself to the BlipNet. Figure 11-3 is a picture of a single BlipNode unit.

Figure 11-3. A single BlipNode

BlipManager Application

The BlipManager tool is used to configure and administer the BlipNet system. As shown in Figure 11-4, the BlipManager gives you a visual representation of all the BlipNodes on your network.

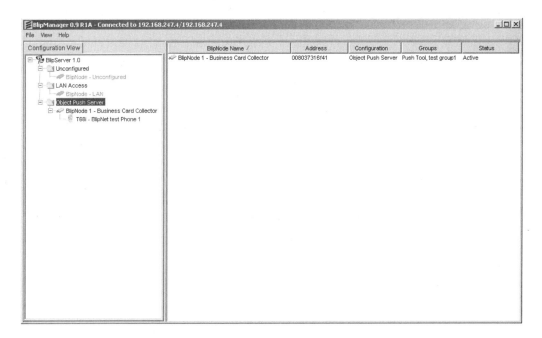

Figure 11-4. The BlipManager application

Out of the box, the BlipManager comes with the following features:

- Device filtering

- Security administration

- Node administration

With the device filtering feature, you can block certain Bluetooth devices from using the BlipNet. You can create this filter based upon the client device's address or the device's class (i.e., laptop, cell phone, headset), or based upon the available services on the device. The security administration feature allows you to assign PINs for individual nodes, or for the entire BlipNet. Using the node administration features of the BlipManager, you can administer an individual node or create a group of nodes and administer them collectively. The node administration features also give you the ability to activate and deactivate the profiles on your nodes. Using this feature, it is very easy to configure multiple enterprise Bluetooth applications on the same BlipNet network. For instance, in a grade school environment, all the BlipNodes at the entrance of the school can be configured to use only the Object Push Profile so that parents and visitors are greeted with some information about the school. However, in the teacher's lounge, the BlipNodes can be connected to the same network, but have only the LAN Access Profile activated so that teachers can get wireless Internet access.

BlipNet API Overview

The BlipNet 1.1 API consists of 6 packages and 40 classes and interfaces that allow you to create enterprise Bluetooth applications. Here's a list of the BlipNet packages:

- `com.ericsson.blipnet.api.blipnode`

- `com.ericsson.blipnet.api.blipserver`

- `com.ericsson.blipnet.api.bluetooth`

- `com.ericsson.blipnet.api.event`

- `com.ericsson.blipnet.api.obex.pushobjects`

- `com.ericsson.blipnet.api.util`

The `com.ericsson.blipnet.api.blipnode` package contains classes that deal directly with individual BlipNodes, like `BlipNodeHandle`. Conversely, the package `com.ericsson.blipnet.api.blipserver` contains classes that deal with the BlipServer such as `BlipServer` and `BlipServerConnection`. If you are looking for classes that pertain to Bluetooth-specific things like `BluetoothAddress` and `ClassOfDevice`, then they are found in the package `com.ericsson.blipnet.api.bluetooth`.

Almost every application will use one or more of the interfaces contained in the `com.ericsson.blipnet.api.event` package. This package contains all the interfaces for listeners and events within the BlipNet. For instance, if you implement the `BlipServerEventListener` interface, then you can receive callbacks from the JVM when `BlipNodeEvents`, `ConnectionEvents`, and `ObexEvents` are occurring. The `com.ericsson.blipnet.api.event` package also includes the `ObexProgressListener` interface, which you can use to determine the progress of an OBEX object transfer.

When dealing with clients that support the Object Push Profile, the classes that form the com.ericsson.blipnet.api.obex.pushobjects package come in handy. This package contains classes such as ObexFile and ObexGenericObject that help you when you're sending or receiving OBEX objects. For obvious reasons the com.ericsson.blipnet.api.util was designed to be a utility package, but at the moment it only contains a single class for icons: BlipNetIcons.

CROSS-REFERENCE   *See Appendix D for a complete list (with descriptions) of all the classes and interfaces of the BlipNet 1.1 API.*

Now that you have a good understanding of the BlipNet architecture and its APIs, let's look at an example demonstrating how to create an enterprise Bluetooth application using the Ericsson BlipNet.

The Bluetooth Device Tracker

A Bluetooth device tracker is an extremely useful enterprise Bluetooth application, but it's really an invaluable tool to anyone in the retail business. Why? Have you ever been to a grocery store where the peanut butter is in aisle two, but the jelly is located in aisle twelve? Or even worse, the coffee and the cream are eight aisles apart.

In the near future, almost every mobile phone will be Bluetooth enabled, so a Bluetooth device tracker will help a grocery store manager to answer the following questions:

- Are customers wandering around aimlessly?

- Do consistent buying patterns exist?

- Which are the frequently traveled aisles?

- Are the aisles arranged properly?

- How long are customers in the store?

All these factors impact customer satisfaction and directly affect whether or not if the customer will return.

Tracking.java is a simple enterprise Bluetooth application that allows you to track Bluetooth devices using the Ericsson BlipNet. Of course, before you run Tracking.java, you have to have at least two BlipNodes connected to your BlipServer (otherwise, it would be pointless to track devices with only a single node). Another prerequisite is that a user name and password to the BlipServer must already be created. In this example, the user name is Tracking and the password is Tracy. You also need to assign the BlipNodes that you want to perform device tracking to a group. In this example the group is called First_Floor.

NOTE *Of course, you can create user names, passwords, and groups using the BlipManager application.*

In order to run the application (and to track every discoverable Bluetooth device), just execute the following statement, at the command line:

```
java Tracking First_Floor
```

If you want to track specific Bluetooth clients, then you need to provide their Bluetooth address at the command line, separated by spaces:

```
java Tracking First_Floor 001122334455 007e3ba4780f 0065ca98bd2e
```

This application starts off by calling the method initBlipServerConnection() in the constructor. In turn, initBlipServerConnection() obtains a BlipServerConnection object by calling the static method getConnection() from the BlipServer class. The parameters to this method include the user name and password that you've created, as well as the hostname of the BlipServer:

```
BlipServer.getConnection("Tracking", "Tracy", "localhost");
```

Afterwards, a BlipServerEventFilter is created by calling the getEventFilter() method:

```
BlipServerEventFilter blipServerEventFilter =
                        getEventFilter(discoverBlipNodeGroup, terminalsToTrack);
```

Finally, we're going to add an event listener to the BlipServerConnection instance by calling its addEventListener() method.

```
blipServerConnection.addEventListener(new TrackingEventListener(),
                                    blipServerEventFilter);
```

The addEventListener() method requires a BlipServerEventListener and (optionally) a BlipServerEventFilter. At this point, we already have an instance of a BlipServerEventFilter on hand, so we create a new instance of our inner class TrackingEventListener. TrackingEventListener is a subclass of BlipServerEventAdapter, which, in turn, is an implementation of BlipServerEventListener.

When Bluetooth devices are detected, the events are passed to the inner class, and the inner class then prints out on the command line what's going on. The code for Tracking.java is shown in Listing 11-1.

Listing 11-1. Tracking.java

```
package com.ericsson.blipnet.samples;

import com.ericsson.blipnet.api.event.*;
import com.ericsson.blipnet.api.blipserver.*;
import com.ericsson.blipnet.api.bluetooth.BluetoothAddress;
import com.ericsson.blipnet.api.blipserver.BlipNode;

import java.util.Hashtable;

public class Tracking {
    private BlipServerConnection blipServerConnection;
    private Hashtable terminalLastSeenOnThisBlipNode = new Hashtable();

    public Tracking(String discoverBlipNodeGroup,
                    BluetoothAddress[] terminalsToTrack) {

        // Get a connection to the server
        initBlipServerConnection();

        BlipServerEventFilter blipServerEventFilter =
                getEventFilter(discoverBlipNodeGroup, terminalsToTrack);

        try {
            // Register the event listener with the generated filter
            blipServerConnection.addEventListener(new TrackingEventListener(),
                                                blipServerEventFilter);
        } catch (BlipServerConnectionException e) {
            System.out.println("Error attaching listener");
            e.printStackTrace();
```

```
                System.exit(-1);
            }

        }


        private void initBlipServerConnection() {
            try {
                blipServerConnection = BlipServer.getConnection("Tracking",
                                                    "Tracy", "localhost");
            } catch (BlipServerConnectionException e) {
                System.out.println("Error connecting to server");
                e.printStackTrace();
                System.exit(-1);
            } catch (BlipServerAccessException e) {
                e.printStackTrace();
                System.out.println("Error registering user - Have You created " +
                        "a username/password for this application in BlipManager?");
                System.exit(-1);
            }
        }


        private BlipServerEventFilter getEventFilter(String discoverBlipNodeGroup,
                                            BluetoothAddress[] terminals) {
            // List of BlipNodeIds used for tracking - is built from input
            // in-line parameters entered at start up of Tracking application.
            BluetoothAddress[] blipNodeAddressList = null;

            BlipNode[] inquiryOnlyBlipNodes = null;
            try {
                inquiryOnlyBlipNodes = blipServerConnection.getBlipNodes
                        (discoverBlipNodeGroup, "Discover Devices", false, false);
            } catch (BlipServerConnectionException e) {
                System.out.println("Could not get BlipNode handles " +
                    "for the BlipNode Group: "+ discoverBlipNodeGroup + "\n" + e);
                System.exit(-1);
            }

            // Are there any BlipNodes in the specified group ?
            if (inquiryOnlyBlipNodes.length > 1) {
                blipNodeAddressList =
                        new BluetoothAddress[inquiryOnlyBlipNodes.length];
                for (int i = 0; i < blipNodeAddressList.length; i++) {
                    blipNodeAddressList[i] =
```

```
                        inquiryOnlyBlipNodes[i].getBlipNodeID();
        }
    } else {
        System.out.println("Have You inserted at least 2 BlipNodes " +
                    "in the group (" + discoverBlipNodeGroup + ") ?");
        usage();
    }


    System.out.println("BlipNodes used for tracking (from group '" +
                        discoverBlipNodeGroup + "'):");
    for (int i=0; i<blipNodeAddressList.length; i++) {
        System.out.println("* " +
                blipNodeAddressList[i].toString().toUpperCase());
    }


    if (null != terminals) {
        System.out.println("\nTerminals being tracked: ");
        for (int i=0; i<terminals.length; i++) {
            System.out.println("* " +
                terminals[i].toString().toUpperCase());
        }
    } else {
        System.out.println("* Tracking all discoverable devices.");
    }
    System.out.println("----------------\n");



    return new BlipServerEventFilter(null,
                                new int[] {Event.TERMINAL_DETECTED},
                                blipNodeAddressList, terminals);

}

private class TrackingEventListener extends BlipServerEventAdapter {
    public void handleConnectionEvent(ConnectionEvent e) {
        switch (e.getEventID()) {
            case Event.TERMINAL_DETECTED:
                BluetoothAddress terminalID = e.getTerminalID();
                BluetoothAddress blipNodeID = e.getBlipNodeID();
                if (terminalLastSeenOnThisBlipNode.containsKey(terminalID)) {
                    // Terminal has already been discovered before,
                    // so has it moved?
                    if (!terminalLastSeenOnThisBlipNode.
                                    get(terminalID).equals(blipNodeID)) {
```

```
                        System.out.println("Terminal: " + terminalID + " (" +
                                    e.getTerminalFriendlyName() +
                                    ") moved from BlipNode: " +
    ((BluetoothAddress) terminalLastSeenOnThisBlipNode.remove(terminalID)) +
                                    " to BlipNode:" + blipNodeID);
                        terminalLastSeenOnThisBlipNode.put(terminalID,
                                                    blipNodeID);
                } else {
                    // Terminal stays on the same BlipNode.
                    // Do not do anything.
                }
            } else {
                // This is the first this terminal is seen on the system
                System.out.println("Terminal: " + terminalID + " (" +
                                    e.getTerminalFriendlyName() +
                                    ") discovered for the first time on" +
                                    " BlipNode: " + blipNodeID);
                terminalLastSeenOnThisBlipNode.put(terminalID,
                                                    blipNodeID);
            }
            break;
        default:
            System.out.println("Error - only TERMINAL_DETECTED " +
                                "events should be received! \nReceived " +
                                "event:" +
                                Event.FRIENDLY_NAMES[e.getEventID()]);
        }
    }
}


private static BluetoothAddress[] parseTerminalList(final String[] args) {
    int numberOfTerminals = args.length - 1;

    // List of BlipNodeIds used for tracking - is built from
    // input in-line parameters entered at start up of Tracking application.
    BluetoothAddress[] trackTheseTerminals = null;

    if (numberOfTerminals > 0) {
        trackTheseTerminals = new BluetoothAddress[numberOfTerminals];
        for (int inputParameterCount=0; inputParameterCount <
                        numberOfTerminals; inputParameterCount++) {
            try {
                // Make sure it is a valid TerminalID (BluetoothAddress)
```

```
                        trackTheseTerminals[inputParameterCount] =
                            new BluetoothAddress(args[inputParameterCount+1]);
            } catch (IllegalArgumentException iae) {
                System.out.println("TerminalId: " +
                                    args[inputParameterCount] +
                                    " is invalid. A valid id, e.g. " +
                                    "112233445566\n" + iae);
                usage();
            }
        }
    }
    return trackTheseTerminals;
}


private static void usage() {
    System.out.println("The tracking application requires at least 2 " +
                        "BlipNodes, please use BlipManager to specify the " +
                        "BlipNodeIds in the group.");
    System.out.println("Specify the group name as first input parameter:");
    System.out.println("> Tracking MyGroup");
    System.out.println("Thereby the BlipNodes (specified in the " +
                        "BlipManager) in the group 'MyGroup' will be used. " +
                        "These BlipNodes must be");
    System.out.println("configured as 'Inquiry Only' BlipNodes. Use at " +
                        "least two BlipNodes in the group.");
    System.out.println("When no Terminal Ids are specified all " +
                        "discoverable devices will be tracked.");
    System.out.println("-------------------");
    System.out.println("If only specific terminal is to be tracked, the " +
                        "Terminal Ids can be specified after the group " +
                        "name, e.g.:");
    System.out.println("> Tracking MyGroup 001122334455 000102030405");
    System.out.println("Thereby the same BlipNodes as above be used " +
                        "for tracking,");
    System.out.println("and only the terminals with Ids 001122334455 " +
                        "000102030405 will be tracked (terminal list can " +
                        "be continued).");
    System.out.println("-------------------");
    System.out.println("In BlipManager a username/password pair must be " +
                        "defined for the Tracking-application. Under " +
                        "'BlipServer Properties',");
    System.out.println("'Applications'; Create a new user with " +
                        "username/password: Tracking/Tracking.");
```

```
            System.exit(-1);
    }


    public static void main(String[] args) {
        // Must specify at least a BlipNode Group
        if (args.length<1) {
            usage();
        }

        BluetoothAddress[] trackTheseTerminals = parseTerminalList(args);

        System.out.println("** Starting Tracking application **");
        System.out.println("------------------");

        Tracking tracker = new Tracking(args[0], trackTheseTerminals);

        System.out.println("Tracking application started");

    }

}
```

NOTE *Please see the Tracker.java example in the "examples" directory of the BlipNet SDK for a more detailed code explanation of the Tracker example.*

Summary

This chapter gave you an introduction to the concept of enterprise Bluetooth applications. At this point, you should understand the scenarios where enterprise Bluetooth applications are best suited and the components that are needed to create them. As you have seen, enterprise Bluetooth applications cannot be built with just a single Bluetooth device and an API.

Using the Ericsson BlipNet, developers have the API, tools, and infrastructure in place in order to create scalable and robust enterprise Bluetooth applications. In the final chapter of this book, we'll examine how to network Bluetooth devices in a decentralized manner and create a Jini federations among Bluetooth devices.

CHAPTER 12

Bluetooth and Jini

WELL, YOU'VE MADE IT TO THE last chapter of the book. By now, you should be fully aware of the capabilities of Bluetooth technology with respect to Java. As we stated in Chapter 4, the basics of any Bluetooth application consist of

- Stack initialization

- Device management

- Device discovery

- Service discovery

- Service registration

- Communication

 CROSS-REFERENCE *See Chapter 4 for more details on the basics of a Bluetooth application.*

Now perhaps you've heard of Jini as well. If you haven't used it before, then you should be at least aware that it's a networking technology. Jini also happens to be a service-oriented technology like Bluetooth (i.e., after you join the network, you are able to consume or provide services).

So, if you want to know how to use Bluetooth and Jini together, then this is the chapter for you! Before we go any further, let's first clearly define the following:

- What is Jini?

- How does Jini work?

After we answer those two questions, we can look at what it'll take to combine Jini and Bluetooth together. We'll also look at a device that already integrates Bluetooth and Jini together: the PsiNaptic PsiNode.

What Is Jini Network Technology?

Jini network technology was created by Sun Microsystems to enable networked devices to communicate and share services with little or no human intervention. In part, this was in response to their (correct) perception that the rapidly increasing complexity of the network environment would cause current practices in network management to fail completely. Jini set out to solve the following problems with distributed computing:

- Networks are unreliable. Connections to other computers may disappear unexpectedly.

- The latency of a network is variable. Delays in sending and receiving information are dependent on factors such as the physical medium, traffic on the network, and information routing algorithms.

- Bandwidth is not constant. Like latency, there is often no guarantee of transmission capacity.

- Networks are insecure. This is especially true of heterogeneous networks where the devices exchanging information cannot control the path that the information takes.

- Network topologies are variable. This is most obvious in mobile networks when devices move between network access points. Now and in the near future, multimode devices will move between network types (e.g., from a cellular network to a wireless local area network to a wired desktop network).

- Administration of networks is not uniform. Multiple networks provide their own sets of rules, protocols, access, authorization, and security protocols, all controlled by different organizations and individuals. Accessing and securing resources across these networks will be complicated because of inconsistent administration practices.

- Access and transportation costs are variable.

- Many different devices with different configurations, capabilities, and operating systems will participate in the network.

Jini federations are agnostic to the type of connection between the devices participating in the network. It doesn't matter if the participants are connected physically or wirelessly; the only requirement is that the connections are TCP/IP based.

> **NOTE** *Jini also supports members in a federation with non–TCP/IP-based connections through surrogates.*

The functionality of members in a Jini federation can be summarized in six mechanisms:

- Lookup

- Discovery

- Join

- Leasing

- Transactions

- Events

Lookup

Lookup is a Jini service that acts much like a directory. For instance, if a printer wants to provide printer services to a Jini federation, then it must register that service with a Lookup Service. Conversely, if you are participating in a Jini federation, and you want to print, you must check the Lookup Service to see if any printer services are available.

NOTE   *As you can see, finding services in Jini has a central-ized approach by going through a Lookup Service. Bluetooth has a decentralized approach to finding services since you need to perform a search on each device in your piconet to find what services are available.*

Discovery

The process of finding a suitable Lookup Service in a Jini federation is referred to as *discovery*.

NOTE   *The concept of discovery in Jini is radically different compared to that in Bluetooth. In Jini, discovery is simply finding a Lookup Service. In Bluetooth, discovery allows you to find Bluetooth devices as well as the services that they offer.*

Join

Once a Lookup Service has been found, a service may join that Lookup Service by providing one or more Java objects. The *Join protocol* defines the mechanism to accomplish this.

Leasing

The use of a resource in a Jini federation is granted for a specific amount of time. This concept is known as a *lease*. The duration of the lease may be fixed by the grantor or negotiated. To maintain the use of a service (including services joined to Lookup Services), the lease must be renewed periodically. This allows for the expiration and cleanup of services that are no longer required, or whose owners have left the federation.

Transactions

A *transaction* allows a set of operations to be grouped in such a way that they either all succeed or all fail. To the members of the federation, the group of operations in the transaction appear to function as a single unit.

Events

An object residing on a device may register an interest in an *event* occurring in another object residing on a different device in the federation and receive notification when the event occurs. Thus, events provide a mechanism for maintaining consistency of state information in the federation.

How Jini Works

So, let's first define a Jini ServiceItem. A ServiceItem is comprised of a service object and some attributes. The only real restriction on ServiceItem objects is that they be serializable.

There are typically three entities involved in a Jini federation:

- *Service Providers* are the entities that provide a Java-based software service. The service can be pretty much anything and doesn't necessarily have anything to do with the device that hosts the provider. For instance, a Jini-enabled printer can provide a printer service in a Jini federation, but there's nothing stopping it from providing a random number generator service to the federation as well.

- *Service Consumers* are clearly the entities that have an interest in using the services that are available in the Jini federation.

- *Lookup Services (LUS)* are the Jini services that act on behalf of Service Providers to host their services. This is also the "directory" that Service Consumers use in order to find services in the federation.

Before the federation is formed, these entities must exist (see Figure 12-1).

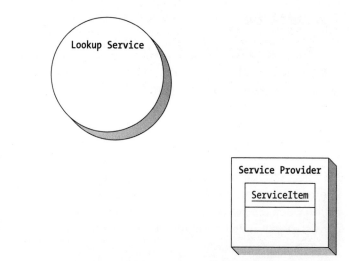

Figure 12-1. These three entities must exist before a Jini federation is established. The federation itself hasn't been formed because the entities don't know anything about each other yet.

Discovering a Lookup Service

In order to get the ball rolling, the clients (Service Providers or Service Consumers) must discover a Lookup Service.

 NOTE *A Jini federation can have more than one Lookup Service.*

Jini defines three discovery mechanisms:

- Multicast announcement from a Lookup Service

- Multicast request from a client

- Unicast request from a client

A Lookup Service can use multicast announcements periodically to advertise its presence on the network. Interested clients, Service Providers or Service Consumers in particular, can use the information provided in an announcement to communicate with the Lookup Service.

Clients use multicast requests to discover a Lookup Service. A Lookup Service receiving a request responds directly to that client. Once the address of a Lookup Service is known, a client sends a unicast request directly to the Lookup Service.

The Lifecycle of a Service Provider

Now, let's assume that a Lookup Service is making periodic multicast announcements. A Service Provider hears an announcement, and receives from the Lookup Service its `ServiceRegistrar`. A `ServiceRegistrar` is a Java object that is simply the public interface to the Lookup Service. It allows a client to register services, look up services, and request notification of changes in the Lookup Service. This interaction is shown in Figure 12-2.

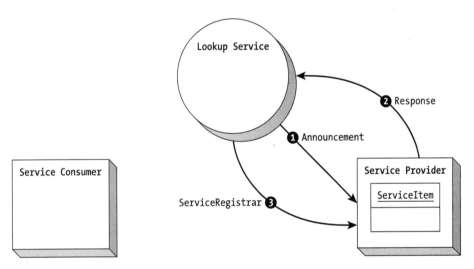

Figure 12-2. The Service Provider discovers the Lookup Service and receives its `ServiceRegistrar` *object. The* `ServiceRegistrar` *is used to interact with the Lookup Service via its public methods.*

In the final step of the discovery process, the Service Provider receives the `ServiceRegistrar` object, which it can use to register its `ServiceItem` with the Lookup Service.

Leasing a ServiceItem and Joining a Federation

When a Service Provider registers its `ServiceItem` as shown in Figure 12-3, it also specifies a lease duration for the service. If the registration is successful, the Lookup Service will keep the service registered for at least that length of the lease requested, or provide a duration of its own. It's up to the Service Provider to renew the lease as required. After the `ServiceItem` is registered with the Lookup Service, the Service Provider has joined the federation.

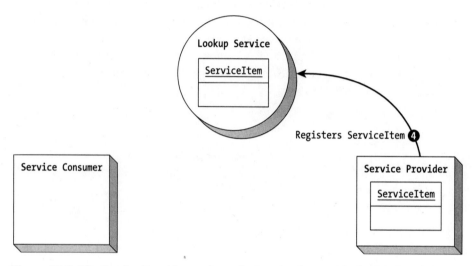

Figure 12-3. The Service Provider registers its `ServiceItem` *with the Lookup Service.*

> **NOTE** *The leasing mechanism is an important part of Jini technology because it allows devices to clean up unused resources. If a lease expires (or if it can't be renewed because the lease grantor or holder has left the federation), the associated resource can be released.*

Now that we have a federation with a Service Provider in it, it's time to look at things from the Service Consumer's perspective.

The Lifecycle of a Service Consumer

The Service Consumer also starts its life cycle by discovering a Lookup Service. It uses the same discovery mechanisms that a Service Provider uses. The Service Consumer can use any of the three discovery mechanisms, but in this scenario, let's say that the Service Consumer is using a multicast request to find a Lookup Service. This is illustrated in Figure 12-4.

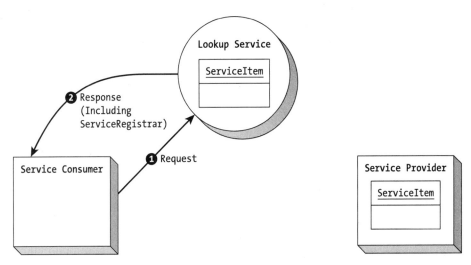

Figure 12-4. The Lookup Service receives a multicast request from the Service Consumer and responds with a unicast message containing the ServiceRegistrar object.

The Service Consumer device makes a number of periodic multicast requests. When a Lookup Service receives a request, it responds with a simple message that contains its ServiceRegistrar object. At this point the Service Consumer is part of the federation.

With the ServiceRegistrar in hand, the Service Consumer can use its lookup methods to look for useful services.

The lookup methods of the ServiceRegistrar object require a ServiceTemplate object as an argument. This template may contain nothing more than an array of class types. It's that simple! You get back either the service object itself, or a special object (ServiceMatches) containing all the services that matched your template. This process is illustrated in Figures 12-5 and 12-6.

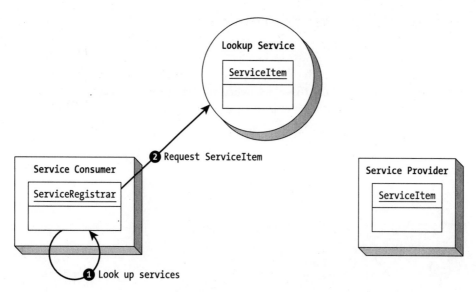

Figure 12-5. The Service Consumer uses the local ServiceRegistrar object to look up services that are registered in the Lookup Service.

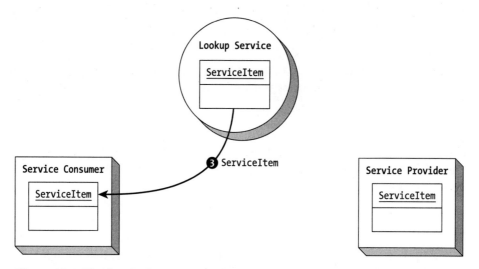

Figure 12-6. The ServiceItem requested is returned to the Service Consumer and can be used locally.

NOTE *Though not crucial to understanding how the Service Consumer gets a service, it's useful to know that a requested service is marshalled on the Lookup Service before being passed to the Service Consumer. Basically, the service object is flattened and serialized, and then served as a file to the Service Consumer. Once received, the Service Consumer's JVM unmarshalls the object into an instantiation of the service object.*

Once the Service Consumer has the desired ServiceItem, it can use the service locally. "Under the covers" the service may communicate back to the Service Provider as shown in Figure 12-7.

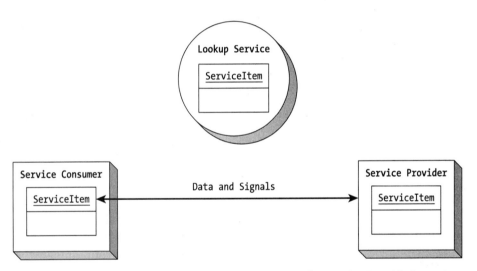

Figure 12-7. Once activated on the Service Consumer, the Service Provider's service may communicate directly with the Service Provider device as part of the service offered.

Integrating Jini and Bluetooth

Now that you have a clear understanding of the basics of a Jini federation, let's examine the possible scenarios of what's involved when integrating Jini and Bluetooth together.

All-Bluetooth Jini Federation

As the name implies, in an all-Bluetooth Jini federation, all the devices participating in the federation are Bluetooth enabled. For such a scenario to take place, the Bluetooth devices must discover each other and form a piconet. Since a requirement of a Jini federation is that the connections between the devices be TCP/IP based, the Bluetooth devices in an all-Bluetooth Jini federation would be connecting with either of the following TCP/IP-based Bluetooth profiles:

- Dial-Up Networking Profile

- LAN Access Profile

- Personal Area Networking Profile

 NOTE *Invariably, a manufacturer could make an all-Bluetooth Jini device without providing any of the preceding Bluetooth profiles in its product. For instance, the manufacturer can satisfy the TCP/IP requirement by simply implementing the BNEP protocol. The major drawback, however, is that those devices will be totally incompatible with devices from other manufacturers.*

After the piconet has been established and the IP addresses have been assigned, the Jini federation can be formed. At this point, this federation is just like any other Jini federation. If other Bluetooth devices want to join the federation, they must first join the piconet, obtain an IP, and then join the Jini federation. Since the IP network is running over Bluetooth, this federation is wireless. An example of an all-Bluetooth Jini federation is shown in Figure 12-8.

Figure 12-8. In an all-Bluetooth Jini federation, all the devices participating in the federation must be Bluetooth enabled. This federation is wireless.

Hybrid Bluetooth Jini Federation

In a hybrid Bluetooth Jini federation, one or more devices are Bluetooth enabled. Note however that all the devices are physically connected by traditional TCP/IP connections, and the federation is not wireless (unless the TCP/IP network is WLAN). There are no special precautions that need to be taken care of, so this federation is formed in the usual manner. Any of the devices in the federation can be Bluetooth enabled, but it makes sense that either the Service Provider or the Service Consumer have Bluetooth capability so it can act as a bridge between the Jini federation and an outside Bluetooth piconet elsewhere. A hybrid Bluetooth Jini federation is shown in Figure 12-9.

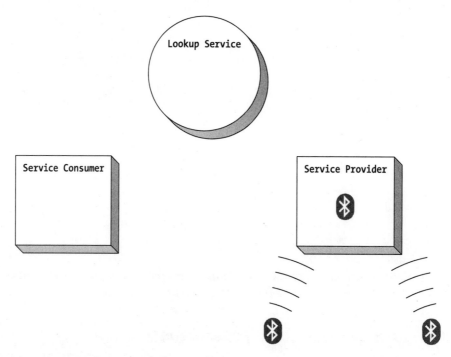

Figure 12-9. In a hybrid Bluetooth Jini federation, at least one of the devices participating in the federation must be Bluetooth enabled. This federation is not (necessarily) wireless, and the Jini–Bluetooth-enabled device acts as a bridge between the Jini federation and an external Bluetooth piconet.

A Jini-Bluetooth-Enabled Device: The PsiNaptic PsiNode

Dallas Semiconductor has a product line of sensors that can be connected to a two-wire bus (power and ground) called 1-Wire. They have a Java development platform and reference design called Tiny Internet Interface (TINI) that includes a 1-Wire interface. PsiNaptic Inc. has combined the TINI chipset with an Ericsson Bluetooth module in a reference design platform that they have named, PsiNode. The PsiNode platform is capable of acting as a Jini Lookup Service host and is a perfect solution for creating a low-cost, small-footprint, remote 1-Wire sensor/controller. A picture of the PsiNode is shown in Figure 12-10.

Figure 12-10. The PsiNode development platform. The Ericsson Bluetooth module is covered by two metal plates, and is connected to the Dallas Semiconductor TINI microcontroller.

NOTE *Any ordinary TINI device (i.e., a non–Bluetooth-enabled TINI) can function as a Jini Lookup Service in a Jini federation. PsiNaptic also makes software for this purpose (called JMatos), and you can get it from their Web site* (http://www.psinaptic.com).

The Benefits of Bluetooth and Jini

So what are the advantages of integrating Bluetooth and Jini into devices? In the case of mobile devices, an all-Bluetooth Jini federation allows devices to form "smarter" networks. A Jini federation allows Bluetooth devices to interoperate with more flexibility, without being constrained by the limits of Bluetooth profiles. More importantly, a Jini federation brings to the table the concepts of events, transactions, and leasing, which allows for more fault-tolerant and robust Bluetooth applications.

In a hybrid Bluetooth Jini federation, Bluetooth devices that are not capable of joining the federation and using its services can interact with the bridge device and consume the services of the federation. Conversely, the bridge device can provide wireless services to the Jini federation by interacting with an external Bluetooth piconet.

Summary

In this chapter, we gave you an overview of the principles and concepts of Jini network technology. We also presented an overview of the "hows" and "whys" for integrating Bluetooth and Jini together in order to create some really cool wireless applications. Both Jini and Bluetooth complement each other for creating networked applications. Jini brings to the table advanced networking capabilities such as leasing and distributed events, while Bluetooth allows the members of the network to be small, power efficient, and wireless.

Appendixes

javax.bluetooth

THIS APPENDIX CONTAINS ALL THE fields and method signatures of the classes, interfaces, and exceptions that comprise the javax.bluetooth package of the JSR-82 API.

Class BluetoothConnectionException

```
// fields
static int FAILED_NOINFO
static int NO_RESOURCES
static int SECURITY_BLOCK
static int TIMEOUT
static int UNACCEPTABLE_PARAMS
static int UNKNOWN_PSM

// constructors
BluetoothConnectionException(int error)
BluetoothConnectionException(int error, java.lang.String msg)

// methods
int getStatus()
```

Class BluetoothStateException

```
// constructors
BluetoothStateException()
BluetoothStateException(java.lang.String msg)
```

Class DataElement

```
// fields
static int BOOL
static int DATALT
static int DATSEQ
static int INT_1
static int INT_16
static int INT_2
static int INT_4
static int INT_8
static int NULL
static int STRING
static int U_INT_1
static int U_INT_16
static int U_INT_2
static int U_INT_4
static int U_INT_8
static int URL
static int UUID

// constructors
DataElement(boolean bool)
DataElement(int valueType)
DataElement(int valueType, long value)
DataElement(int valueType, java.lang.Object value)

// methods
void addElement(DataElement elem)
boolean getBoolean()
int getDataType()
long getLong()
int getSize()
java.lang.Object getValue()
void insertElementAt(DataElement elem, int index)
boolean removeElement(DataElement elem)
```

Class DeviceClass

```
// constructors
DeviceClass(int record)

// methods
int getMajorDeviceClass()
int getMinorDeviceClass()
int getServiceClasses()
```

Class DiscoveryAgent

```
// fields
static int CACHED
static int GIAC
static int LIAC
static int NOT_DISCOVERABLE
static int PREKNOWN

// methods
boolean cancelInquiry(DiscoveryListener listener)
boolean cancelServiceSearch(int transID)
RemoteDevice[] retrieveDevices(int option)
int searchServices(int[] attrSet, UUID[] uuidSet, RemoteDevice btDev,
                    DiscoveryListener discListener)
java.lang.String selectService(UUID uuid, int security, boolean master)
boolean startInquiry(int accessCode, DiscoveryListener listener)
```

Interface DiscoveryListener

```
// fields
static int INQUIRY_COMPLETED
static int INQUIRY_ERROR
static int INQUIRY_TERMINATED
static int SERVICE_SEARCH_COMPLETED
static int SERVICE_SEARCH_DEVICE_NOT_REACHABLE
static int SERVICE_SEARCH_ERROR
static int SERVICE_SEARCH_NO_RECORDS
static int SERVICE_SEARCH_TERMINATED
```

```
// methods
void deviceDiscovered(RemoteDevice btDevice, DeviceClass cod)
void inquiryCompleted(int discType)
void servicesDiscovered(int transID, ServiceRecord[] servRecord)
void serviceSearchCompleted(int transID, int respCode)
```

Interface L2CAPConnection

```
// fields
static int DEFAULT_MTU
static int MINIMUM_MTU

// methods
int getReceiveMTU()
int getTransmitMTU()
boolean ready()
int receive(byte[] inBuf)
void send(byte[] data)
```

Interface L2CAPConnectionNotifier

```
// method
L2CAPConnection acceptAndOpen()
```

Class LocalDevice

```
// methods
java.lang.String getBluetoothAddress()
DeviceClass getDeviceClass()
int getDiscoverable()
DiscoveryAgent getDiscoveryAgent()
java.lang.String getFriendlyName()
static LocalDevice getLocalDevice()
static java.lang.String getProperty(java.lang.String property)
ServiceRecord getRecord(javax.microedition.io.Connection notifier)
boolean setDiscoverable(int mode)
void updateRecord(ServiceRecord srvRecord)
```

Class RemoteDevice

```
// constructor
protected RemoteDevice(java.lang.String address)

// methods
boolean authenticate()
boolean authorize(javax.microedition.io.Connection conn)
boolean encrypt(javax.microedition.io.Connection conn, boolean on)
boolean equals(java.lang.Object obj)
java.lang.String getBluetoothAddress()
java.lang.String getFriendlyName(boolean alwaysAsk)
static RemoteDevice getRemoteDevice(javax.microedition.io.Connection conn)
int hashCode()
boolean isAuthenticated()
boolean isAuthorized(javax.microedition.io.Connection conn)
boolean isTrustedDevice()
```

Interface ServiceRecord

```
// fields
static int AUTHENTICATE_ENCRYPT
static int AUTHENTICATE_NOENCRYPT
static int NOAUTHENTICATE_NOENCRYPT

// methods
int[] getAttributeIDs()
DataElement getAttributeValue(int attrID)
java.lang.String getConnectionURL(int requiredSecurity, boolean mustBeMaster)
RemoteDevice getHostDevice()
boolean populateRecord(int[] attrIDs)
boolean setAttributeValue(int attrID, DataElement attrValue)
void setDeviceServiceClasses(int classes)
```

Class ServiceRegistrationException

```
// constructors
ServiceRegistrationException()
ServiceRegistrationException(java.lang.String msg)
```

Class UUID

```
// constructors
UUID(long uuidValue)
UUID(java.lang.String uuidValue, boolean shortUUID)

// methods
boolean equals(java.lang.Object value)
int hashCode()
java.lang.String toString()
```

javax.obex

THIS APPENDIX CONTAINS ALL THE fields and method signatures of the classes, interfaces, and exceptions that comprise the javax.obex package of the JSR-82 API.

Interface Authenticator

```
// methods
PasswordAuthentication onAuthenticationChallenge(java.lang.String description,
                    boolean isUserIdRequired, boolean isFullAccess)
byte[] onAuthenticationResponse(byte[] userName)
```

Interface ClientSession

```
// methods
HeaderSet connect(HeaderSet headers)
HeaderSet createHeaderSet()
HeaderSet delete(HeaderSet headers)
HeaderSet disconnect(HeaderSet headers)
Operation get(HeaderSet headers)
long getConnectionID()
Operation put(HeaderSet headers)
void setAuthenticator(Authenticator auth)
void setConnectionID(long id)
HeaderSet setPath(HeaderSet headers, boolean backup, boolean create)
```

Interface HeaderSet

```
// fields
static int APPLICATION_PARAMETER
static int COUNT
static int DESCRIPTION
static int HTTP
```

```
static int LENGTH
static int NAME
static int OBJECT_CLASS
static int TARGET
static int TIME_4_BYTE
static int TIME_ISO_8601
static int TYPE
static int WHO

// methods
void createAuthenticationChallenge(java.lang.String realm, boolean userID,
                                    boolean access)
java.lang.Object getHeader(int headerID)
int[] getHeaderList()
int getResponseCode()
void setHeader(int headerID, java.lang.Object headerValue)
```

Interface Operation

```
// methods
void abort()
HeaderSet getReceivedHeaders()
int getResponseCode()
int getResponseCode()
```

Class PasswordAuthentication

```
// constructor
PasswordAuthentication(byte[] userName, byte[] password)

// methods
byte[] getPassword()
byte[] getUserName()
```

Class ResponseCodes

```
// fields
static int OBEX_DATABASE_FULL
static int OBEX_DATABASE_LOCKED
static int OBEX_HTTP_ACCEPTED
static int OBEX_HTTP_BAD_GATEWAY
static int OBEX_HTTP_BAD_METHOD
static int OBEX_HTTP_BAD_REQUEST
static int OBEX_HTTP_CONFLICT
static int OBEX_HTTP_CREATED
static int OBEX_HTTP_ENTITY_TOO_LARGE
static int OBEX_HTTP_FORBIDDEN
static int OBEX_HTTP_GATEWAY_TIMEOUT
static int OBEX_HTTP_GONE
static int OBEX_HTTP_INTERNAL_ERROR
static int OBEX_HTTP_LENGTH_REQUIRED
static int OBEX_HTTP_MOVED_PERM
static int OBEX_HTTP_MOVED_TEMP
static int OBEX_HTTP_MULT_CHOICE
static int OBEX_HTTP_NO_CONTENT
static int OBEX_HTTP_NOT_ACCEPTABLE
static int OBEX_HTTP_NOT_AUTHORITATIVE
static int OBEX_HTTP_NOT_FOUND
static int OBEX_HTTP_NOT_IMPLEMENTED
static int OBEX_HTTP_NOT_MODIFIED
static int OBEX_HTTP_OK
static int OBEX_HTTP_PARTIAL
static int OBEX_HTTP_PAYMENT_REQUIRED
static int OBEX_HTTP_PRECON_FAILED
static int OBEX_HTTP_PROXY_AUTH
static int OBEX_HTTP_REQ_TOO_LARGE
static int OBEX_HTTP_RESET
static int OBEX_HTTP_SEE_OTHER
static int OBEX_HTTP_TIMEOUT
static int OBEX_HTTP_UNAUTHORIZED
static int OBEX_HTTP_UNAVAILABLE
static int OBEX_HTTP_UNSUPPORTED_TYPE
static int OBEX_HTTP_USE_PROXY
static int OBEX_HTTP_VERSION
```

Class ServerRequestHandler

```
// constructor
protected ServerRequestHandler()

// methods
HeaderSet createHeaderSet()
long getConnectionID()
void onAuthenticationFailure(byte[] userName)
int onConnect(HeaderSet request, HeaderSet reply)
int onDelete(HeaderSet request, HeaderSet reply)
void onDisconnect(HeaderSet request, HeaderSet reply)
int onGet(Operation op)
int onPut(Operation op)
int onSetPath(HeaderSet request, HeaderSet reply, boolean backup, boolean create)
void setConnectionID(long id)
```

Interface SessionNotifier

```
// methods
javax.microedition.io.Connection acceptAndOpen(ServerRequestHandler handler)
javax.microedition.io.Connection acceptAndOpen(ServerRequestHandler handler,
                                                Authenticator auth)
```

Java Bluetooth Development on the PalmOS Platform

THE PURPOSE OF THIS APPENDIX IS to demonstrate how to get started using the Impronto Developer Kit 1.0 for PalmOS (the Palm DK).

 NOTE *For more updated information, please consult the Palm DK user guides.*

Supported Bluetooth Protocols

The Palm DK supports the following Bluetooth protocols:

- RFCOMM

- L2CAP

- SDP

- OBEX

System Requirements

Here are the system requirements for the Palm DK:

- Pentium-based PC with at least 64MB of RAM

- Microsoft Windows 2000 service pack 1 (or higher)

- Minimum 35MB of free disk space

- JDK 1.3.1

- PalmOS device with PalmOS 4.0 (or higher)

- Palm Bluetooth SDIO card (or) Sony Bluetooth Memory Stick

Now, developing ordinary, stand-alone Java applications on the PalmOS can be a little cumbersome because you need to create your application, compile it, build a PRC, and deploy (i.e., HotSync) it on the PDA. It gets even more cumbersome if you develop wireless Java applications because you'll need to create two applications (client and server code) and deploy to two PDAs. Because of this, it is highly recommended that you also get the following:

- PalmOS emulator 3.5, with PalmOS 4.0 ROM (or higher) and Palm's Bluetooth stack

- TDK Bluetooth Palm Developers Kit (includes TDK Bluetooth hardware).

This configuration is shown in Figure C-1.

Figure C-1. With the TDK Bluetooth Developer's Kit and the PalmOS emulator, you can develop, deploy, and test your Java Bluetooth applications all within the environment of your development machine.

Included Software

The following items are included in the Impronto Developer Kit 1.0 for PalmOS:

- IBM WebSphere Micro Environment for PalmOS (the J9 KVM)

- Apache ANT build tool

- Java Bluetooth APIs

- Demo applications

Installation

Installation is pretty simple. In order to run the installer, just execute devkit.exe, and follow the on-screen instructions. The installation of the Impronto Developer Kit will also install WebSphere Micro Environment.

To complete your installation, install the necessary .prc files on your PDA. The Impronto Developer Kit files are

- idev_midp_j9.prc

- idev_racs.prc

- idev_utils.prc

- idev_wrap.prc

The J9 VM .prcs are named

- cdlc15.prc

- j9_vm_bundle.prc

- j9pref.prc

- midp15.prc

After you have completed your installation, verify that everything is correct by running the sample application: MIDP-Chat. A screenshot of this application is shown in Figure C-2.

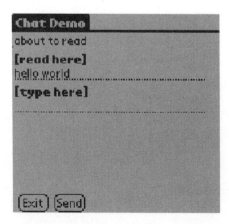

Figure C-2. The MIDP-Chat application

BlipNet 1.1 API

THIS APPENDIX, PRESENTED HERE with permission from Ericsson, contains descriptions of all the fields and method signatures of the classes, interfaces, and exceptions that comprise the BlipNet 1.1 API.[1]

 NOTE *For more information about BlipNet, see* http://www.ericsson.com/blipnet.

Class BlipNetIcons

```
public class BlipNetIcons extends java.lang.Object
```

```
//Package
com.ericsson.blipnet.api.util
```

```
//Fields
static int BLIPMANAGER_ICON
static int BLIPNODE_ALARM_ICON
static int BLIPNODE_ICON
static int BLIPNODE_LOCKED_ICON
static int BLIPNODE_NOT_WORKING_ICON
static int BLIPNODE_SWUPGRADE_ICON
static int BLIPSERVER_ICON
static int COMPUTER_DESKTOP_ICON
static int COMPUTER_LAPTOP_ICON
static int COMPUTER_PDA_ICON
static int COMPUTER_SERVER_ICON
static int LAN_ACCESS_AVAIL_ICON
static int PHONE_CELLULAR_ICON
static int PHONE_SMARTPHONE_ICON
static int SESSION_LAP_ICON
```

---

1. Copyright © L.M. Ericsson A/S, Bluetooth Networks

```
static int SESSION_OPP_ICON
static int UNKNOWN_DEVICE_ICON
```

```
//Methods
static getIcon(ClassOfDevice classOfDevice, boolean javax.swing.ImageIcon
largeIcon)
```

Returns an ImageIcon illustrating the specified Class of Device.

```
static javax.swing.ImageIcon  getIcon(int iconId, boolean largeIcon)
```

Returns a ImageIcon.

Interface BlipNode

```
public interface BlipNode extends java.io.Serializable
```

A BlipNode object contains information about a BlipNode.

```
//Package
com.ericsson.blipnet.api.blipserver
```

```
//Methods
java.lang.String getBlipNodeFriendlyName()
```

Returns the friendly name of the BlipNode.

```
java.lang.String getBlipNodeGroupConfigurationName()
```

Returns the Configuration group of the BlipNode.

```
java.lang.String getBlipNodeGroupName()
```

Returns the group name of the BlipNode.

```
BluetoothAddress getBlipNodeID()
```

Returns the Bluetooth device address of the BlipNode.

```
java.lang.String getBlipNodeIP()
```

Returns the IP address of the BlipNode.

```
java.lang.String getUser()
```

Returns the user of the BlipNode if it was reserved at the time this BlipNode object was created.

```
boolean isBlipNodeConnected()
```

Checks whether the BlipNode is connected to the server at the time this BlipNode object was created.

Interface BlipNodeCause

```
public interface BlipNodeCause
```

This interface defines the cause values returned in BlipNode events.

```
//package
com.ericsson.blipnet.api.blipnode
```

```
//Fields
static int CAUSE_BASEBAND_ERROR
```

Baseband error in BlipNode.

```
static int CAUSE_BLIPNODE_BLIPSERVER_PROTOCOL_ERROR
```

BlipNode-BlipServer protocol error.

```
static int CAUSE_DHCP_ERROR_LAP
```

DHCP error (LAN Profile).

```
static int CAUSE_HOST_STACK_ERROR
```

Host stack error.

```
static int CAUSE_HOST_TIMEOUT
```

Host timeout.

static int `CAUSE_INSUFFICIENT_TERMINAL_CAPABILITIES`

Insufficient terminal capabilities.

static int `CAUSE_INTERNAL_ERROR`

Signifies an internal error in the BlipNode which causes a reboot.

static int `CAUSE_LOSS_OF_SIGNAL`

Loss of signal.

static int `CAUSE_MAX_CONNECTIONS_REACHED`

Max connections reached.

static java.lang.String[] `CAUSE_NAMES`

Friendly names for the cause values.

static int `CAUSE_PAGE_TIMEOUT`

Page timeout.

static int `CAUSE_RELAY_AGENT_TO_DHCP_CLIENT_SWITCH`

Relay Agent/DHCP Client switch (rebooting).

static int `CAUSE_SESSION_NOT_CREATED`

Session not created.

static int `CAUSE_SYSTEM_ENDED_CONNECTION`

System ended connection.

static int `CAUSE_UNEXPECTED_TERMINAL_BEHAVIOR`

Unexpected terminal behavior.

static int `CAUSE_USER_ENDED_CONNECTION`

User ended connection.

Interface BlipNodeEvent

`public interface BlipNodeEvent extends Event`

An event which indicates that a BlipNode-related action occurred in the server.

```
//Package
com.ericsson.blipnet.api.event
```

```
//Methods
boolean equals(java.lang.Object obj)
```

Returns true if content of object is equal to this.

`java.lang.String getApplicationName()`

Returns the name of the user/application which has (un)locked the BlipNodeHandle for the BlipNode specified in this event.

`java.lang.String getBlipNodeFriendlyName()`

Returns the friendly name of the BlipNode which initiated this event.

`java.lang.String getBlipNodeIP()`

Returns the IP address of the BlipNode which initiated this event.

`java.lang.String getBlipNodeSoftwareVersion()`

Returns the software version of the BlipNode which initiated this event.

`int getCause()`

Returns the cause of the event.

Interface BlipNodeHandle

`public interface BlipNodeHandle`

A BlipNodeHandle provides an application access to a physical BlipNode. A BlipNodeHandle is obtained through a BlipServerConnection.

When an application has acquired a `BlipNodeHandle`, that application has exclusive access to the physical BlipNode until the handle is released by calling `release()`.

If the BlipNode disconnects from the server, the handle will be released by the server causing a `BlipNodeHandleReleasedException` to be thrown when an application tries to use the handle.

```
//Package
com.ericsson.blipnet.api.blipnode
```

```
//Methods
void addToBlipNodeDenyList(BluetoothAddress terminalID)
```

Adds the specified device ID to the local deny list on this BlipNode.

```
void addToInquiryFilter(BluetoothAddress terminalID, int timeout)
```

Adds the specified terminal to the inquiry filter in this BlipNode.

```
void changeInquiryLength(int inquiryLength)
```

Dynamically configures the length of time (in units of 1.28 s) in which the BlipNode performs inquiry before restarting inquiry or switching to Scan.

```
void changeLinkEstablishmentMode(boolean
automaticLinkEstablishmentOn, boolean nameLookupOn)
```

Dynamically switch the BlipNode in and out of automatic link establishment mode.

```
void changeScanLength(int scanLength)
```

Dynamically configures the length of time (in units of 1.28 s) in which terminals are able to detect the BlipNode during inquiry or paging.

```
void changeScanMode(ScanMode scanMode)
```

Dynamically changes the Scan mode on the BlipNode.

```
void clearBlipNodeDenyList()
```

Clears the local deny list on this BlipNode.

```
void disconnectLink(BluetoothAddress terminalID, int inquiryFilterTime)
```

Disconnects the specified terminal from this BlipNode if it is connected.

```
void establishLink(BluetoothAddress terminalID, ClassOfDevice terminalCOD)
```

Attempts to establish a link to the specified terminal.

```
void establishLink(PageData p)
```

Attempts to establish a link to the terminal specified in the paging data.

```
void exchangeBusinessCards(BluetoothAddress terminalID)
```

Initiates a business card exchange between the specified terminal and the BlipNode if the terminal is connected to the BlipNode.

```
Link[] getActiveLinks()
```

Returns a list of links that are currently active on the BlipNode.

```
BluetoothAddress[] getBlipNodeDenyList()
```

Retrieves a list of terminals in this BlipNode's deny list.

```
BluetoothAddress getBlipNodeID()
```

Returns the Bluetooth device address of the BlipNode connected to this handle.

```
void pullBusinessCard(BluetoothAddress terminalID)
```

Attempts to pull the business card from the specified terminal.

```
void push(ObexPushObject pushObject, BluetoothAddress terminalID)
```

Pushes the specified object to the specified terminal if it is connected to the BlipNode.

```
void push(ObexPushObject pushObject, BluetoothAddress terminalID,
ObexProgressListener listener)
```

Pushes the specified object to the specified terminal if it is connected to the BlipNode.

```
void pushBusinessCard(BluetoothAddress terminalID)
```

Pushes this BlipNode's business card to the specified terminal if the terminal is connected to the BlipNode.

```
void release()
```

Releases the BlipNodeHandle for use by other applications.

```
void removeFromBlipNodeDenyList(BluetoothAddress terminalID)
```

Removes the specified device from the local deny list on this BlipNode.

```
void removeSession(BluetoothAddress terminalID, Session  sessionType)
```

Removes the specified session from this BlipNode if the session exists.

```
void setBlipNodeDenyList(BluetoothAddress[] terminalIDs)
```

Sets the local deny list on this BlipNode to the specified list.

```
void setBusinessCard(java.lang.String businessCard)
```

Configures the business card of this BlipNode.

Class BlipNodeHandleInUseException

```
public final class BlipNodeHandleInUseException extends BlipServerException
```

Thrown by BlipServerConnection when an application attempts to get a handle for a BlipNode which is already used by another application.

```
//Package
com.ericsson.blipnet.api.blipnode

//Constructors
BlipNodeHandleInUseException()
BlipNodeHandleInUseException(java.lang.String s)
BlipNodeHandleInUseException(java.lang.String s,
java.lang.Throwable e)
```

Class **BlipNodeHandleReleasedException**

public final class BlipNodeHandleReleasedException extends
BlipServerException

Thrown by BlipNodeHandle when an application attempts to execute a method on
a released BlipNodeHandle.

    The handle may have been released either by the application itself or by the
server (due to a reboot of the BlipNode).

//Package
com.ericsson.blipnet.api.blipnode

//Constructors
BlipNodeHandleReleasedException()
BlipNodeHandleReleasedException(java.lang.String s)
BlipNodeHandleReleasedException(java.lang.String s,
java.lang.Throwable e)

Class **BlipNodeNotConnectedException**

public final class BlipNodeNotConnectedException extends
BlipServerException

Thrown by a BlipServerConnection when an application tries to get
a BlipNodeHandle for a BlipNode which is not connected to the server.

//Package
com.ericsson.blipnet.api.blipnode

//Constructors
BlipNodeNotConnectedException()
BlipNodeNotConnectedException(java.lang.String s)
BlipNodeNotConnectedException(java.lang.String s,
java.lang.Throwable e)

Class **BlipServer**

public final class BlipServer extends java.lang.Object

Factory class for getting BlipServerConnections.

```
//Package
com.ericsson.blipnet.api.blipserver

//Constructors
BlipServer()

//Methods
static getConnection(java.lang.String username, BlipServerConnection
java.lang.String password, java.lang.String serverHost)
```

Returns a BlipServerConnection to the specified server using default values for port number and service name.

```
static getConnection(java.lang.String username, BlipServerConnection
java.lang.String password, java.lang.String serverHost, int serverPort,
java.lang.String serverServiceName)
```

Returns a BlipServerConnection to the specified server.

Class BlipServerAccessException

```
public class BlipServerAccessException extends BlipServerException
```

Thrown by a BlipServerConnection when an application tries to access the server with invalid username or password. The reason for denying access can be wrong username/password or access from a host other than the host associated with this account.

```
//Package
com.ericsson.blipnet.api.blipserver

//Constructors
BlipServerAccessException(java.lang.String s)
BlipServerAccessException(java.lang.String s, java.lang.Throwable e)
```

Interface BlipServerConnection

```
public interface BlipServerConnection
```

A BlipServerConnection is used to attach BlipNode event listeners to the server, and to get handles for connected BlipNodes.

```
//Package
com.ericsson.blipnet.api.blipserver
```

```
//Methods
void addEventListener(BlipServerEventListener listener)
```

Adds the specified listener to the BlipServer.

```
void addEventListener(BlipServerEventListener listener,
BlipServerEventFilter filter)
```

Adds the specified listener to the BlipServer.

```
java.lang.String[] getBlipNodeConfigurationGroupNames()
```

Returns a list of the configuration names which are currently defined in the server.

```
java.lang.String[] getBlipNodeGroupNames()
```

Returns a list of BlipNode group names which are currently defined in the server.

```
BlipNodeHandle getBlipNodeHandle(BluetoothAddress blipNodeID)
```

Returns a handle to the BlipNode with the specified ID if it is connected to the server, or null if the BlipNode is not connected or the handle is already in use by another application.

```
BlipNodeHandle getBlipNodeHandleFromGroup(java.lang.String blipNodeGroupName)
```

Returns a handle to the first available BlipNode from the specified BlipNode group.

```
BlipNode[] getBlipNodes(java.lang.String groupName,java.lang.String
blipNodeGroupConfigurationName,boolean includeReservedBlipNodes,
boolean includeDisconnectedBlipNodes)
```

Returns a list of BlipNodes which match the specified criteria.

```
BluetoothAddress getConnectedBlipNode(BluetoothAddress terminalID)
```

Returns the Bluetooth device address of the BlipNode to which the specified terminal is connected.

```
BluetoothAddress[] getConnectedTerminals()
```

Returns a list of terminals currently connected to the server.

byte[] getObexObject(java.io.File file)

Returns the contents of the specified file if the file is found on the server.

void releaseBlipNodeHandle(BluetoothAddress blipNodeID)

Releases the handle to the specified BlipNode if the handle was reserved by this user.

void removeEventListener(BlipServerEventListener listener)

Removes the specified listener from the server.

Class BlipServerConnectionException

public final class BlipServerConnectionException extends BlipServerException

Thrown by a BlipServerConnection if the connection to the server is lost.

//Package
com.ericsson.blipnet.api.blipserver

//Constructors
BlipServerConnectionException(java.lang.String s, java.lang.Throwable e)

Class BlipServerEventAdapter

public abstract class BlipServerEventAdapter extends java.lang.Object implements BlipServerEventListener

An abstract adapter class for receiving events from the BlipServer. The methods in this class are empty. The class exists as convenience for creating listener objects which only listens to a certain class of events.

// package
com.ericsson.blipnet.api.event

```
//Constructors
BlipServerEventAdapter()

//Methods
void handleBlipNodeEvent(BlipNodeEvent e)
```

Called by the BlipServer event dispatcher when a `BlipNodeEvent` occurs.

```
void handleConnectionEvent(ConnectionEvent e)
```

Called by the BlipServer event dispatcher when a `ConnectionEvent` occurs.

```
void handleObexEvent(ObexEvent e)
```

Called by the BlipServer event dispatcher when an `ObexEvent` occurs.

Class BlipServerEventFilter

```
public final class BlipServerEventFilter extends java.lang.Object
implements java.io.Serializable
```

This class is used to filter notification of events for client applications which implement `BlipServerEventListener`.

```
//Package
com.ericsson.blipnet.api.event

//Constructors
BlipServerEventFilter(int[] eventClasses, int[] eventIDs,
BluetoothAddress[] blipNodeIDs, BluetoothAddress[] terminalIDs)
```

Constructs a `BlipServerEventFilter`.

```
//Methods
boolean contains(Event event)
```

Checks whether the listener attached to this filter should be notified of the specified event.

```
boolean containsBlipNodeID(BluetoothAddress blipNodeID)
```

Checks whether the specified BlipNode ID is included in this filter.

```
boolean containsEventClass(int eventClass)
boolean containsEventID(int eventID)
boolean containsTerminalID(BluetoothAddress terminalID)
```

Checks whether the specified terminal ID is included in this filter.

```
BluetoothAddress[] getBlipNodeIDs()
```

Returns a copy of the blipNodeIDs of the BlipServerEventFilter.

```
int[] getEventClasses()
```

Returns a copy of the eventClasses of the BlipServerEventFilter.

```
int[] getEventIDs()
```

Returns a copy of the eventTypes of the BlipServerEventFilter.

```
BluetoothAddress[] getTerminalIDs()
```

Returns a copy of the terminalIDs of the BlipServerEventFilter.

Interface BlipServerEventListener

```
public interface BlipServerEventListener
```

This interface should be implemented by client classes wishing to listen to events generated by the BlipServer.

```
//Package
com.ericsson.blipnet.api.event
```

```
//Methods
void handleBlipNodeEvent(BlipNodeEvent e)
```

Called by the BlipServer event dispatcher when a BlipNodeEvent occurs.

```
void handleConnectionEvent(ConnectionEvent e)
```

Called by the BlipServer event dispatcher when a ConnectionEvent occurs.

```
void handleObexEvent(ObexEvent e)
```

Called by the BlipServer event dispatcher when an ObexEvent occurs.

Class BlipServerException

```
public class BlipServerException extends java.lang.Exception
```

Superclass for all exceptions which can be thrown by the BlipServer.

```
//Package
com.ericsson.blipnet.api.blipserver
```

```
//Constructors
BlipServerException()
BlipServerException(java.lang.String s)
BlipServerException(java.lang.String s, java.lang.Throwable e)
```

Class BluetoothAddress

```
public final class BluetoothAddress extends java.lang.Object implements
java.io.Serializable
```

The BluetoothAddress class models a Bluetooth Device Address (BD_ADDR). This is a 48 bit unsigned integer, often written in hexadecimal.

Objects of the BluetoothAddress class are immutable—once created they cannot change.

This class provides the equals and hashCode methods for use in connection with the Collection classes.

```
//Package
com.ericsson.blipnet.api.Bluetooth
```

```
//Constructors
BluetoothAddress(byte[] bluetoothAddress)
```

Constructs a BluetoothAddress object from a byte[].

```
BluetoothAddress(java.lang.String bluetoothAddress)
```

Constructs a BluetoothAddress object from a String.

```
//Methods
boolean equals(java.lang.Object obj)
```

Compares this BluetoothAddress with an Object and returns true if they are equal.

```
byte[] getBytes()
int hashCode()
```

Returns a hashCode for this BluetoothAddress.

```
java.lang.String toString()
```

Returns a String representation of this BluetoothAddress.

Class ClassOfDevice

```
public final class ClassOfDevice extends java.lang.Object implements
java.io.Serializable
```

The ClassOfDevice class models a class of device. This is a 24 bit unsigned integer, often written in hexadecimal.

Objects of the ClassOfDevice class are immutable—once created they cannot change.

This class provides the equals and hashCode methods for use in connection with the Collection classes.

```
//Package
com.ericsson.blipnet.api.Bluetooth
```

```
//Fields
static java.lang.String AV
static java.lang.String AV_CAMCORDER
static java.lang.String AV_CAR_AUDIO
static java.lang.String AV_GAMING_TOY
static java.lang.String AV_HANDS_FREE
static java.lang.String AV_HEADPHONES
static java.lang.String AV_HEADSET
```

```
static java.lang.String AV_HIFI
static java.lang.String AV_LOUDSPEAKER
static java.lang.String AV_MICROPHONE
static java.lang.String AV_PORTABLE_AUDIO
static java.lang.String AV_SET_TOP_BOX
static java.lang.String AV_SHORT
static java.lang.String AV_VCR
static java.lang.String AV_VIDEO_CAMERA
static java.lang.String AV_VIDEO_CONF
static java.lang.String AV_VIDEO_DISPLAY
static java.lang.String AV_VIDEO_MONITOR
static java.lang.String BLIPNODE_CLASS_OF_DEVICE
static java.lang.String COMPUTER
static java.lang.String COMPUTER_DESKTOP
static java.lang.String COMPUTER_HANDHELD
static java.lang.String COMPUTER_LAPTOP
static java.lang.String COMPUTER_PALM_SIZED
static java.lang.String COMPUTER_SERVER_CLASS
static java.lang.String COMPUTER_SHORT
static java.lang.String COMPUTER_WEARABLE
static java.lang.String IMAGING
static java.lang.String IMAGING_CAMERA
static java.lang.String IMAGING_DISPLAY
static java.lang.String IMAGING_PRINTER
static java.lang.String IMAGING_SCANNER
static java.lang.String IMAGING_SHORT
static java.lang.String LAN_ACCESS_POINT
static java.lang.String LAN_ACCESS_POINT_FIFTH
static java.lang.String LAN_ACCESS_POINT_FIRST
static java.lang.String LAN_ACCESS_POINT_FOURTH
static java.lang.String LAN_ACCESS_POINT_FULLY
static java.lang.String LAN_ACCESS_POINT_NO_SERVICE
static java.lang.String LAN_ACCESS_POINT_SECOND
static java.lang.String LAN_ACCESS_POINT_SHORT
static java.lang.String LAN_ACCESS_POINT_SIXTH
static java.lang.String LAN_ACCESS_POINT_THIRD
static java.lang.String PERIPHERAL
static java.lang.String PERIPHERAL_COMBO
static java.lang.String PERIPHERAL_DIGITIZER
static java.lang.String PERIPHERAL_GAMEPAD
static java.lang.String PERIPHERAL_JOYSTICK
static java.lang.String PERIPHERAL_KEYBOARD
static java.lang.String PERIPHERAL_POINTING_DEV
```

```
static java.lang.String PERIPHERAL_REMOTE
static java.lang.String PERIPHERAL_SENSING_DEV
static java.lang.String PERIPHERAL_SHORT
static java.lang.String PHONE
static java.lang.String PHONE_CELLULAR
static java.lang.String PHONE_CORDLESS
static java.lang.String PHONE_ISDN
static java.lang.String PHONE_SHORT
static java.lang.String PHONE_SIMCARD
static java.lang.String PHONE_SMART_PHONE
static java.lang.String PHONE_WIRED
static java.lang.String UNKNOWN
static java.lang.String UNKNOWN_SHORT
```

```
//Constructors
ClassOfDevice(boolean limitedDisc, boolean positioning, boolean networking,
boolean rendering, boolean capturing, boolean objectTransfer, boolean audio,
boolean telephony, boolean information, java.lang.String majorClass,
java.lang.String minorClass)
```

Constructs a `ClassOfDevice` object.

```
ClassOfDevice(byte[] classOfDevice)
```

Constructs a `ClassOfDevice` object from a byte[].

```
ClassOfDevice(java.lang.String classOfDevice)
```

Constructs a `ClassOfDevice` object from a string.

```
//Methods
boolean equals(java.lang.Object obj)
```

Compares this `ClassOfDevice` with an `Object` and returns true if they are equal.

```
byte[] getBytes()
```

Returns the byte representation of this `ClassOfDevice` object.

```
int getIconId()
```

Returns the Icon Id for the Class of Device.

`java.lang.String getMajorTypeText()`

Returns the Class of Device Major type as a Long text description.

`java.lang.String getMajorTypeText(boolean longText)`

Returns the Class of Device Major type as a text description.

`java.lang.String getMinorTypeText()`

Returns the Class of Device Minor type as a text description.

`int hashCode()`

Returns a hashCode for this Class Of Device.

`boolean isAudioSet()`

Examines the Audio bit of the Class Of Device.

`boolean isCapturingSet()`

Examines the Capturing bit of the Class Of Device.

`boolean isInformationSet()`

Examines the Information bit of the Class Of Device.

`boolean isLimitedDiscoverableSet()`

Examines the Limited Discoverable bit of the Class Of Device.

`boolean isNetworkingSet()`

Examines the Networking bit of the Class Of Device.

`boolean isObjectTransferSet()`

Examines the Object Transfer bit of the Class Of Device.

`boolean isPositioningSet()`

Examines the Positioning bit of the Class Of Device.

```
boolean isRenderingSet()
```

Examines the Rendering bit of the Class Of Device.

```
boolean isTelephonySet()
```

Examines the Telephony bit of the Class Of Device.

```
java.lang.String toString()
```

Returns a String representation of this Class Of Device.

Interface ConnectionEvent

```
public interface ConnectionEvent extends Event
```

An event indicating that a connection-related action has occurred in the server.

```
//Package
com.ericsson.blipnet.api.event
```

```
//Methods
boolean equals(java.lang.Object obj)
```

Returns true if content of object is equal to this.

```
int getCause()
```

Returns the cause of this event.

```
int getSessionType()
```

Returns the type of session that this event is related to.

```
ShortUuid[] getShortUUIDs()
```

Returns an array of short UUIDs representing the services supported by the terminal to which this event is related.

```
java.lang.String getTerminalClassOfDevice()
```

Returns the class of device of the terminal to which this event is related.

```
java.lang.String getTerminalFriendlyName()
```

Returns the friendly name of the terminal to which this event is related.

```
BluetoothAddress getTerminalID()
```

Returns the Bluetooth device address of the terminal to which this event is related.

```
java.lang.String getTerminalIP()
```

Returns the IP address of the terminal to which this event is related.

Class EricssonMelody

```
public final class EricssonMelody extends java.lang.Object implements
ObexPushObject
```

An ObexPushObject implementation of an Ericsson Melody. This class wraps the given melody string in a format understandable by an Ericsson Mobile Phone.

```
//Package
com.ericsson.blipnet.api.obex.pushobjects
```

```
//Constructors
EricssonMelody(java.lang.String melody)
```

Constructs an Ericsson Melody push object with a default name (NONAME.EMY).

```
EricssonMelody(java.lang.String melody, java.lang.String name)
```

Constructs an Ericsson Melody push object with the name specified.

```
//Methods
byte[] getObexBody()
```

Returns the body of this ObexPushObject.

```
java.lang.String getObexName()
```

Returns the name of this ObexPushObject.

```
java.lang.String getObexType()
```

Returns the mime-type of this `ObexPushObject`.

Interface Event

```
public interface Event extends java.io.Serializable
```

The superclass of all events. This interface defines common event methods and contains event ID definitions for all events.

```
//Package
com.ericsson.blipnet.api.event
```

```
//Fields
static int BLIPNODE_ALARM
```

Indicates that a critical condition has occurred in a BlipNode connected to the server.

```
static int BLIPNODE_DEREGISTERED
```

Indicates that a BlipNode has disconnected from the server.

```
static int BLIPNODE_EVENT
```

Event class of BlipNode-related events.

```
static int BLIPNODE_LOCKED
```

Indicates that an application has acquired the lock on a BlipNode.

```
static int BLIPNODE_REGISTERED
```

Indicates that a BlipNode has connected to the server.

```
static int BLIPNODE_RELEASED
```

Indicates that an application has released its lock on a BlipNode.

```
static int BLIPNODE_STARTUP_FAILED
```

Indicates that a BlipNode attempted to connect to the server, but the startup failed for some reason.

```
static int BLIPNODE_SW_UPGRADE_COMPLETE
```

Indicates that a BlipNode software upgrade has been completed successfully.

```
static int BLIPNODE_SW_UPGRADE_FAILED
```

Indicates that a BlipNode software update failed.

```
static int BLIPNODE_SW_UPGRADE_STARTED
```

Indicates that a BlipNode software upgrade has been initiated.

```
static int BLIPNODE_WAITING_FOR_CONFIGURATION
```

Indicates that a BlipNode has registered with the server, but no configuration exists for that BlipNode.

```
static java.lang.String[] CLASS_NAMES
static int CONNECTION_EVENT
```

Event class of Connection-related events.

```
static java.lang.String[] FRIENDLY_NAMES
static int OBEX_BUSINESS_CARD_EXCHANGE_COMPLETED
```

Indicates successful completion of a business card exchange.

```
static int OBEX_BUSINESS_CARD_EXCHANGE_FAILED
```

Indicates a failed attempt to exchange business cards with a terminal.

```
static int OBEX_BUSINESS_CARD_PULL_COMPLETED
```

Indicates successful completion of a business card pull.

`static int OBEX_BUSINESS_CARD_PULL_FAILED`

Indicates a failed attempt to pull business card from a terminal.

`static int OBEX_EVENT`

Event class of OBEX-related events.

`static int OBEX_OBJECT_RECEIVED`

Indicates that an OBEX object has been received and stored by the server.

`static int OBEX_PUSH_COMPLETED`

Indicates successful completion of an OBEX push.

`static int OBEX_PUSH_FAILED`

Indicates a failed attempt to push an OBEX object to a terminal.

`static int OBEX_PUSH_PROGRESS`

Indicates progress in an ongoing OBEX push.

`static int TERMINAL_DETECTED`

Indicates that a terminal was detected in inquiry.

`static int TERMINAL_LINK_ESTABLISH_FAILED`

Indicates a failed attempt to establish a Bluetooth link to a terminal.

`static int TERMINAL_LINK_ESTABLISHED`

Indicates that a Bluetooth link to a terminal has been established.

`static int TERMINAL_LINK_LOST`

Indicates that a Bluetooth link to a terminal has been disconnected.

`static int TERMINAL_SESSION_CREATE_FAILED`

Indicates a failed attempt to create a session with a terminal.

```
static int TERMINAL_SESSION_CREATED
```

Indicates that a session has been created with a terminal.

```
static int TERMINAL_SESSION_REMOVED
```

Indicates that a session with a terminal has been removed.

```
//Methods
boolean equals(java.lang.Object obj)
```

Returns true if content of object is equal to this.

```
BluetoothAddress getBlipNodeID()
```

Returns the Bluetooth device address of the BlipNode to which this event is related.

```
int getEventClass()
```

Returns the event class of this event.

```
int getEventID()
```

Returns the ID of this event.

```
java.lang.String getMessage()
```

Returns the message associated with this event if any.

```
int hashCode()
java.lang.String toString()
```

Returns a String representation of this event.

Interface InquiryResultEvent

```
public interface InquiryResultEvent extends ConnectionEvent
```

An event indicating that a terminal has been detected by a BlipNode in Inquiry Only Mode.

```
//Package
com.ericsson.blipnet.api.event
```

```
//Methods
PageData getPageData()
```

Returns the Paging data needed for direct paging of this terminal.

Interface Link

```
public interface Link extends java.io.Serializable
```

The Link interface provides methods to retrieve snapshot information about a specific BlipNode-Terminal link.

```
//Package
com.ericsson.blipnet.api.Bluetooth
```

```
//Methods
boolean equals(java.lang.Object obj)
```

Compares this LinkImpl with an Object and returns true if they are equal.

```
BluetoothAddress getBlipNode()
```

Returns the BluetoothAddress of the BlipNode using this session.

```
int[] getCurrentSessions()
```

Returns an array of active sessions on this link.

```
BluetoothAddress getTerminal()
```

Returns the BluetoothAddress of the terminal using this session.

```
boolean isSessionActive(long sessionType)
```

Tells whether the indicated session type is active.

```
java.lang.String toString()
```

Implements the toString method.

Class NoSuchSessionException

`public class NoSuchSessionException extends java.lang.RuntimeException`

Thrown by a `BlipNodeHandle` to indicate that an attempt was made to close a non-existing session.

```
//Package
com.ericsson.blipnet.api.blipnode
```

```
//Constructors
NoSuchSessionException()
NoSuchSessionException(java.lang.String message)
NoSuchSessionException(java.lang.String message,
java.lang.Throwable cause)
NoSuchSessionException(java.lang.Throwable cause)
```

Interface ObexEvent

`public interface ObexEvent extends Event`

An event indicating that an OBEX-related action has occurred in the BlipServer.

```
//Package
com.ericsson.blipnet.api.event
```

```
//Methods
boolean equals(java.lang.Object obj)
```

Returns true if content of object is equal to this.

`java.lang.String getMimeType()`

Returns the mime-type of the OBEX object to which this event is related.

`int getObexResponseCode()`

Returns the OBEX Response Code associated with this event (if any).

`java.io.File getPath()`

Returns the path of the file to which this event is related.

```
BluetoothAddress getTerminalID()
```

Returns the Bluetooth device address of the terminal to which this event is related.

Class ObexFile

```
public final class ObexFile extends java.lang.Object implements
ObexPushObject
```

Implements an OBEX push object containing a file.

```
//Package
com.ericsson.blipnet.api.obex.pushobjects
```

```
//Constructors
ObexFile(java.io.File file)
```

Constructs an OBEX push object representing the specified file.

```
ObexFile(java.io.File file, byte[] b)
```

Constructs an OBEX push object containing the bytes of the specified byte[] and with the specified filename.

```
//Methods
java.lang.String getAbsoluteFileName()
byte[] getObexBody()
```

Returns the body of this ObexPushObject.

```
java.lang.String getObexName()
```

Returns the name of this ObexPushObject.

```
java.lang.String getObexType()
```

Returns the mime-type of this ObexPushObject.

```
void setObexType(java.lang.String mimeType)
```

Class ObexGenericObject

public class ObexGenericObject extends java.lang.Object implements
ObexPushObject

Implements a generic OBEX push object.

//Package
com.ericsson.blipnet.api.obex.pushobjects

//Constructors
ObexGenericObject(byte[] bytes)

Constructs an OBEX push object representing the specified file.

ObexGenericObject(byte[] bytes, java.lang.String obexType)

Constructs an OBEX push object containing the bytes of the specified byte[] and
with the specified filename.

ObexGenericObject(java.lang.String obexName, byte[] bytes)

Constructs an OBEX push object containing the bytes of the specified byte[] and
with the specified filename.

ObexGenericObject(java.lang.String obexName, byte[] bytes,
java.lang.String obexType)

Constructs an OBEX push object containing the bytes of the specified byte[] and
with the specified filename.

//Methods
byte[] getObexBody()

Returns the body of this ObexPushObject.

java.lang.String getObexName()

Returns the name of this ObexPushObject.

java.lang.String getObexType()

Returns the mime-type of this `ObexPushObject`.

```
void setObexType(java.lang.String mimeType)
```

Interface ObexProgressEvent

```
public interface ObexProgressEvent extends Event
```

An event indicating progress of an ongoing OBEX push. This type of event is only sent to `ObexProgressListeners`.

```
//Package
com.ericsson.blipnet.api.event
```

```
//Methods
boolean equals(java.lang.Object obj)
```

Returns true if content of object is equal to this.

```
int getBytesCompleted()
```

Returns the number of bytes received so far.

```
java.lang.String getObexName()
```

Returns the name of the OBEX object to which this event is related.

```
int getObjectSize()
```

Returns the total size of the object to which this event is related.

```
BluetoothAddress getTerminalID()
```

Returns the Bluetooth device address of the terminal to which this event is related.

```
int hashCode()
```

Interface ObexProgressListener

```
public interface ObexProgressListener
```

This abstract class should be extended to create an event listener for listening to ObexProgressEvents while pushing content to a terminal.

```
//Package
com.ericsson.blipnet.api.event
```

```
//Methods
void newProgress(ObexProgressEvent e)
```

This method is called by the BlipServer whenever new push progress information is available.

Interface ObexPushObject

```
public interface ObexPushObject extends java.io.Serializable
```

The ObexPushObject class defines a common interface for OBEX objects which are going to be pushed to a terminal.

```
//Package
com.ericsson.blipnet.api.obex.pushobjects
```

```
//Methods
byte[] getObexBody()
```

Returns the body of this ObexPushObject.

```
java.lang.String getObexName()
```

Returns the name of this ObexPushObject.

```
java.lang.String getObexType()
```

Returns the mime-type of this ObexPushObject.

Class ObexServerHostedFile

```
public final class ObexServerHostedFile extends java.lang.Object
implements ObexPushObject
```

An `ObexServerHostedFile` is an OBEX push object which will be read from the server's local storage when the object is pushed to a terminal. The advantage of a server hosted file compared to a regular `ObexFile` is that the contents of the file are not transferred across the network when pushing the file. This may be desirable when pushing very large objects.

```
//Package
com.ericsson.blipnet.api.obex.pushobjects
```

```
//Constructors
ObexServerHostedFile(java.io.File file)
ObexServerHostedFile(java.io.File file, java.lang.String obexType)
```

```
//Methods
boolean fileExists()
java.io.File getFileDescriptor()
byte[] getObexBody()
```

Returns the body of this `ObexPushObject`.

```
java.lang.String getObexName()
```

Returns the name of this `ObexPushObject`.

```
java.lang.String getObexType()
```

Returns the mime-type of this `ObexPushObject`.

Interface PageData

```
public interface PageData extends java.io.Serializable
```

A `PageData` object contains all data needed to do a link establishment after an inquiry. Using the data in this object, link establishment time will be shortened. Used when BlipNode is in INQUIRY RESULT mode and the application does the link establishment via the BlipServer API.

//Package
com.ericsson.blipnet.api.bluetooth

Interface RemoteBlipServerEventListener

public interface RemoteBlipServerEventListener extends java.rmi.Remote

Defines the handle Event method for notifying event listeners of BlipServer events. The interface is used internally by the BlipServer API, and *should never* be implemented by client applications.

//Package
com.ericsson.blipnet.api.event

//Methods
void handleEvent(Event event)

Interface RemoteObexProgressListener

public interface RemoteObexProgressListener extends java.rmi.Remote

Defines the newProgress method for notifying event listeners of Push progress events. The interface is used internally by the BlipServer API, and *should never* be implemented by client applications.

//Package
com.ericsson.blipnet.api.event

//Methods
void newProgress(ObexProgressEvent e)

Class ScanMode

public final class ScanMode extends java.lang.Object implements java.io.Serializable

The ScanMode class encapsulates the different Scan Modes supported by the BlipNode.

```
//Package
com.ericsson.blipnet.api.Bluetooth
```

```
//Fields
static java.lang.String[] FRIENDLY_NAMES
```

Friendly names of the defined Scan Modes.

```
static int INQUIRY_AND_PAGE_SCAN_DISABLED
```

Inquiry Scan: Disabled, Page Scan: Disabled.

```
static int INQUIRY_AND_PAGE_SCAN_ENABLED
```

Inquiry Scan: Enabled, Page Scan: Enabled.

```
static int INQUIRY_SCAN_ENABLED
```

Inquiry Scan: Enabled, Page Scan: Disabled.

```
static int PAGE_SCAN_ENABLED
```

Inquiry Scan: Disabled, Page Scan: Enabled.

```
//Constructors
ScanMode(int value)
```

Constructs a ScanMode object representing a valid Scan Mode.

```
//Methods
boolean equals(java.lang.Object obj)
int getScanMode()
```

Returns the scan mode represented by this object.

```
int hashCode()
java.lang.String toString()
```

Class Session

```
public final class Session extends java.lang.Object implements
java.io.Serializable
```

The Session class encapsulates the session types supported by the BlipServer.

```
//Package
com.ericsson.blipnet.api.Bluetooth
```

```
//Fields
static java.lang.String[] FRIENDLY_NAMES
```

Friendly names of the defined session types.

```
static long LAP_CLIENT
```

LAN Access Profile (LAP) Client session type.

```
static long LAP_SERVER
```

LAN Access Profile (LAP) Server session type.

```
static long OPP_CLIENT
```

Object Push Profile (OPP) Client session type.

```
static long OPP_SERVER
```

Object Push Profile (OPP) Server session type.

```
//Constructors
Session(long sessionType)
```

Constructs a Session object representing the specified session type.

```
//Methods
boolean equals(java.lang.Object obj)
long getSessionType()
```

Returns the type of this Session object.

```
int hashCode()
java.lang.String toString()
```

Class ShortUuid

```
public final class ShortUuid extends java.lang.Object implements
java.io.Serializable
```

The ShortUuid class models a Bluetooth universal unique identifier. This is a 16 bit unsigned integer, often written in hexadecimal.

Objects of the ShortUuid class are immutable—once created they cannot change.

This class provides the equals and hashCode methods for use in connection with the Collection classes.

```
//Package
com.ericsson.blipnet.api.bluetooth
```

```
//Fields
static int DIALUP_NETWORKING_SERVICE_CLASS_ID
```

Short UUID for the Dialup Networking Profile.

```
static int LAN_ACCESS_USING_PPP_SERVICE_CLASS_ID
```

Short UUID for the LAN Access Using PPP Profile.

```
static int OBEX_OBJECT_PUSH_SERVICE_CLASS_ID
```

Short UUID for the OPP Profile.

```
static int SERIAL_PORT_SERVICE_CLASS_ID
```

Short UUID for the Serial Port Profile.

```
static int SERVICE_DISCOVERY_SERVER_SERVICE_CLASS_ID
```

Short UUID for the Service Discovery Server Profile.

```
static int WAP_OVER_BLUETOOTH_CLIENT_SERVICE_CLASS_ID
```

Short UUID for the WAP over Bluetooth Client.

```
static int WAP_OVER_BLUETOOTH_SERVER_SERVICE_CLASS_ID
```

Short UUID for the WAP over Bluetooth Server.

```
//Constructors
ShortUuid(byte[] shortUuid)
```

Constructs a ShortUuid object from a byte[].

```
ShortUuid(int shortUuid)
```

Constructs a ShortUuid object from an int.

```
ShortUuid(java.lang.String shortUuid)
```

Constructs a ShortUuid object from a String.

```
//Methods
boolean equals(java.lang.Object obj)
```

Compares this ShortUuid with an Object and returns true if they are equal.

```
byte[] getBytes()
```

Returns the byte representation of this ShortUuid object.

```
int getInt()
int hashCode()
```

Returns a hashCode for this ShortUuid.

```
java.lang.String toString()
```

Returns a String representation of this ShortUuid.

```
java.lang.String toString4MalSignal()
```

Class TerminalNotConnectedException

```
public class TerminalNotConnectedException extends
java.lang.RuntimeException
```

Thrown by a BlipNodeHandle when a request for action is made towards a terminal which is not connected.

```
//Package
com.ericsson.blipnet.api.blipnode
```

```
//Constructors
TerminalNotConnectedException()
TerminalNotConnectedException(java.lang.String message)
TerminalNotConnectedException(java.lang.String message,
java.lang.Throwable cause)
TerminalNotConnectedException(java.lang.Throwable cause)
```

Class WapServiceIndication

```
public final class WapServiceIndication extends java.lang.Object implements
ObexPushObject, java.io.Serializable
```

The WapServiceIndication class models the WAP Service Indication. This service provides the ability to send notifications to end-users in an asynchronous manner. Such notifications may, for example, be about new e-mails, changes in stock prices, news headlines, advertising, reminders of, for example, low prepaid balance, and so forth.

The WAP Service Indication contains a short message and a URI indicating a service. The message is presented to the end-user upon reception, and the user is given the choice to either start the service indicated by the URI immediately, or postpone the Service Indication for later handling. If the Service Indication is postponed, the client stores it and the end-user is given the possibility to act upon it at a later point of time.

Objects of the WapServiceIndication class are immutable—once created they cannot change.

```
//Package
com.ericsson.blipnet.api.obex.pushobjects
```

```
//Fields
static byte DELETE
```

The WAP Service Indication(s) received on the terminal with a given ID must be deleted.

```
static byte SIGNAL_HIGH
```

Indicates that the WAP Service Indication must be presented as soon as the implementation (of the terminal) allows that to be carried out in a non-user-intrusive manner, or earlier if considered appropriate (which may result in a user-intrusive behavior).

```
static byte SIGNAL_LOW
```

Indicates that the WAP Service Indication must be postponed without user intervention.

```
static byte SIGNAL_MEDIUM
```

Indicates that WAP Service Indication must be presented as soon as the implementation allows that to be carried out in a non-user-intrusive manner.

```
static java.lang.String TOKENIZED_MEDIA_TYPE
```

Defines the tokenized form of the WAP Service Indication Media Type.

```
//Constructors
WapServiceIndication (java.lang.String uri, java.lang.String id,
byte action, java.lang.String contents)
```

Constructs a WapServiceIndication.

```
WapServiceIndication(java.lang.String uri, java.lang.String id,
java.lang.String contents)
```

Constructs a WapServiceIndication.

```
WapServiceIndication(java.lang.String uri, java.lang.String id,
java.lang.String expires, byte action, java.lang.String contents)
```

Constructs a WapServiceIndication.

```
WapServiceIndication(java.lang.String uri, java.lang.String id,
java.lang.String expires, java.lang.String contents)
```

Constructs a `WapServiceIndication`.

```
//Methods
boolean equals(java.lang.Object obj)
```

Compares this `WapServiceIndication` with an `Object` and returns true if they are equal.

```
byte[] getObexBody()
```

Returns the body of this `ObexPushObject`.

```
java.lang.String getObexName()
```

Returns the name of this `ObexPushObject`.

```
java.lang.String getObexType()
```

Returns the mime-type of this `ObexPushObject`.

```
int hashCode()
```

Returns a `hashCode` for this `WapServiceIndication`.

```
java.lang.String toString()
```

Returns a `String` representation of this `WapServiceIndication`.

Class `WapServiceLoading`

```
public final class WapServiceLoading extends java.lang.Object implements
ObexPushObject, java.io.Serializable
```

The `WapServiceLoading` class models the WAP Service Loading. This service provides the ability to cause a user agent on a terminal to load and execute a service, that, for example, can be in the form of a WML deck. The Service Loading contains an URI indicating the service to be loaded by the user agent without user intervention when appropriate.

Objects of the WapServiceLoading class are immutable—once created they cannot change.

```
//Package
com.ericsson.blipnet.api.obex.pushobjects
```

```
//Fields
static byte CACHE
```

Indicates that the WAP service content is loaded in the same way as for EXECUTE-LOW, but instead of executing the service in the same way as for EXECUTE-LOW it is placed in the cache of the client.

```
static byte EXECUTE_HIGH
```

Indicates that the WAP service content is loaded and executed in the same way as for EXECUTE-LOW but may result in an user-intrusive behavior.

```
static byte EXECUTE_LOW
```

Indicates that the WAP service content is fetched from either an origin server or from the client's cache, if available.

```
static java.lang.String TOKENIZED_MEDIA_TYPE
```

Defines the tokenized form of the WAP Service Loading Media Type.

```
//Constructors
WapServiceLoading(java.lang.String uri)
```

Constructs a WapServiceLoading.

```
WapServiceLoading(java.lang.String uri, byte action)
```

Constructs a WapServiceLoading.

```
//Methods
boolean equals(java.lang.Object obj)
```

Compares this WapServiceLoading with an Object and returns true if they are equal.

`byte[] getObexBody()`

Returns the body of this `ObexPushObject`.

`java.lang.String getObexName()`

Returns the name of this `ObexPushObject`.

`java.lang.String getObexType()`

Returns the mime-type of this `ObexPushObject`.

`int hashCode()`

Returns a `hashCode` for this `WapServiceLoading`.

`java.lang.String toString()`

Returns a `String` representation of this `WapServiceLoading`.

Index

About Apress

Apress, located in Berkeley, CA, is a fast-growing, innovative publishing company devoted to meeting the needs of existing and potential programming professionals. Simply put, the "A" in Apress stands for *The Author's Press™*. Apress' unique approach to publishing grew out of conversations between its founders, Gary Cornell and Dan Appleman, authors of numerous best-selling, highly regarded books for programming professionals. In 1998 they set out to create a publishing company that emphasized quality above all else. Gary and Dan's vision has resulted in the publication of over 70 titles by leading software professionals, all of which have *The Expert's Voice™*.

Do You Have What It Takes to Write for Apress?

Apress is rapidly expanding its publishing program. If you can write and you refuse to compromise on the quality of your work, if you believe in doing more than rehashing existing documentation, and if you're looking for opportunities and rewards that go far beyond those offered by traditional publishing houses, we want to hear from you!

Consider these innovations that we offer all of our authors:

- **Top royalties with *no* hidden switch statements**
  Authors typically receive only half of their normal royalty rate on foreign sales. In contrast, Apress' royalty rate remains the same for both foreign and domestic sales.

- **Sharing the wealth**
  Most publishers keep authors on the same pay scale even after costs have been met. At Apress author royalties dramatically increase the more books are sold.

- **Serious treatment of the technical review process**
  Each Apress book is reviewed by a technical expert(s) whose remuneration depends in part on the success of the book since he or she too receives royalties.

Moreover, through a partnership with Springer-Verlag, New York, Inc., one of the world's major publishing houses, Apress has significant venture capital and distribution power behind it. Thus, we have the resources to produce the highest quality books *and* market them aggressively.

If you fit the model of the Apress author who can write a book that provides *What The Professional Needs To Know™*, then please contact us for more information:

editorial@apress.com